ROUTLEDGE LIBRARY EDITIONS: DISCOURSE ANALYSIS

Volume 3

SITUATIONS AND SPEECH ACTS

SITUATIONS AND SPEECH ACTS
Toward a Formal Semantics of Discourse

DAVID A. EVANS

LONDON AND NEW YORK

First published in 1985 Garland Publishing, Inc.

This edition first published in 2017
by Routledge
2 Park Square, Milton Park, Abingdon, Oxon OX14 4RN

and by Routledge
711 Third Avenue, New York, NY 10017

Routledge is an imprint of the Taylor & Francis Group, an informa business

© 1985 David A. Evans

All rights reserved. No part of this book may be reprinted or reproduced or utilised in any form or by any electronic, mechanical, or other means, now known or hereafter invented, including photocopying and recording, or in any information storage or retrieval system, without permission in writing from the publishers.

Trademark notice: Product or corporate names may be trademarks or registered trademarks, and are used only for identification and explanation without intent to infringe.

British Library Cataloguing in Publication Data
A catalogue record for this book is available from the British Library

ISBN: 978-1-138-22094-2 (Set)
ISBN: 978-1-315-40146-1 (Set) (ebk)
ISBN: 978-1-138-22467-4 (Volume 3) (hbk)
ISBN: 978-1-138-22470-4 (Volume 3) (pbk)
ISBN: 978-1-315-40178-2 (Volume 3) (ebk)

Publisher's Note
The publisher has gone to great lengths to ensure the quality of this reprint but points out that some imperfections in the original copies may be apparent.

Disclaimer
The publisher has made every effort to trace copyright holders and would welcome correspondence from those they have been unable to trace.

Situations and Speech Acts

Toward a Formal Semantics of Discourse

David A. Evans

Garland Publishing, Inc. ■ New York & London
1985

Library of Congress Cataloging-in-Publication Data

Evans, David A. (David Andreoff), 1948–
  Situations and speech acts.

  (Outstanding dissertations in linguistics)
  Thesis (Ph.D.)—Stanford University, 1981.
  Bibliography: p.
  1. Speech acts (Linguistics) 2. Discourse analysis.
3. Semantics. I. Title. II. Series.
P95.55.E93 1985   401.41   85-13152
ISBN 0-8240-5446-6 (alk. paper)

© 1985 by David A. Evans
All rights reserved

The volumes in this series are printed on
acid-free, 250-year-life paper.

Printed in the United States of America

PREFACE

It is the goal of this dissertation to develop an approach to speech acts that has the virtue of being straight-forward, explicit, formal, and flexible enough to accomodate many of the more general problems of interactive verbal communication. The principal problem that informs the design of this project is simply stated: How does an utterance come to be interpreted in some and not other ways on a particular occasion of use? And further: How does utterance interpretation change the discourse situation, in terms of the information it introduces and the constraints it effects? To answer these questions, if only partially, it is necessary to ask and answer other questions about the structure of situations, the competence of speakers, and the rules that govern discourse.

Obviously, such questions do not admit of facile answers. Though some of the solutions presented are limited in scope, the problem of speech acts, which is central to the problem of language use, is kept in constant focus. While much that is developed here is programmatic and can represent only the modest beginnings of a formal theory of discourse, the foundations for a semantic theory of speech acts are laid.

Here, it should be noted, I take semantics to refer to the representation of meaning, not merely truth-values. While an entire chapter is devoted to the detailed analysis of several discourse situations in terms of truth conditions, the principal point there for a theory of speech acts is that truth value questions are but a small and incomplete facet of linguistic interpretation.

The thesis itself — that it is possible to give a formal theory of speech acts in terms of the semantics of the situations in which discourse occurs — is presented in several chapters, each of which can be viewed as relatively independent.

Chapter 1 sets the stage for the discussion of speech acts by introducing situation semantics, and, in particular, the special role of discourse situations in a typology of situation-types. The effects of speech acts are discussed and an orientation toward speech act theory is presented. It is assumed that the reader is familiar with traditional work on speech acts in the philosophical, linguistic, psychological, and artificial intelligence literature, so, although a representative set of references is given, no historical review or systematic exegesis is attempted. Examples of the kinds of phenomena that fall within the scope of speech acts are offered, along with the desiderata for a complete theory.

Chapter 2 addresses two assumptions that frame the theory developed here, namely that the problem of representing speaker intentionality is incidental to the representation of speech act effect and that it is possible to describe such effects exhaustively in terms of the end-states of discourse situations. Here, speech acts are understood to include the effects of utterances on the structure of the discourse situation at all levels of interaction, including, for example, conversational moves. Some speech act types, which play a role in Chapters 3 and 4, are given, designed to illustrate the kind of information that competent speakers must possess if they are to engage successfully in interactive discourse.

Chapter 3 presents a streamlined theory of speech acts that, in a four stage process, utilizes information in the utterance itself, in the discourse situation, and in the inventory of speech act types to generate an interpretation of utterance meaning. Provision is made for sub-utterance phenomena to give rise to speech acts. The role of more general planning mechanisms is discussed in connection with the decisions an addressee must make when faced with several or ambiguous choices of speech act interpretation.

Chapter 4 tests the predictions of the theory in several hypothetical discourse situations, focusing on the interaction of truth conditions with utterance interpretation. The first example repeats the case presented in Stalnaker (1978) involving constatives and multiple addressees. The second examines a case exhaustively discussed in Goffman (1976) involving the relationship between the use of *Do you have the time?* and possible responses. The third is designed to address the question *What counts as a lie?* raised by Coleman and Kay (1981), by presenting an analysis of several discourse situations in which the characteristic effects of lies are seen as deriving from a variety of discourse phenomena. In all cases, the theory of speech acts developed in this thesis is sensitive to interpretations that arise from various aspects of the use of utterances.

Chapter 5 summarizes the thesis, discusses the limitations of the theory, and suggests directions for future research. The principal conclusion is that it is possible to give a formal semantic treatment to many aspects of speech act interpretation but that a complete theory of natural language discourse requires components that involve non-linguistic as well as more properly linguistic cognitive processes.

Footnotes and all references are collected at the end of the dissertation. Three appendices are included to facilitate reference to some of the key concepts developed in the theory presented here. The first appendix (A) contains a very limited set of definitions; the second (B) gives all the speech act types that are used, organized under families of types; and the third (C) recapitulates the formal components of the theory.

ACKNOWLEDGMENTS

One of the rewards of writing a dissertation is the opportunity it presents to thank the many individuals who contributed both tangibly and intangibly to its creation. Ideas, unlike Athena, do not spring to life full-grown, but require the nuture of many hands over many years.

Whatever achievement this work represents, it would be meaningless and empty without the love of my wife, Lynnae. Of all the blessings I have known the greatest have been her constancy, patience, understanding, and affection during our life together. Without her I am nothing; with her I am more than myself.

During the writing of this dissertation, our daughter, Brynn, was ever-present, providing an anchor for the reality that threatened, at times, to slip away. Unaffected by the weightiness of the matters that preoccupied me, she persisted in reminding me of our humble, pre-linguistic beginnings, and of the enormity of the achievement that even child discourse represents.

And ever-present, too, were thoughts of my own beginnings and of the family into which I was born. My great fortune as a child and youth was to have lived with my parents, Eleanor and Joseph Evans, and grandparents, Marie and Andrea Andreoff, in a secure and happy home. Though I can never repay the kindness and support they have always shown me, as a small token of my love, I dedicate this dissertation to them.

I can imagine no more conscientious and thoughtful dissertation committee than the one which supervised my work. Jon Barwise, through his encouragement of my fledgling ideas and his persistent tolerance of my false-starts and misunderstandings, is most responsible for my having written this dissertation. Had I not met him when I did, I would still be scratching my head over the perplexities of discourse, unable to see trees in the midst of a forest. Tom Wasow has been an unfailing friend during my years as a graduate student, and has been a model of intellectual honesty and personal integrity. I will consider myself a worthy scholar and a noble human being if I succeed in being half the person I have always known Tom to be. Terry Winograd has often acted as a sounding board for my ideas and has never failed to ask the difficult questions that separate clarity from confusion. And Herb Clark has sharpened my understanding of speech acts in lively discussions and through his perceptive criticism. All the members of my committee indulged the idiosyncracies of my approach to the problem of speech acts, and graciously accommodated my harried schedule. I shall be ever grateful to them for the help they have given me.

I owe an intellectual debt, as well, to Gerald Gazdar, whose clarity and intelligence in dealing with issues of pragmatics served both to inspire me and to focus my attention on formal treatments of discourse-based phenomena.

I would also like to acknowledge the great support, through friendship and occasional collaboration, I have received from my friends at SRI International, Jerry Hobbs, Armar Archbold, and Jane Robinson. I took my first steps on the road to discourse analysis with Jerry as a guide, and have a richer understanding of the computational facets of natural language interaction as a result. Armar Archbold has spent numerous evenings listening to my ideas, helping me find the gaps in my thinking. And Jane Robinson has encouraged me through her kindness and grace in more ways than she can ever know. I would like to thank as well all the members of the SRI TINLUNCH discussion group for stimulation, entertainment, and good humor, all for the price of a roast beef sandwich.

Finally, I thank all those who at various times nudged me along the path which has lead to this point, especially Louis Lunte, Joachim Bark, Julius Moravcsik, Will Leben, Clara Bush, and Elizabeth Traugott. All have added to my understanding of the world and my understanding of myself, and all have wished me well.

I must certainly claim that I alone am responsible for the shortcomings of this dissertation, but I cannot alone take credit for its successes. Every person here has contributed to whatever good there may be in this work.

TABLE OF CONTENTS

Preface i
Acknowledgements iv
List of Figures vii
CHAPTER 1   SITUATIONS AND SPEECH ACTS
  1.0. Introduction 1
  1.1. Situations and Situation-Types 2
  1.2. Discourse Situations 7
  1.3. Speech Acts 15
  1.4. Desiderata for a theory of Speech Acts 19
CHAPTER 2   SPEECH ACT TYPES
  2.0. Introduction 20
  2.1. Effect and Intentionality 21
  2.2. Moves in Discourse Situations 29
  2.3. Some Speech Act Types 38
CHAPTER 3   A THEORY OF SPEECH ACT INTERPRETATION
  3.0. Introduction 51
  3.1. Interpretive Constituents 52
  3.2. Illocutionary Mode Functions 66
  3.3. Reconciliation with Context 72
  3.4. Matching Types and Implementing Choices 88
CHAPTER 4   SPEECH ACTS, MEANING, AND TRUTH
  4.0. Introduction 101
  4.1. Orientation in the World 103
  4.2. Assertion and Truth 113
  4.3. Questions and Responses 129
  4.4. Lies 146

CHAPTER 5   SUMMARY AND EVALUATION
  5.0. Introduction 160
  5.1. The Thesis Summarized 161
  5.2. The Thesis Evaluated 166
  5.3. Directions for Future Research 171

NOTES 175
BIBLIOGRAPHY 187
APPENDIX A: Definitions of Concepts 194
APPENDIX B: The Speech Act Types 199
APPENDIX C: The Formal Apparatus 207

LIST OF FIGURES

FIGURE 1   A Finite State Diagram for Moves
in Two-person Discourse   30

FIGURE 2   An Overview of the Speech Act
Interpretation Process   100

FIGURE 3   An Overview of Levels of Interpretation   140

FIGURE 4   A Schematization for the Interpretation
of *Do you have the time?*   142

CHAPTER 1   SITUATIONS AND SPEECH ACTS

1.0.   INTRODUCTION

This chapter has four goals. First, an apparatus for describing situations, viz. a situation semantics à la Barwise and Perry (1981a), is presented, along with a brief discussion of some of the motivation for using situations as the basis of meaning representation, and some of the theoretical consequences of such an orientation. The notion of situation-type is explicated, accompanied by formal definitions, and forms the basis of the semantics of discourse developed later. Second, it is argued that discourse constitutes a distinguished situation, a discourse situation, which has properties that affect linguistic interpretation at all levels. Third, speech acts are described in terms of their effects on discourse situations, and it is argued that current theories treating speech acts are inadequate to deal with the variety of speech act phenomena encountered in actual discourse. Finally, desiderata for a formal theory of speech acts are presented.

1.1. SITUATIONS AND SITUATION-TYPES

Before presenting the brief introduction to situation semantics that this chapter requires, it is worth considering some of the factors that motivate the use of situations as distinguished descriptive entities. To do this, it is useful to consider, further, the difference between a <u>scene</u> and a <u>situation</u>.

When we look out upon the world, a scene presents itself to our view. The scene consists of objects with properties, standing in relationships. The situation of which the scene is a part, contains us, the observers, and all that is observed.

But the situation contains much more than what we observe. As though obeying the Law of Plenitude,[1] it contains all the objects that are there, and all their properties and relationships, not just the ones on which we fix our attention. The scene we view represents a small subset of the elements of the situation and is, in a sense, an artifact of the observation process: we cannot attend to all the elements of a situation, but only to a handful, in the time the scene is accessible to us. This limitation is a limitation in our cognitive capacity, not a limitation inherent in situations under observation (at least down to the atomic level[2]).

Now, a scene is part of not just one situation, but of an infinite number of situations. This multitude of situations reflects the infinite number of possible partitionings of the space-time environment in which the scene is set. Still, the facts of the scene are not etiolated by this plethora of embedding possibilities: what is true of the scene is true regardless of the situation containing it. This feature of scenes gives them a powerful ability to characterize the superset situations of which they are parts. And it is this feature that is exploited in situation semantics.

The object of situation semantics is to provide a formal characterization of situations, taking objects, properties, and relations as primitives. One of the most useful means of describing situations is through <u>situation-types</u>, which can be thought of, intuitively, as minimal scenes: highly limited information about situations. The situation-type in the semantic theory can be regarded as the analog of the activated network in psychological theory, and is designed to capture certain facts of cognitive processing.

When we observe a situation, or think about it, or talk about it, we are forced to choose some features and exclude others. If we look out into a yard and fix our attention on a nearby tree, the surrounding shrubs, grass, and objects of all kinds wash into a blur. We are aware of the tree, its leaves, its shape, its color, perhaps, but of only a handful of the many relationships the tree has to its environment. Nevertheless, the features of the tree that we bring into focus are true, independent of the many other ways the tree and its environment might be related. And what we know about the tree from our limited observation provides us with accurate information about some aspects of all the situations of which the tree is a part.

In situation semantics, we define a situation-type to be a partial function characterizing various kinds of situations. More precisely, if we let A represent the set of objects, $\{ a_0, a_1, a_2, ... \}$, and R the set of sets of n-place relations, $\{ R^0, R^1, R^2, ... \}$, with R^0 being the set of 0-place relations (one of which might give, for example, the state of it raining); R^1, the set of properties, or 1-place relations (including, for example, the property of being green); R^2, the set of 2-place relations (including, for example, the relation of one person hitting another person); etc.; then we can define a situation-type, s, to be a partial function that returns the values 0, 1, or *undefined* for any relation and set of objects depending on whether that relation holds of that set of objects for the situations of which s is the type. We write:

$$(1) \qquad s(r^n, a_1, ... , a_n) = 1 \qquad \text{iff } a_1, ... , a_n \text{ are in the relation } r^n$$
$$\text{in the set of situations given by } s,$$
$$s(r^n, a_1, ... , a_n) = 0 \qquad \text{iff } a_1, ... , a_n \text{ are not in the}$$
$$\text{relation } r^n \text{ in the set of situations}$$
$$\text{given by } s, \text{ and otherwise}$$
$$s(r^n, a_1, ... , a_n) = \text{undefined.}$$

Suppose, for example, that we are looking at a room containing, along with its unexceptional furnishings, a red balloon and a green telephone. If we let a_0 designate the room, a_1, the balloon, and a_2, the telephone, and assume that **contain** is a 2-place relation, and that **be-red** and **be-green** are properties (1-place relations), then the following situation-types can be given:[3]

$$(2) \qquad s(\textbf{contain}, a_0, a_1) = 1$$
$$s(\textbf{contain}, a_0, a_2) = 1$$
$$s(\textbf{be-red}, a_1) = 1$$
$$s(\textbf{be-red}, a_2) = 0$$

This captures some of the (partial) information we have about the situations that have this room as a part. Of course, we could list many other facts about these situations, including the following:

$$(3) \quad s(\text{contain}, a_1, a_0) = 0$$
$$s(\text{be-green}, a_1) = 0$$
$$s(\text{be-green}, a_0) = \text{undefined}$$

The virtue of the situation-type is that it enables us to encode accurate information about situations without requiring that we know everything about the situations. And there seems to be in situation-types a natural way of representing the meanings of sentences.

As argued in Barwise and Perry (1981b), there is an essential difference in sentences of the following type that cannot be captured in post-Fregean approaches to semantics that take the interpretation (=reference) of a sentence to be its truth-value:

(4) *Aristotle said that the meaning of a sentence is proportional to its length.*

(5) *Cicero thought that silence is golden.*

Though both (4) and (5) are false, their subject matter is very different. Furthermore, their embedded sentences contribute to the interpretation of the whole by representing some situation that we must understand if we are to determine the attitude being expressed and, ultimately, the truth conditions on the whole. We would want a semantics of English to have a way of representing the differences in (4) and (5) explicitly, while offering us the possibility of evaluating the statements made as equally false. This is possible if we let these sentences determine situation-types, since the situation-types associated with (4) and (5) will be quite distinct.

These examples underscore two orientations lurking in situation semantics which should be made explicit. The first is philosophical; the second, psychological. The philosophical commitment situation semantics makes is to a strong realism. There is no distinction between the objects of situation-types (partial functions) and the objects of situations (slices of space-time). In the psychological realm, this commitment is translated into an antiphenomenalism. When we see a tree, it is the tree itself that we see, not some pattern of sensations.

In terms of linguistics, this leaves us in a very interesting position. Since words are the names of objects and relationships, and since sentences designate situation-types, which are partial characterizations of situations, the object of inquiry in linguistics should be nothing less than the situations of the actual universe. Grammatical rules can be regarded as a means of encoding relationships, so a failure of grammar results in ill-formedness not so much because of language rule violation as because it creates a situation-type for which there is no corresponding situation in our experience.

There is, of course, an element of Whorfianism in this position, with attendant chicken-and-egg problems. Does the situational structure of the world constrain cognition, or does some cognitive predisposition affect and limit our perception of the structure of the world? Do language rules reflect the situational environments in which they develop, or does a tradition of arbitrary grammatical form become associated with some possible situations in the world and not others, inhibiting our ability to view the world ingenuously?

Situation semantics does not address these issues directly; it is, after all, a descriptive formalism. Indeed, it leaves the question open while accommodating linguistic determinism.

For example, the situation-type

(6)   s(**want, Brynn, the-ball**) = 1

gives just those situations in which the person designated by *Brynn* (i.e., **Brynn**) is in a **want** relationship to the person or object designated by *the ball* (i.e., **the-ball**). Whether or not there are, in fact, situations that have this type is an empirical matter. Conventionally, in situation semantics, the problem is whether or not **S**, the set of situations having s as their type, is contained in **W**, the set of situations that obtain in the world. If $S \subseteq W$, then (6) gives the type of a set of real situations; if not, then (6) gives the type of a set of imaginary situations.

The linguistic problem raised by this example is how the interpretation of the use of an utterance (or inscription) of the form

(7)   *Brynn wants the ball.*

can have a situation-type such as (6) as a part. Consider just the lexical issues. *Brynn* must be associated with a particular individual, **Brynn**; *the ball* must be associated with a particular individual or object, **the-ball**; and *want* must be associated with the relation, **want** (which we might assume, here, gives the relationship normally understood as desiring to have or hold for a limited time, rather than other relationships subsumed under the English word *want*, such as lacking, or needing, or desiring to eat, etc.)

But this, of course, overly simplifies the matter. If (7) is a real utterance, then it is issued by someone, to someone, in the service of some intention. Its interpretation might involve distinguishing the word *Brynn* from the individual **Brynn**, if, for example, it is produced as part of an exercise in elocution. Or, its interpretation might involve distinguishing the state of a fact about the world, as encoded in (6), from the statement of a reason for a particular action, say, moving to get the ball; or from a request to an addressee to get the ball. Or, its interpretation might involve recognizing that Brynn is a certain kind of individual, say, a child, and that the utterance is designed to accompany the action of Brynn's reaching for the ball, as a means of teaching the child the meaning of the word *want*.

The point that this rather long discursis seeks to make is just this. Sentences can stand for situation-types, real or imaginary, but the use of sentences (as utterances) occurs only in real situations in which they are a means to an end. This requires that the situation-types given by the sentences, in order to be interpreted correctly, always be embedded in the situation that gives rise to their use. This, in turn, requires that we accord the circumstances of the use of sentences a distinguished status, in short, that we have a special means of representing discourse situations.

1.2.   DISCOURSE SITUATIONS

There are a number of reasons why discourse situations should have a distinguished role in any theory of language use.

First, we should emphasize that natural language is not like artificial language — a point that has too often been ignored in recent linguistic work. The meanings of words, if such units can be defined, are not fixed precisely, but are complex functions of their uses in particular instances. This makes them "fuzzy" as primes, and ultimately indeterminate. If we attempt to define a word (or any other meaningful unit of human communication) it must be in terms of the constraints it exercises on just those situations in which its use has an interpretation.

Consider how a word might be defined in terms of its possible uses. By using the word *car* in an utterance, in a particular discourse situation, we intend by its use to do something that is semi-determinate in that situation, namely, if used referentially, to call attention to some object in the domain of discourse that either bears the name *car* or is disambiguated from other candidate objects by the use of the name *car*; or if used attributively, to suggest that some object in the domain of discourse which is distinguished from other candidate objects at the time of utterance has at least some features that justify the use of the word *car* as a descriptive device; or if used iconically, to direct the addressee to the fact of the utterance, that is, its form, shape, sound, etc., in a way that allows the addressee to isolate it from surrounding text. And we could continue this list to include other aspects of the use of words.

Second, as many studies on child language development and isolated or neglected children have shown, children do not develop language merely because they are exposed to it. The children of deaf/mute parents who have access to T.V. and radio in their homes (and who hear and watch T.V. regularly) do not necessarily learn or use the spoken language they regularly hear. Instead, they develop a rich ability to communicate in the non-spoken language of their parents. The point here is obvious: it is not the rules of language that are being learned as much as the rules of discourse situations, in which communication can take place. The details and complexities of form which seem dominant in adult language obscure the fact that, ultimately, only the situation in which the interaction takes place is being manipulated. Children learn from situations, not from words. (It is worth noting that recent work in child language development has paid much more attention to the whole discourse situation giving rise to communication than simply the surface utterances (words) involved (cf. Ochs and Schieffelin (1979) and Ervin-

Tripp and Mitchell-Kernan (1977)).)

Third, as an intuitive proof, consider the difference between expressing one's thoughts, face-to-face, to a cooperative interlocutor, and writing those thoughts in the form of a short note or essay. Not only are the tasks different (in one case we must attend to the addressee and make our words conform to his needs at the moment; in the other we must imagine and interpret both roles of speaker and addressee, simultaneously), but the words we use, the rules we observe, are different too. The differences are due in part to the different constraints on achieving our desired effect in these two ways. Expressing an idea on a single occasion to a particular individual involves different problems than expressing the same idea to an unknown addressee (potentially, anyone), who may encounter the written expression of our thoughts on any occasion.

What these three reasons have in common is their dependence on the notion of semiotic effects relative to a situation. The use of a word (e.g., *car*) can result in many interpretations, but all are governed by a set of rules applying to the use of words (as opposed, say, to the making of noises). Those rules develop out of patterns that are repeated again and again in actual situations involving communication. Children learning language do not encounter radios or T.V. sets in primary communicational situations; rather, they encounter their keepers (parents), and become familiar with the patterns of interaction their keepers employ. There is no interaction with one-way radios or T.V. sets, just as there is no immediate interaction with the addressee of a memo, letter, or essay. It requires a special act of abstraction to communicate effectively in situations that have no interlocutors, and in such situations we discover, indirectly, the elements that are an integral part of discourse.

We might list some of the features of discourse situations that distinguish them from other situations as follows:

(8) a. There is a speaker
     b. There is at least one addressee
     c. All parties to the situation recognize that they are in a discourse situation.
     d. The purpose is semiotic (meaning that the speaker engages in symbolic representation of situations for a purpose, designed so the addressee(s) can discover the purpose)
     e. The process is rule-governed[4]

These points seem obvious enough, but their effect is profound. The only concrete phenomenon over which a speaker has control is the production of utterances, yet by following rules peculiar to discourse he can use utterances to manipulate belief states in his addressee(s) and thereby bring about changes in his environment. Of course, effects are achieved and belief states are manipulated only because the addressee cooperates, actually co-participates, in the discourse situation. The situation that a speaker and addressee find themselves in is similar to all other situations involving mutual activity, but is distinguished by having all the characteristics given in (8). These characteristics represent the framing facts of a discourse situation.

A complete set of framing facts exists in every non-defective discourse situation. For purposes of abstraction, we might regard a discourse situation in which a transition between the speaker and addressee roles of the interlocutors is taking place as temporarily defective in that an essential framing fact is undetermined, but in all the examples involving speech act effects that we might consider, this aspect of discourse situations is irrelevant. Furthermore, where one participant is utilizing rules or conventions that are not shared by the other(s), for the purposes of abstraction, we can regard the discourse situation's framing facts as consisting of the sets of rules employed by each participant.

There are, of course, other facts that are part of any discourse situation, and these will consist of two kinds, immediate and derived. Immediate facts include what one sees, hears, smells, etc., in the physical environment — those facts that are directly accessible to perception — of which all the participants can be aware. In addition, we can consider the direct effects of utterances — including the meanings of the subparts of the utterance, and their speech act effects — to be part of the set of immediate facts. Derived facts, on the other hand, are any facts introduced to the discourse situation through processes of inferencing that begin with framing facts or immediate facts. For example, if it is a fact that a is the speaker, and b the addressee, in a discourse situation, we might infer that a believes he is the speaker in that discourse situation; and we might utilize this inference in yet other inferences about what a should do or think if he does, in fact, hold such a belief. But while such an inference might seem natural and even essential under normal conventions of interaction, it is in no way necessary. The speaker might not believe that he is the speaker is a discourse situation that includes b: he might think he is talking to himself; or he might be speaking deliriously to an imaginary interlocutor. So, while derived facts may be very important constituents of the discourse situation, we should be cautious, in writing rules, to distinguish between them and the other, more immutable framing and immediate facts.

Acknowledging the importance of this distinction, we could index the facts of any discourse situation according to their type, and could require that all rules (inferencing schemata, etc.) be clearly labeled as to the type of facts they take as input and the type they produce as output. For the most part, in the development of the theory of speech acts presented in this thesis and in the numerous examples given where the facts of the discourse situation are important, the differences in types of facts are not critical. Where such distinctions do affect the theory or its framework, they are maintained.

In general, we should strive to keep the number of facts in the discourse situation to a minimum, specifically, to the smallest subset of facts — of the set of total facts that could be maintained about the discourse situation — that enables the discourse interaction to proceed. We should attempt to account for utterance interpretations on the basis of the least amount of information that is extraneous to the utterance and the framing facts of the discourse situation.

Some of the framing facts, (8a.) - (8c.), can be formalized with the aid of situation-types. Let A be a set of individuals, and let \$ and @ be distinguished variables ranging over A that, for a given discourse situation, D, designate the current speaker and the current addressee, respectively. A discourse situation exists among the members of A iff

$$\text{(9)} \quad \text{i.} \quad (\forall a_i \in A) \ d(\text{believe}, a_i, \varphi) = 1,$$
$$\text{where } \varphi := d(\text{be-in}, a_i, D) = 1;$$
$$\text{ii.} \quad (\exists! a_j \in A) \ \text{s. t. } d(\text{have-value}, \$, a_j) = 1; \text{ and}$$
$$\text{iii.} \quad (\exists a_k \in A) \ \text{s. t. } d(\text{have-value}, @, a_k) = 1.[5]$$

This tells us that a discourse situation, D, with type d, exists among the members of A if and only if ((9i.)) each individual in A believes himself to be in the discourse situation, D; ((9ii.)) there is a unique speaker in D who is one of the individuals in A; and ((9iii.)) there are one or more addressees in D who are among the individuals in A. Note that this leaves open the possibility that some individuals may be neither speaker nor addressee, yet still be part of the discourse situation. This possibility is exploited in situations where primary addressees are distinguished from co-participants not being addressed. Furthermore, nothing in this definition prevents the speaker from taking himself to be the addressee.

Clearly, this formulation represents an idealization, since in actual discourse situations more than one person can be speaker at the same time. Such cases can be captured here by regarding each situation with a single speaker as a separate discourse situation, overlapping in time, and perhaps even addressee constituency, with the other situations with single speakers. At such times, we might think of D as splitting or fracturing into parts, with each having one of the competing speakers as nuclear elements.

To avoid, for the moment, the complexities — both conceptual and representational — that this aspect of actual discourse introduces, we can limit our consideration of discourse situations to strictly two-person sets. This results in no loss of generality for most of the discourse situations that are treated here and in subsequent sections.

Repeating (9), then, for this restricted case, we can list all the framing facts given by (8a.) - (8c.) for the situation in which individual a is speaking to individual b, as follows:

(10)   a. $d(believe, a, (a \in D)) = 1$
       b. $d(believe, a, (b \in D)) = 1$
       c. $d(believe, b, (a \in D)) = 1$
       d. $d(believe, b, (b \in D)) = 1$
       e. $d(\$ = a) = 1$
       f. $d(@ = b) = 1$

In fact, (10) encodes a great deal of redundancy of mutual belief which can be eliminated by an interpretation of what the discourse situation-type, d, represents. We want d to give us the facts of the discourse situation, hence we can assume that a discourse situation already exists, with its usual framing requirements. We want also to be able to interpret the discourse situation omnisciently, so that any fact of the discourse situation will be known to each participant. A metarule could be used to translate all instances of knowledge into instances of mutual belief, as well. For example, if

(11)   a. $(a \in D)$
       b. $(b \in D)$
       c. $d(\$ = a) = 1$
       d. $d(@ = b) = 1$

represent the facts of the discourse situation, we might want to generate

(12)   a. $d(believe, a, (\$ = a)) = 1$
       b. $d(believe, b, (\$ = a)) = 1$
       c. $d(believe, a, (@ = b)) = 1$

d. $\quad$ d(believe, b, $((a = b)) = 1$
e. $\quad$ d(believe, a, φ) = 1,
$\qquad$ where $\varphi := $ d(believe, b, ((12a.) & (12c.))) = 1
f. $\quad$ d(believe, b, ψ) = 1,
$\qquad$ where $\psi := $ d(believe, a, ((12b.) & (12d.))) = 1
g. $\quad$ d(believe, a, (a∈D)) = 1
h. $\quad$ d(believe, a, (b∈D)) = 1
i. $\quad$ d(believe, b, (a∈D)) = 1
j. $\quad$ d(believe, b, (b∈D)) = 1

More generally, for our two-person case, we could write:

(13) **Metarule of Mutual Belief**
$\qquad$ If f is a fact of the discourse situation consisting of participants a and b, then the following are also facts of the discourse situation:
$\qquad$ a. $\quad$ d(believe, **a**, f) = 1
$\qquad$ b. $\quad$ d(believe, **b**, f) = 1

However, there are several undesirable consequences of such a rule. First, since (13a.) and (13b.) are themselves facts of the discourse situation, the rule allows an infinite recursion on mutual beliefs, which makes every discourse situation infinite. Second, following the first point, such a rule violates the principle that we should introduce as few facts as possible to guarantee the interpretation of utterances. Unless there is some kind of interpretation that cannot be made on the basis of finite degrees of mutual belief, such a rule is unjustifiably over-powered.

There may be advantages to a restricted version of the metarule in (13), however, to allow for processes of inferencing requiring the assumption of mutual belief.[6] We could modify the metarule to apply (optionally) only to framing facts or immediate facts of the discourse situation, and to generate only derived facts. This would partially account for the normal assumptions of limited mutual beliefs we make in discourse situations, without making such mutual beliefs necessary for all discourse situations. Furthermore, the recursion is blocked because the output of the rule cannot be used as input. Rewriting (13):

(13') **Metarule of Mutual Belief (Optional)**
$\qquad$ If f is a framing fact or immediate fact of the discourse situation consisting of participants a and b, then the following are derived facts of the discourse situation:
$\qquad$ a. d(believe, **a**, f) = 1
$\qquad$ b. d(believe, **b**, f) = 1

$$\text{c. } d(\text{believe, a, } \varphi) = 1,$$
$$\text{where } \varphi := d(\text{believe, b, } (13'a.)) = 1$$
$$\text{d. } d(\text{believe, b, } \psi) = 1,$$
$$\text{where } \psi := d(\text{believe, a, } (13'b.)) = 1$$

With this metarule, we can generate all the facts given in (10) (and more); and can take the framing facts of the discourse situation to be given, simply, as in (11).

The other characteristics under (8), viz. (8d.) and (8e.), also need to be incorporated in the set of framing facts, perhaps as a series of conventions as, for example, in Bach and Harnish (1979). Some of the assumptions at this level are quite familiar and unexceptional, for instance, the assumption that speaker and addressee share a language, or share some kind of community (if only their mutual humanity), or share a great deal of common knowledge about the world. But some are more problematic, and, indeed, are part of the focus of this work, including the assumption that speaker and addressee share a series of rules governing language use, and a means of representing the state of the discourse situation and the effects of utterances on the discourse situation.

There are other aspects of discourse that can vary from situation to situation, but that should have status as framing facts in the situations where they occur. Generally, these variable framing facts correspond to sets of mutual belief about the structure and purposes of the particular interaction being engaged in.

We might think of some of these as falling under "discourse genre," with each genre consisting of a set of rules governing conduct and goal structure appropriate to that discourse type. Intuitively, participating in a lecture involves us in very different activity, with different expectations, than participating in a debate, or in "cocktail" talk. In a lecture the addressee has no turn at talk; in a debate, highly regulated turns; in cocktail conversation, freely accessible, short turns. A lecture fails if it does not create a well-structured whole; a debate, if it presents only one side of an issue; a cocktail conversation, if it becomes too detailed or well-defined. Part of our competence as mature speakers involves knowing what kind of discourse we are engaged in, what structure it has, and how we as participants should behave.

There are other kinds of mutual beliefs that greatly affect the form that individual discourse situations take, including knowledge that participants have of shared personal experiences or of topics of current relevance. We offer congratulations or condolences not only at gatherings that pointedly call for such expressions, but also when we encounter someone for the first time after we have learned of his triumph or bereavement. As a society we tend to speak to parents or parents-in-law or children in different registers, but with our own parents, parents-in-law, and children we choose some words, phrases, and topics to avoid, some to exploit, depending on highly individual histories of past encounters and knowledge of personal preference.

All of these factors are part of the factual content of the discourse situation in which they occur, and any may be relevant in interpreting an utterance in that discourse situation. But the content is not static: new information is added as a result of the interpretation of utterances, which may even have the effect of invalidating or modifying old information; or the physical circumstances of the environment in which the discourse is taking place may change (obvious to some of the participants) effecting an unspoken change in the state of mutual knowledge.[7]

The position taken here is that a discourse situation, D, will consist of nothing more or less than its content, viz. the set of facts of the situation. Any utterance that occurs can be given an interpretation only to the extent that it exploits information that is part of the discourse situation (including, of course, information that the utterance itself introduces.) Clearly, all of the information about a discourse situation may not be useful in interpreting an utterance, and indeed, it might be necessary to block some information from contributing to an interpretation. But, for the purposes of the theory developed here, no distinction will be made between information of current relevance and the content of the discourse situation, in general.

This position is tolerable only because the theory presented here is not a complete theory of language use, but only a theory of speech acts. A theory of language use would have to address the problems associated with, for example, topic, focus, pronoun resolution, and coherence — problems that go beyond a theory of speech acts. I do not wish to suggest that a theory of speech acts should not be informed, or even directly shaped, by consideration of these aspects of language use, rather, I wish merely to state that within the framework of a "first-pass" formalization of speech act theory, such considerations are secondary.

1.3.   SPEECH ACTS[8]

A discourse situation changes as the result of the interpretation of an utterance. New information is added; old information may be modified or deleted. It is assumed here, first, that changes to the discourse situation occur discretely, to whatever level of finegrainedness we might wish, and second, that changes resulting from utterance interpretation are rule-governed and are based on the content of the utterance and the content of the discourse situation. We might represent this as in (14), where D_i gives the discourse situation at time i, and I gives the interpretation of the utterance U.[9]

$$(14) \quad D_{i+1} = I(U, D_i)$$

The expression $I(U, D_i)$ represents the effect of the utterance U in context D_i, and is what the theory developed here takes to be a speech act.

Note that (14) does not commit us to a representation of the discourse situation that is monotonically increasing in factual content. While many utterances will result in a new discourse situation that has the immediately prior discourse situation as a proper subset (i.e., where it is the case that $D_i \subseteq D_{i+1}$), not all utterances will have this effect. For example, retractions or refutations might have the effect of removing propositions that characterized the old discourse situation (while, of course, introducing new information as well). In such cases, D_i and D_{i+1} will overlap to some extent, but will not be in a sub-set – super-set relationship.

Up to this point the term *utterance* has been used in all generality: we might have thought of it as including grunts and groans as well as entire filibusters. Yet, involuntary noises and long-winded speeches are not meaningfully subsumed under one category, certainly not under *utterance*. At the same time, it would be arbitrary and perhaps misleading to limit utterances to sentences, or single clauses, or constituent phrases, or single words, or phones. To retain some flexibility while eliminating the adventitious and the interminable we might use the following definition:

> (15)   An <u>utterance</u> is a sound or sequence of sounds (words) produced in a discourse situation, designed by the speaker to be given an interpretation (by one or more addressees), that produces a (non-trivial) change in the discourse situation.

We want to allow utterances at the level of single phones in order to accommodate such phenomena as illustrated in the following:

(16) [a and b observing a prize-winning cow being given a
       bushel of clover]
       a: *Fine feed for a cow!*
       b: *What about its feet?*
       a: *No. [d]. [d]. Feed. Not feet.*

Here, a sound is articulated and designed to be recognized as a particular sound (in contrast to another similar sound), to facilitate comprehension of a target word.

Still, the notion *utterance* does little to add clarity to the structure of discourses. Utterances do not even function as the usual vehicles of speech acts: there is no convenient one-to-one mapping between utterances and speech acts, just as there is no one-to-one mapping between sentences and speech acts.

To review briefly the arguments supporting this observation, consider first that small class of utterances that do seem to overlap precisely with some of the speech acts they can perform, aptly, the "performatives." A typical example is

(17) *I apologize.*

But while this can effect an apology, so can the two utterances

(18) *I did a terrible thing. I'm very sorry.*

Of course, there are more complex cases where effects cannot be achieved in single utterances, but result only from an accumulation of related effects across a stretch of discourse, as in a refutation or a verbal proof. One cannot make a refutation with the words *I refute X* as one might make an assertion with the words *I assert X*.

Finally, there are speech act-like effects that can occur in the process of utterance production, as the sub-parts of utterances. Some of the best examples involve the use of referring expressions that serve not only to indicate referents but also to reveal speaker attitudes, for example

(19) *I told the guy at the door to watch out, but the idiot wouldn't listen.*[10]

Note that the use of *the idiot* is marked[11] — the unmarked *he* would have done just as well as a co-referent — and involves a characterization of the individual referred to. Note also that the context in which *the idiot* occurs does not admit possible co-referents freely: *the person*, for example, is distinctly infelicitous here.

Other members of this last class include "amalgams" (Lakoff (1974)) such as

(20) *I met* **you'll never guess who** *at the ballpark yesterday.*

Again, the speaker does something in the course of the production of an utterance that effects a change in the discourse situation by effecting a change in his relationship to the addressee, namely by expressing an attitude to the course of introducing a referent. Notice that this kind of linguistic *Doppelgänger* is highly context sensitive: its identity as a referring expression comes in part from the *wh*-word, but also from cannonical word order and selectional restrictions on *meet*. To take another example, in the following,

(21) a. *I did it for* **you'll never guess who.**
      b. *I did it for* **you'll never guess why.**

we can understand the phrase in (21a.) to refer to an individual; in (21b.), to a reason. This double-duty is made possible by the ambiguous role of the *for* phrase in this construction. But these kinds of phrases cannot appear freely in all possible NP positions. We do not find amalgams in fronted or topicalized positions, as the following illustrate:

(22) a. *I met John at the ballpark.*
      b. *I met you'll never guess who at the ballpark.*
      c. *John, I met at the ballpark.*
      d. **You'll never guess who, I met at the ballpark.*[12]

The point that these examples serve to make is that significant incrementations to the content of the discourse situation can be made as a result of the interpretation of smaller than utterance segments as well as larger than utterance stretches of discourse. To accommodate this aspect of discourse we should revise (14) as follows:

(23) $D_{i+1} = I(f_u, D_i)$

Here, U, in the expression $I(U, Di)$, has been replaced by f_u, which stands for some constituent (not necessarily proper) subpart of an utterance that can be given an interpretation effecting a change in the content of the discourse situation. As before, the expression $I(f_u, D_i)$ represents the speech act.

It might seem that, while representing the effects of subutterance speech act phenomena, (23) cannot be used to represent the effects of suprautterance phenomena. But this is false. Suprautterance phenomena do not manifest themselves at a single stroke, rather are possible only because of an accumulation of effects that culminate in the achievement of the whole. For example, in making a refutation a speaker must build an argument in a step-by-step fashion, each part of which must be introduced to the discourse situation via a speech act of a "lesser" type. To take a simple-minded example, consider the following:

(24) *You have stated that $2+2=3$. But take any two individual objects and any other two individual objects and place them in a row. Then count them, say, from left to right. What do you get? Not 3 but 4. Therefore, $2+2$ cannot equal 3.*

Though a thorough analysis of this text is beyond the scope of this section, and transcends a theory of speech acts as well, it should be obvious that the individual utterances in (24) each serve to contribute to a focused goal. The command *take any two objects...* is a request to the addressee to construct a hypothetical situation-type having certain properties. Later imperatives similarly request that operations be performed on the hypothetical situation-type, with certain clear results. The question *What do you get?* is not literal, but serves to underscore the result of the operation: the answer is the evidence needed to defeat the premise.

Each utterance up to that point is a necessary but insufficient part of the whole refutation. Each can be regarded as establishing some of the preconditions (in the discourse situation) that must obtain before a refutation can be effected. But, while in one sense the whole of (24) is the refutation, only the penultimate utterance, which makes explicit the necessary contradiction, completes the refutation, and so can be viewed as the constituent (f_u) that effects the speech act.

The crucial point is that the condition of the discourse situation — its content — is the co-determining factor enabling a speech act to be achieved. If the preconditions for a speech act are met, a single utterance, or its subpart, can trigger the whole effect. Any theory that encompasses speech act phenomena must be sensitive to the interaction of single constituents with the current state of the discourse situation.

1.4. DESIDERATA FOR A THEORY OF SPEECH ACTS

It is the goal of this work to account for the production of speech acts through the interaction of utterance interpretation and discourse situation content. The theory developed is not proposed as a final solution, but as a first-attempt solution upon which to build, hence the approach is straightforward.

However, this theory, indeed any theory, should be informed both by the data of actual discourse and by the pretheoretic features that should be part of any formal system. Some of these are given in the following list:

(25) **Desiderata**: Any complete theory of speech acts should be
- (i.) formal: giving explanations and making predictions;
- (ii.) capable of assigning multiple speech act interpretations to an utterance;
- (iii.) capable of capturing sub-utterance as well as supra-utterance phenomena;
- (iv.) explicit about the kinds of inferencing it requires and the rules that govern such inferencing;
- (v.) computationally feasible (utilizing, as much as possible, simple mechanisms);
- (vi.) specific about the role of extra-theoretic information or processes in accounting for speech act interpretation;
- (vii.) capable of representing and utilizing contextual information in giving derivations for speech acts;
- (viii.) sensitive to the role of non-verbal and prosodic information in discourse;
- (ix.) flexible enough to account for indirect as well as direct speech acts; and
- (x.) generalizable to situations involving multiple speakers and multiple addressees.

It goes without saying that no traditional speech act theory satisfies these criteria. It is hoped that the theory presented in the following chapters will accommodate most, if not all, of the points in this list.

CHAPTER 2   SPEECH ACT TYPES

2.0.   INTRODUCTION

This chapter discusses two assumptions that are crucial to the theory developed in this work. The first assumption is that the component of intentionality that is part of traditional speech act theories need not be represented directly in order to account for the phenomena of speech acts in discourse. It is argued that the range of possible speaker intentions, vis-a-vis a discourse situation, is strictly delimited by the rules governing moves in discourse and constraints on the end-states that utterances can effect, hence can be pragmatically and semantically determined. The second assumption is that part of the competence of individual speakers consists of having an inventory of <u>speech act types</u>, which encode not only the effects of speech acts on discourse situations but also the preconditions that enable speech acts to occur. These speech act types consist, principally, of propositions giving relationships among speaker, addressee, and interpretations of utterance constituents, which together represent the meaning of an utterance in a particular situation; and of conditions on the discourse situation in which they are used.

2.1. EFFECT AND INTENTIONALITY

A word should be addressed, at this point, to the question of utterance effect, especially as this problem has a long history in the speech acts literature. The traditional distinction of effects due to linguistics causes was articulated in Austin (1962) as a trichotomy: locutionary, illocutionary, and perlocutionary. Austin's locutionary act encompasses several phenomena including the production of sounds, the production of words, and the production of constituents with a sense and reference. His illocutionary act consists of the use of the locutionary act in saying something, that is, in performing one of the functions of language. And his perlocutionary act represents the effects, both intended and unintended, that result from saying something.

To use a hackneyed example, if a utters the words *It is hot* to b, intending thereby to get b to open a window, and b, in fact, opens a door, we can make the following distinctions:

(26)   i.   The locutionary act consists of a's speaking the words *It is hot*, where *it* refers to the conditions of the immediate environment, as perceived by a, and *hot* refers to air temperature.

      ii.   The illocutionary acts consist of a's representing his condition of being hot to b (viz. <u>asserting</u> that he is hot) and <u>requesting</u> that b act so as to ameliorate his condition; in short, of a's indirectly asking b to make it cooler.

      iii.   The perlocutionary act consists of b's opening a door as a result of being informed of a's discomfort. (And perhaps, also, a's feeling of relief, physically from the heat, and psychologically, because his misfired intention did not appreciably affect the result.)

Yet, if we examine this, and other examples, more closely, it is clear that the intended distinctions do not have clear boundaries separating them.[1]

To begin with the locutionary-illocutionary boundary, we encounter problems when we try to distinguish the mere recognition of the sense and reference of the words used from the effects produced by recognizing the speaker's intention in using a particular sense and reference. Part of this problem is due to the tacit assumption (made by Austin, and others) that words have senses and references independent of use, so that in recognizing a word — a parsing of a string of phonemes

— one automatically recognizes the other lexical features of the word, including its sense and reference (or, for those who believe that certain syntactic structures, or co-occurrence with other lexical items, determines sense and reference, its possible senses and references). But this is clearly false. Recognizing a referent correctly requires that we recognize the speaker's intentions. For example, the definite referring expression

> (27) *the first president of the United States*

might be used to refer to

> (28) George Washington

or to

> (29) George Washington, from the time he was 56 until he was 64

or to

> (30) anyone who fits the description *first president of the United States* (perhaps not George, if new historical data is unearthed)

or to

> (31) Chester Ludlow (who is playing George Washington in a local theatrical production).

Finding either some individual to substitute for (27), or some representation of an individual to satisfy the description in (27), requires that we divine the speaker's intention, especially if we believe that the speaker had alternative ways of expressing himself.

Part of the knowledge we must bring to bear in deducing the meaning behind the use of these words is the knowledge that in the vast majority of the situations in which we have heard (27) used, we have been correct in assuming that the speaker in those situations would have accepted (28) as the name of the referent. But we must also know that the ultimate resolution of the question of intended meaning of an expression like (27) depends on the circumstances of the situation in which it is used, specifically, on the types of changes to the discourse situation that could result from its use.

For example, while (28) - (31) represent more or less textbook kinds of uses of (27) as a referring expression, occurrences of (27) can have other functions, as in the dialogue below.

(32)   a: *The second president of the United States was known as the father of his country.*
       b: *The first president of the United States.*

In this instance, b's use of (27) has little or nothing to do with its conventional interpretation, rather can be given an interpretation because of the context in which it occurs, and because we recognize (32) to be a type of discourse situation which allows certain kinds of transformations of content. Indeed, it is not the whole expression but only the second word which serves to focus the speaker's intentions. Furthermore, it is not clear what the sense of the words in b's response should be. Is it part of the sense of these words that they be recognizable as words, in particular, as the same words — save one, the correction — that a just used? Without belaboring this point it should be obvious that there is no facile way of giving the neutral sense(s) of words, just as there is no way of giving a concrete referent for a referring expression independent of its context of use.

At the other boundary, between the illocutionary and perlocutionary, we encounter problems in delimiting the effects that a speaker can intend. We might want to allow the use of a sentence such as

(33)   *I'm going to shoot you.*

to constitute a threat or a warning (under appropriate circumstances), but not a "scaring." Even if a speaker uses (33) with the hope and intention that the addressee be frightened, and even if that design is realized in every detail, we are reluctant to attribute the addressee's becoming frightened to some immediate effect of interpretation. Upon hearing (33), if an addressee were not frightened, though he understood (33) as a threat, we could not say that he failed to interpret it correctly. If, on the other hand, he did not recognize that (33) could be a threat, but became frightened because, say, he saw a gun pointed at him, we would say that he failed to interpret the utterance correctly.

What we must do is separate the effects that arise as a result of general inferences that can be drawn about situations — such as the inference that a situation in which someone threatens you with a gun can lead to a situation in which you are dead — from the effects that arise as a result of inferences that are specific to discourse situations.[2]

As an example of some specific effects, consider the difference in status of statements (in general), and responses (answers) to questions. At any point in a discourse a speaker can make a statement, for instance, an assertion, and expect his interlocutors to attribute a belief in the assertion to him. If he later asserts something that appears to entail the contradiction of his earlier assertion, his interlocutors might point this out as contradictory or inconsistent. But while the speaker is apparently responsible for maintaining a belief in his assertion (at least for the purposes of the discourse situation), his interlocutors are not. It is neither odd or inconsistent for two participants in a discourse situation to make contradictory assertions: we attribute belief in one proposition to one of them, and belief in the opposite to the other. The semiotic covenant is not strained by these circumstances. But in question-answer pairs the situation is quite different. If a sincerely asks b a question (a request for information), and b sincerely responds with a statement, both a and b are committed to a belief in the response, at least for the purposes of the discourse situation. If a is dissatisfied or mistrustful of b's response, he is responsible for making his reservations known, or for maintaining a charade in which he acts as though he fully accepts b's response; certainly, he can expect b to act as though he (a) believes the response.

We might distinguish the types of effects here by saying that in the first case the speaker asserts a proposition, in the second that the speaker (respondent) informs his interlocutor of a proposition. In an act of assertion a speaker goes on record as believing the proposition asserted; in an act of informing, both the speaker and the addressee(s) go on record as believing the proposition.

Now, in actual discourse situations, a statement can be taken either way by the addressee. That is, the addressee can either believe the proposition stated or not — an effect which is outside the control of the speaker, hence solely perlocutionary. But in certain types of discourse situations (e.g., upon receiving an answer to a question) the addressee must behave as though he does believe the stated proposition, or risk introducing unexpected incoherence. Compare the following (where we assume both a and b to be speaking sincerely, and to be in the same time-zone):

(34) a: *I have to leave at six o'clock. What time is it?*
    b: *Three o'clock.*
    a: *Since it's three o'clock, I can stay.*

(35) a: *I have to leave at six o'clock. What time is it?*
b: *Three o'clock.*
a: *Since it's six o'clock, I can't stay.*

Whether b believes a's first statement or not, b has no reason to doubt that a believes it. After b's response to a's question, b has every reason to expect a to act as though he believed it was three o'clock. In dialogue (35), b might respond by saying *I said it was three o'clock, not six.* Unless a misheard b, a's final statement is incoherent.

At issue here is not whether a could make the response in (35) — clearly, he could — but, rather, what can count as a legitimate (coherent) response under the assumption of cooperation. If b were to ask *What do you mean?*, after hearing a's response, a could not reply, *I expected you to be able to understand* (assuming that there are no other conditions of the discourse situation that could be exploited for an interpretation). If there is an explanation that is supported by a's understanding of the discourse situation, but not b's, then a has an obligation to introduce the information necessary to bring b's understanding into conformity with his. In short, a does not have license to make statements that are understandable only in the context of some private model of the discourse situation, though that may best serve his intentions.[3]

Nevertheless, it is only through our private models that the discourse situation can be manipulated. Our understanding of an utterance will conform to that of our interlocutor only to the extent that we share rules of interpretation and, more to the point, an understanding of the discourse situation, that is, the relevant context of utterance interpretation. So a general constraint on discourse situations must be the constraint imposed by the ethereal nature of speech and by the human systems that process it: the actual discourse situation will be the intersection of the set of facts that are remembered by and in focus for each participant. This is a constraint of <u>congruence</u> of models, and it serves to limit the extent of speaker intention.

As in the case of locutionary-illocutionary distinctions, which seemed to grow fuzzy when the problem of neutral meaning (sense/reference) was raised, illocutionary-perlocutionary distinctions blur under the constraints of some discourse situations.

The questions that these points introduce turn on the role of speaker intention and the extent to which recognition of speaker intention is to be regarded as a reflex of the linguistic act of interpretation of utterance meaning. Traditionally, intention and meaning merge in illocutionary acts. While it is difficult to find a straightforward definition of an illocutionary act in the speech acts literature, the following paraphrase of Searle (1969:48ff) serves as a point of departure:

> (36) A **Speech Act** is the use of an utterance directed at an addressee in the service of a set of intentions, namely,
>
> i. the intention to produce a certain illocutionary effect in the addressee;
>
> ii. the intention to produce this effect by getting the addressee to recognize the intention to produce the effect; and
>
> iii. the intention to produce this recognition by means of the addressee's knowledge of the rules governing the utterance.

Here *speech act* can be understood as *illocutionary act*, that aspect of the utterance that produces *illocutionary* effects. Illocutionary effects are related to intentions, which are realized in their recognition. Recognition of intention, in turn, is affected by rules governing the utterance.

This definition does nothing to disentangle speaker intention from effect, indeed, it binds the two tightly together. But this need not involve us in the dilemma that the only means of revealing intentions is to have them recognized. The key constraint in (36) seems to be in part (iii.): the utterance is rule-governed.

Searle gives examples of the kinds of rules he has in mind in his felicity conditions (preparatory, sincerity, propositional content, and essential), but there are many circumstances that can go beyond these. To take a classical performative as an example, the rules governing the felicitous use of

> (37) *I declare this court to be in session.*

require, among other things, that the speaker be legally empowered to open court, that the speaker be in (his/her own) court at the time of utterance, that certain officers of the court be in station, etc., before (37) can be understood as effecting the commencement of a legal proceeding. Once these conditions obtain, the uttering of (37) achieves its goal.

The effects of the use of (27) can be recast in a similar light. Presumably, the effect of having an addressee think of George Washington when a speaker uses (27) to refer to George Washington is possible only because the addressee recognizes that, in the circumstances of its use, the inference from (27) to George Washington is not blocked. Similarly, the effect of the use of (27) by b in (32), which can be interpreted as correcting a — as well as informing a of an apparent error;

accepting a's statement with the amended phrase; requesting a response from a; and continuing the conversation, generally — is possible only because the addressee recognizes that the inference from (27) to George Washington _is_ blocked. Put another way, the inference that the speaker means to refer to George Washington does not result in inconsistencies in the discourse situation in the first case, but does in the second.

What is achieved in these cases is constrained by what can be achieved given the circumstances of utterance use. This is an aspect of discourse situations that goes beyond the locutionary-illocutionary-perlocutionary distinction.

This position can be summarized as a general principle of discourse situations:

> (38) **Constraint on Intention**
> A speaker can intend to achieve only those effects that are legitimately sanctioned by the rules of the discourse situation.

This constraint is designed to be interpreted positively, not negatively. A paraphrase would be: discourse states can be brought about directly as a result of the existence of rules that enable them, and only those states are the legitimate objects of speaker intention. It would be a misinterpretation to understand (38) as denying that a speaker can have any number of intentions in mind when issuing an utterance.

In effect, (38) relativizes speaker intention to a discourse situation, where a speaker's possible moves are constrained by the "constitutive" (Searle (1969:33ff)) rules of discourse. To use a traditional example, an opponent at chess can move a knight with the intention of attacking a piece, protecting a piece, or blocking or enabling a future move, or stalling for time, or wasting a move, etc., but not with the intention of requesting an adjournment, or signalling that he is hungry, or causing us to become frightened, etc., at least within the scope of the game of chess. Of course, an opponent might move his knight with the intention, say, of requesting an adjournment, and might be understood by us as thereby making such a request, but if this communication succeeds, it is because of inferences that we make that are outside the scope of the game of chess — due, perhaps, to our knowledge of our opponent's playing habits, or the deadlocked state of the game.

Similarly, within a discourse situation a speaker might use (33) to threaten, or promise, or predict, or warn, but not to frighten (directly), because there is no rule within the scope of discourse situations that accommodates "frightenings." When we encounter an utterance like (33), for the purposes of the discourse situation, we can interpret it to be intended to achieve any of the legitimate endstates that can be achieved in a discourse situation and no others. It is quite another matter what we do with the information we derive after giving the utterance its interpretation. If (33) is used as a warning we may be thankful and take defensive action; if as a prediction, we may choose to disregard it entirely; if as a threat, we may indeed become frightened.

The constraint on intention is meaningful only if we have a well-defined set of rules that govern moves in a discourse situation, and a well-defined set of end-states that can be achieved by the use of utterances. If these obtain it should be possible to make speaker intention a reflex of utterance interpretation.

2.2. MOVES IN DISCOURSE SITUATIONS

It is not a goal of this work to list exhaustively the moves that can occur in discourse situations. However, it is worth considering the kinds of moves that would have to be included in any complete list and their relationship to speech act phenomena.

Two points should be made at the outset. First, while there are, no doubt, many moves that are common to all discourse situations, the rules governing moves are greatly variable across cultures and even within cultural groups. Work in ethnomethodology and sociolinguistics during the past fifteen years has established this rather convincingly (cf. Philips (1976), Dore & McDermott (to appear), Goody (1972), Gumperz (1977a, b), and Schiffrin (1977)). Hence we should be aware that any particular set of rules we might adopt, tacitly or overtly, will probably reflect our own dialect's, perhaps even idiolect's, patterns. No theory should be dependent on one fixed set of rules, but should accommodate any possible set. Second, moves effect changes in the discourse situation not only at the level of the text, that is, not only in terms of the information explicitly expressed by the utterance, but also at the level of the move itself. An assertion can introduce information about the object of a speaker's beliefs, but it can also serve to initiate an encounter, or continue or terminate a conversation, or request a response, or mitigate an undesired state that currently obtains, or take a turn. These hypertactic functions are among the most common and obvious effects of the use of utterances, and, except in the work of a few authors, among the most ignored (cf. Labov and Fanshel (1977), Dore (1977), and especially Goffman (1980)). A theory of speech acts should not overlook the role of these moves in framing the interpretations given to utterances.

Recall that the minimum requirements for a discourse situation are given in the framing facts of the situation, as listed in (8). These facts might be regarded as giving a state description at the time of an initial utterance. But they do not capture the interactive dynamism of a discourse situation, and so do not fully capture the information that participants share. A more complete model of the gross structure of a two-person discourse situation might be given as the finite state network in Figure 1.

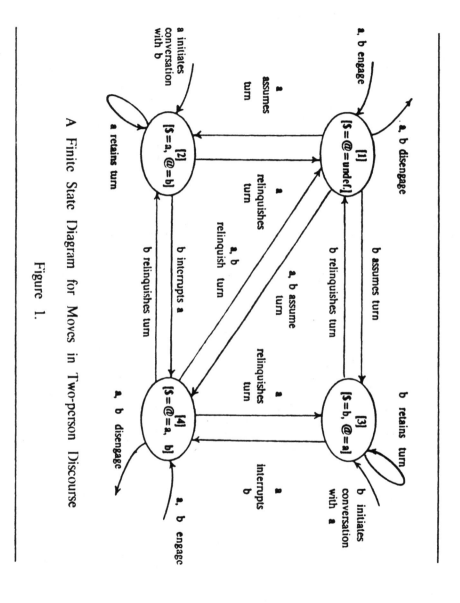

A Finite State Diagram for Moves in Two-person Discourse

Figure 1.

This representation is highly idealized, of course, and omits many of the details of face-to-face conversational interaction. For example, there are a number of crucial steps between any actual physical encounter and the decision to enter into a discourse situation, all of which are collected under the *a, b engage* step here. Furthermore, while there is provision here for one-sided initiation of conversation, there is none for one-sided withdrawal. No doubt other flaws could be listed. However, Figure 1 does serve to illustrate the kind of information that two individuals must share if they are to negotiate a path through a conversational encounter.

Here, each arrow represents a move that has consequences for the discourse situation. Sometimes an arrow corresponds to making an utterance, as when one person interrupts another, or one person takes a turn; and sometimes an arrow corresponds to the absence of action, as when one person stops talking, relinquishing a turn. The effects of moves are given, simply, in terms of changes to the principal framing facts, namely, the identity of the speaker and addressee; but moves combine with other facts in the discourse situation to effect more comprehensive changes, and, indeed, to constrain speech act interpretation.

The interaction of moves at this level and other information about the interpretation of utterances can be used to circumscribe speaker intentions. This can be given as a series of implications, some of which might be as follows:[4]

(39) a. making an assertion then relinquishing a turn
⇒ requesting addressee to take turn and comment
b. making an assertion then retaining turn
⇒ requesting interlocutor not to interrupt
c. asking a question then relinquishing turn
⇒ requesting addressee to take turn and answer
d. asking a question then retaining turn
⇒ requesting interlocutor not to interrupt and either promising to answer question or promising to elaborate question
e. interrupting with backchannel expression[5] then relinquishing turn
⇒ requesting addressee to retain turn and informing addressee that utterance is accepted
f. assuming turn after former speaker has made an assertion and relinquished turn
⇒ promising to comment on assertion (or ask for

clarification)

g. assuming turn after former speaker has asked a
question and relinquished turn
$\Rightarrow$ promising to answer question or state equivocation
(or ask for clarification)

h. producing a fragmentary utterance[6] then relinquishing
turn
$\Rightarrow$ requesting interlocutor to take turn

i. uttering closing expressive then relinquishing turn
$\Rightarrow$ requesting interlocutor to disengage

j. uttering salutatory expressive then relinquishing turn
$\Rightarrow$ requesting interlocutor to engage in conversation

k. assuming turn and uttering salutatory expressive (after
former speaker has uttered salutatory expressive) then
relinquishing turn
$\Rightarrow$ informing addressee of willingness to engage in
conversation and requesting addressee to assume
turn

l. answering question and relinquishing turn
$\Rightarrow$ requesting interlocutor to take turn and
acknowledge or comment or answer

m. refusing to assume turn (after former speaker has
uttered salutatory expressive and relinquished turn)
$\Rightarrow$ requesting interlocutor to disengage

n. refusing to assume turn (after former speaker has
answered question or made assertion and relinquished
turn)
$\Rightarrow$ requesting further answer or expressing
dissatisfaction with answer

As with the finite state diagram above, this list omits many details
and is not comprehensive. It is intended only as an example of the kinds
of relationships that the actions of participants in a discourse situation
entail. But even this limited idealization can help us better understand
the structure of conversational interaction.

Consider the differences in the following two dialogues[7] as an
example:

(40)   [a examining a long manuscript]
a: i.) *Who's gonna type this all for you?*
b: ii.) *Some poor lady I hope.*
iii.) *I did have a typist but it's been a long time since I talked to her.*
iv.) *I could type it myself, see.*
v.) *I've got a great IBM typewriter.*
vi.) *Its only flaw is that it doesn't know how to type by itself.*
vii.) [b pointing to manuscript]   *Isn't it exciting?*
viii.) *No.*
a: ix.) *Yeah.*

(41)   [a examining long manuscript]
a: i.) *Who's gonna type this all for you?*
b: ii.) *Some poor lady I hope.*
iii.) [pause]
iv.) *I did have a typist but it's been a long time since I talked to her.*
v.) [pause]
vi.) *I could type it myself, see.*
vii.) [pause]
viii.) *I've got a great IBM typewriter.*
ix.) [pause]
x.) *Its only flaw is that it doesn't know how to type by itself.*
xi.) [pause]
xii.) [b pointing to manuscript]   *Isn't it exciting?*
xiii.) [pause]
xiv.) *No.*
a: xv.) *Yeah.*

The words spoken in (40) and (41) are the same; their performance is quite different. In (40) we have b answering a's question with a long elaboration that seems designed to amuse; it is fluid and fluent. In (41) we sense first awkwardness, then desperation, and finally, some sardonic resolution.

If we were to describe the dialogues in terms of the moves made and their implications, without, for the moment, considering the content of the utterances, we might derive the following structures:

(42) (corresponding to (40))

i.) <
    a .initiates conversation

    a asks question
       + $\Rightarrow$ a requests b to assume turn and answer
    a relinquishes turn
       + $\Rightarrow$ b promises to answer question or state
                       equivocation or ask for clarification

ii.) <
    b assumes turn

    b answers question
       + $\Rightarrow$ b requests a not to interrupt
    b retains turn

iii.) <
    b makes assertion (elaboration of answer)
       + $\Rightarrow$ b requests a not to interrupt
    b retains turn

iv.) <
    b makes assertion
       + $\Rightarrow$ b requests a not to interrupt
    b retains turn

v.) <
    b makes assertion
       + $\Rightarrow$ b requests a not to interrupt
    b retains turn

vi.) <
    b makes assertion
       + $\Rightarrow$ b requests a not to interrupt
    b retains turn

vii.) <
    b asks question
       + $\Rightarrow$ b requests a not to interrupt and
                       promises to answer question
    b retains turn

viii.) <
    b answers question (makes an assertion)
       + $\Rightarrow$ b requests a to assume turn and comment
    b relinquishes turn
       + $\Rightarrow$ a promises to comment on assertion or
                       ask for clarification

ix.) <
    a assumes turn

    a makes comment/answer

(43)   (corresponding to (41))

a initiates conversation

i.) ⟨

a asks question
+   ⟹ a requests b to assume turn and answer

a relinquishes turn
+   ⟹ ·b promises to answer question or state
equivocation or ask for clarification

b assumes turn

ii.) ⟨

b answers question
+   ⟹ b requests a to assume turn and accept
or comment on answer

b relinquishes turn

iii.) ⟨   +   ⟹ a requests elaboration or expresses
dissatisfaction

a refuses turn

b assumes turn

iv.) ⟨

b makes assertion
+   ⟹ b requests a to assume turn and make
comment

b relinquishes turn

v.) ⟨   +   ⟹ a requests elaboration or expresses
dissatisfaction

a refuses turn

b assumes turn

vi.) ⟨

b makes assertion
+   ⟹ b requests a to assume turn and make
comment

b relinquishes turn

vii.) ⟨   +   ⟹ a requests elaboration or expresses
dissatisfaction

a refuses turn

b assumes turn

viii.) ⟨

b makes assertion
+   ⟹ b requests a to assume turn and make
comment

b relinquishes turn

ix.) ⟨   +   ⟹ a requests elaboration or expresses
dissatisfaction

a refuses turn

x.) <
 b assumes turn

 b makes assertion
  +   ⟹ b requests a to assume turn and make
       comment

xi.) <
 b relinquishes turn
  +   ⟹ a requests elaboration or expresses
       dissatisfaction

 a refuses turn

xii.) <
 b assumes turn

 b asks question
  +   ⟹ b requests a to assume turn and answer
       question

xiii.) <
 b relinquishes turn
  +   ⟹ a requests clarification or refuses to
       accept question

 a refuses turn

xiv.) <
 b assumes turn

 b makes assertion (answers question)
  +   ⟹ b requests a to assume turn and make
       comment

 b relinquishes turn
  +   ⟹ a promises to comment on assertion or
       ask for clarification

xv.) <
 a assumes turn

 a makes assertion

Even with just this skeletal account we can see dramatic differences. (40/42) is a model of cooperation and orderly procedure; (41/43) is a long struggle reflecting either serious miscommunication or deliberate non-cooperation by a. In this latter case, b's problem is to plan utterances and moves that will either satisfy a's requests or persuade a to take a turn.[8] Beginning with more subtle attempts to get a to respond, and failing, b eventually asks an overt question. Only then does a resume the dialogue.

If we couple to this account of the dialogues the information we obtain by considering the semantic content of the utterances, a new level of interpretation emerges. For example, b's question, which calls most directly for a response at one level, can be regarded as expressing an ironic reflection on the entire discourse situation at another: the situation is decidedly not exciting, as b's preemptive answer confesses.

A better way of putting this is that we are capable of giving the utterances an interpretation at other levels because of our understanding of the interaction of the content of the utterances and the roles the utterances play. The move that the utterance represents constrains the speech act it can perform, which, in turn, constrains how its content is to be interpreted in the discourse situation.

Just as it was possible to express the effects of moves in terms of changes in the state of the discourse situation, so, too, we can express the effects of speech acts in terms of specific changes — at the level of the semantic structure of the discourse — which they effect. In order to be more precise, we must consider in detail the end- states that speech acts achieve.

2.3. SOME SPEECH ACT TYPES[9]

At the outset of our exploration of the effects of speech acts we should remind ourselves that we are concerned with effects and conditions vis-a-vis the discourse situation and not vis-a-vis the other situations that might embed the discourse situation. An actor playing a part can make assertions, ask questions, contract obligations (e.g., make promises), etc., without believing the substance of his remarks, or sincerely intending to fulfill his pledges. It would be wrong to designate the effect of the actor's utterances in these cases as *deceptively assert* or *insincerely promise.* To do so would be to evaluate the utterances in terms of the real world circumstances of the actor as speaker and us or other actors as addressees. Rather, we must evaluate the utterances relative to the discourse situation that is being dramatized, and we must understand their type in terms of the changes that they can effect in that discourse situation.

In non-fictional discourse situations we find ourselves sometimes in the position of being actors. We make statements that we don't believe or commitments that we don't intend to fulfill. Still, relative to the discourse situation we behave as though we were sincere and if we depart from the "fiction" we risk incoherence. Our utterances change the discourse situation in precise ways, regardless of our secret intentions; as long as we participate we are constrained both by the actual state of the discourse situation and by the effects of our utterances.

In order to speak precisely about the effects of utterances on discourse situations, we need a device to capture the (partial) information that speech acts add to discourse situations and to express the (partial) constraints on the discourse situations in which speech acts of a certain type can take place. That device is a <u>speech act type</u>.

Formally, a speech act type can be regarded as a partial mapping between discourse situations. A given speech act type, applied to a particular discourse situation, in which the variables of the speech act type are defined and the conditions of the speech act type are met, returns a new discourse situation. Specifically, it returns a new discourse situation containing a finite number of new facts and all the facts of the old discourse situation unchanged except where specified in its conditions.

In practice, we can write speech act types as a list of propositions about the discourse situation, some of which give the constraints on the state of the discourse situation at the time of interpretation and some, the constraints on the discourse situation after the speech act has been effected. This is better explicated via a concrete illustration.

In section 2.1, the point was made that, depending on when it occurs in a discourse situation, a simple statement might be regarded as having very different effects, distinguished as an assert and an inform act. We might represent these two types as follows:

(44) ASSERT φ (D_i)
  1: $d(\underline{say}, \$, \varphi) = 1$
  2: $d(\underline{believe}, \$, \varphi) = 1$
  where φ is a proposition
  and 1, 2 $\in D_{i+1}$

(45) INFORM φ (D_i)
  1: $d(\underline{say}, \$, \varphi) = 1$
  2: $d(\underline{believe}, \$, \varphi) = 1$
  3: $d(\underline{believe}, @, \varphi) = 1$
  where φ is a proposition
  and 1, 2, 3 $\in D_{i+1}$

(44) and (45) can be regarded as the speech act types associated, respectively, with asserting or informing an addressee of a proposition. D_i indicates that the act is performed at the discourse time i, where the discourse situation is in state D_i, which can be thought of, further, as the set of facts of the discourse situation. The numbers *1, 2, 3*, etc., serve as indices to specific propositions. The condition, utilizing the indices, indicates that the propositions are to be considered part of the discourse situation at the next incrementation of discourse time.

These two examples illustrate the general structure of speech act types. The type has a name (e.g., ASSERT φ); a list of propositions that express a relationship among the speaker, addressee, and aspects of the utterance, vis-a-vis the discourse situation; and some conditions reflecting constraints on the constituency of the propositions themselves, and on the content of the discourse situation.

An interpretation of the information in a speech act type, for example, (44) might be given as follows:

"If a speaker uses an utterance (or utterance constituent) as an assertion, then the utterance (or utterance constituent) must be ·interpretable as a representation (i.e., as expressing a proposition), φ, and its effect is to introduce the two propositions *speaker says (that)* φ and *speaker believes (that)* φ into the discourse situation."

Every actual assertion would have all the variables in the speech act type replaced by specific individuals ($ and @) and propositions (φ). But the effect of the assertion *qua* assertion would be no more or less than the addition, to the discourse situation, of the two propositions that the particular speaker says and believes the particular proposition represented by the utterance.

There are several other points about speech act types that should be made at this juncture.

First, the speech act types given here and elsewhere in this thesis are not to be regarded as encapsulations of a speech act theory. They are merely mappings that encode information about states of discourse situations, and represent one facet of a complete theory. Without them speech act interpretation would be impossible, but outside the context of a complex interpretation process, they are meaningless.

Second, the speech act types used in this thesis are to be taken seriously as illustrations of actual speech act types, but, if possible, not taken seriously in all their details. It is well beyond the scope of this dissertation accurately to define and justify even three or four speech act types, let alone the score or so that actually appear here. So, while the speech act types are based on information that comes from discussions of the relevant speech act phenomena that have appeared in the speech acts literature, and on considerations of the particular needs of the current theory, they are incomplete and uncertifiable. Still, they have an important role to play, and should be accepted, tentatively, for expository purposes.

Third, in the speech act types, and in many other aspects of the theory where propositions are given, there is a deliberate departure from some of the conventions now established in situation semantics, largely in the direction of simplification. Since we are concerned with the state of a discourse situation in the here and now of an actual interaction, we can do without indices for place and time on each situation-type expression. To be sure, such indexical reference is indispensible in giving the interpretation of the propositions that may be expressed by the words of an utterance, but that is not the primary concern of a theory that focuses on giving the propositions associated with the use of utterances as speech acts. The propositions determined by the words of the utterance are one step removed from the propositions that derive from the speech act interpretation of the utterance's use.

Fourth, we find in (44) and (45) the first instances of the distinction, mentioned earlier and maintained in later sections, in types of primitive relations. The primitive relations that are based on the illocutionary mode in which utterances are used are underlined to distinguish them from other relations that arise only in discourse situations and should not be confused with glosses of English words except to the extent that the particular meaning of one of these primitives might be subsumed under that of some similar English word. In the case of (44) and (45), <u>say</u> expresses the relationship that obtains between an individual and some proposition when that individual has spoken an utterance whose interpretation gives that proposition. **Believe** expresses the relationship that obtains between an individual and a proposition, and, actually, is identical to the **believe** relation discussed in presenting the framing facts of the discourse situation.

Finally, in choosing to use belief (even in a highly constrained way) as a primitive in the constatives, I have made a philosophical and ontological commitment that reverberates throughout the theory. I am saying, in a sense, that what can be known about an interlocutor's apparent beliefs is the basis of understanding the meaning of the propositions he expresses. This, of course, might be gravely misoriented — the basis of understanding the propositions expressed might lie in perceptions, in (other) knowledge, or in other (perhaps simpler) illocutionary relationships, such as saying. However, it would be the topic of yet another thesis to explore this problem in the detail it deserves; and it is necessary for the theory that some position be taken. Some of the consequences of this position are examined in later chapters.

While both ASSERT φ and INFORM φ have the effect only of adding propositions to the discourse situation, not all constatives have this characteristic. For example, a retraction or a self-contradiction has the effect of deleting propositions from the discourse situation, as well. These types might be given as follows:

(46)   RETRACT φ (D_i)
   1: $d(\underline{say},\ \$,\ \varphi)\ =\ 1$
   2: $d(\underline{say},\ \$,\ \psi)\ =\ 1$
   3: $d(\underline{believe},\ \$,\ \psi)\ =\ 1$
   4: $d(\underline{believe},\ \$,\ \varphi)\ =\ 1$
   5: $d(\underline{believe},\ \$,\ \varphi)\ =\ 0$
      where φ, ψ are propositions
      s. t. $\psi\ \Rightarrow\ d(\underline{believe},\ \$,\ \varphi)\ =\ 0$,
      and 1, 4 $\in\ D_i,\ \notin\ D_{i+1}$

$$\text{and } 2, 3, 5 \in D_{i+1}$$

(47) (SELF-) CONTRADICT φ (D_i)

1: $d(\underline{say}, \$, \varphi) = 1$
2: $d(\underline{say}, \$, \psi) = 1$
3: $d(\underline{believe}, \$, \varphi) = 1$
4: $d(\underline{believe}, \$, \psi) = 1$

where φ, ψ are propositions such that $\psi \Rightarrow$ NOT φ,
and $1, 3 \in D_i$, $\notin D_{i+1}$
and $2, 4 \in D_{i+1}$

The condition of interest in (46) is that the speaker's belief in a proposition must be part of the discourse situation at the time of retraction, and that the effect of the retraction is to remove that belief from the discourse situation. This is achieved by uttering something that indicates that the speaker is specifically focusing on a proposition involving his beliefs, which entails that the proposition given by φ is no longer held. (Typically, this is done by uttering something like, *I don't think φ anymore*, or *I've changed my mind on φ*, etc.) Note that a retraction does not necessarily commit the speaker to a belief in NOT φ.

The condition of interest in (47) involves the removal from the discourse situation of the two propositions containing φ by the uttering of ψ, which entails NOT φ. Here the speaker is committed to a belief in ψ, hence, indirectly, in NOT φ.

Both speech act types contain partial descriptions that match the description for the speech act type ASSERT ψ, i.e., both contain the description for ASSERT ψ as a sub-part. In principle, there is no reason why the use of ψ as a retraction or self-contradiction should not also count as the assertion of ψ. Indeed, it may often be the case, where multiple addressees are involved, where interlocutors may have come and gone during the course of a conversation, that for some of the discourse situations (i.e., two person, speaker-addressee pairs) the use of ψ may not satisfy the preconditions necessary to be evaluated as a retraction or self-contradiction, but would still count as an assertion.

The four speech act types we have considered up to this point all involve the speaker (and sometimes the addressee) in **say** and **believe** relations. These are the principal relations in constatives of all types, where we are concerned with attribution of statement and belief. Note that it would be wrong to say that φ (a proposition representing a state of affairs) is ever made directly a part of any discourse situation. Rather, it is the speaker's stating and believing φ which is the fact of the discourse situation, from which we might choose to deduce putative facts of the world. For example. by asserting

(48) *It is hot.*

with reference to air temperature in the current situation, a speaker expresses a judgment that we could give in terms of the **say** and **believe** relations of an assertion. But the fact that it is hot is not thereby introduced to the discourse situation, and, indeed, it might not be hot. Even if we agree with the speaker's judgment, at most we can make our shared belief part of the discourse situation; the representation itself remains embedded in a relationship of belief.

For it to be hot, there must be a situation with type

(49) $s(\text{be-hot}) = 1$

(assuming **be-hot** to be a 0-place relation) which contains the discourse situation. The speaker's statement is true iff

(50) $(\exists s)$ s. t. $[s(\text{be-hot}) = 1 \text{ and } d \subseteq s \subseteq W]$.

The statement may be false with respect to the world-type, W (hence not a fact of the real world), but true with respect to some (fictional) situation which embeds the discourse situation.

When we consider the truth conditions of utterances we must distinguish among several domains of evaluation, the least of which is the discourse situation. Classically, the question of truth is the question of truth in the real world, but this is at once the most difficult of problems and the least interesting. It is most difficult because of the great limitations on our knowledge of events and states in space-time, and least interesting because most questions of fact that arise in human discourse involve questions of fact relative to some situation that is intended to be congruent with the real world, but which actually is a highly individual fictional world (reflecting not only the partial knowledge the individual has of his real world but also the misconceptions).

Our first concern in a theory of speech acts must be with the truth conditions of discourse situations. Only when these are clearly explicated can we consider the problems that arise when we evaluate the consequences of utterance interpretation, that was made relative to a discourse situation, in the scope of other situations. Some of the problems encountered in moving from discourse situations to other situations are discussed in Chapter 4, where several discourse situations are examined in detail, and the interaction of speech acts and truth conditions is more fully described.

The **say** and **believe** relations reflected in constatives of all types are the primitive relationships we are concerned with in understanding representations of states of affairs.[10] The **believe** relation reveals how a proposition is viewed: it can be regarded as true (*1*) for the purposes of the discourse situation, or false (*0*). The **say** relation reveals the status of the fact of the communication: it is introduced to the discourse situation via discourse as a representation. But, of course, not all speech acts are constatives, and not all the primitive relationships in discourse situations are expressible in terms of **say** and **believe** relations.

A large class of speech acts that involve the primitive relations **request** and **want** are the requestives, which include requests for information, permission, or action. For example, in asking a question, a speaker indicates that he wants an answer, α, which is constrained to be something whose interpretation, when added to the partial set of information represented by the presuppositions of the question, yields a complete proposition. Furthermore, the speaker specifically requests the addressee to supply an answer. But, in addition, by asking the question the speaker indicates that he, himself, does not know an answer and that he believes it is not the case that the addressee does not know an answer. A speech act type showing these effects might be given as follows:

(51) REQUEST INFORMATION (D_i)

1: $d(\underline{\text{want}}, \$, @, \langle\alpha, q(x)\rangle) = 1$
2: $d(\underline{\text{request}}, \$, @, \langle\alpha, q(x)\rangle) = 1$
3: $d(\underline{\text{know}}, \$, \langle\alpha, q(x)\rangle) = 0$
4: $d(\underline{\text{believe}}, \$, \varphi) = 0$

where α is a reply such that $\lambda x[q(x)] \, [[\alpha]]$
is a well-formed and complete expression,
where $\lambda x[q(x)]$ represents the partial information of
the presuppositions of the question,
and $\varphi := d(\underline{\text{know}}, @, \langle\alpha, q(x)\rangle) = 0$,
and 1, 2, 3, 4 $\in D_{i+1}$

The conditions under this type are not intended to represent the complete semantics of questions. There are great many truly difficult problems associated with the semantics of questions, which have supported a large body of literature (cf. for example the bibliography in Belnap and Steel (1976)). Nevertheless, for the discursive purposes of this present section, the conditions as given should suffice.

The **want** and **request** relations here are not glosses for corresponding English words. **Want** is not the intuitively two-place relationship given by *want*, but is a three-place relation that involves the speaker, the addressee, and some highly constrained proposition, represented here as a pair, α (an answer) and $q(x)$ (the set of propositions framing the question). A gloss might be given as "the speaker desires of the addressee that he provide an answer (α) that satisfies the question ($q(x)$)." Similarly, **request** is a three-place relation glossed as "the speaker requests of the addressee that he act in such a way as to provide an answer (α) that satisfies the question ($q(x)$)."

The essential constraint on α is that it be a reply — a signal of some kind, not necessarily verbal — that can be interpreted as supplying the missing information required to complete the set of incomplete propositions representing the presuppositions of the question. Here, and elsewhere, "[[ ]]" is used to indicate the interpretation of the expression enclosed. Naturally, such an interpretation can only be made relative to a time, a place, a particular discourse situation, etc., but for the sake of simplicity, these variables are suppressed.

In a request for permission, a speaker indicates that he wants a reply, α, whose interpretation has the effect of removing the prohibition presupposed in the request. More precisely, the speaker indicates that he wants the addressee to permit the performance of an action or the attainment of a state currently inhibited by the presence of a prohibition. Furthermore, the speaker specifically requests the addressee to grant permission, indicating, in addition, that the speaker believes the addressee has authority to grant permission, that the addressee will not necessarily deny the request, that the speaker believes that the prohibition exists, and that the speaker wants to perform the action or attain the state currently prohibited.

Though this involves a great deal of information, it should be possible to encode it all in a speech act type, as follows:

(52) REQUEST PERMISSION (for γ) (D_i)
   1: $d(\underline{\text{want}}, \$, @, \alpha) = 1$
   2: $d(\underline{\text{request}}, \$, @, \alpha) = 1$
   3: $d(\underline{\text{believe}}, \$, \varphi) = 0$
   4: $d(\underline{\text{believe}}, \$, \psi) = 0$
   5: $d(\underline{\text{believe}}, \$, \xi) = 1$
   6: $d(\underline{\text{want}}, \$, @, \gamma) = 1$
      where α is a reply
      s. t. $[d(\underline{\text{permit}}, @, \$, \gamma) = 1] \in [[\alpha]]$
      and γ is an action or a state,
      and $\varphi := d(\text{be-able-to-do}, @, \xi) = 0$,
      where $\xi := d(\underline{\text{permit}}, @, \$, \gamma) = 1$,

and $\psi := [d(\underline{permit}, @, \$, \gamma) = 0] \notin D_{i+n}, n \geq 1,$
and $\xi := d(exist, \beta) = 1,$
where $\beta := [[d(do, \$, \gamma) = 1] \gg$
$$d(suffer\text{-}neg.\text{-}conseq., \$) = 1],$$
and $1, 2, 3, 4, 5, 6 \in D_{i+1}$

This complex condition begins with the crucial clause, namely, that the granting of permission, to perform the desired action or attain the desired state, be part of the interpretation of the reply, α. The relation **do**, alone and in **be-able-to-do**, should be understood as meaning "act in such a way as to bring about."

Permit is a three-place relation that can be glossed (here) as "the addressee allows the speaker to act in such a way as to bring about γ." Exist can be understood as "be present in the discourse situation." In this case, it is the prohibition, β, that is present, where β stands for something like the proposition that acting to bring about γ leads to negative consequences for the actor. What those consequences are, and what constraints attend particular prohibitions in particular cases, cannot and need not be specified exhaustively in the speech act type. The symbol "$\gg$" here is designed to represent some causal connection, not (material) implication in a truth-functional sense.

The many facts encoded under the speech act type are designed to capture the relevant appropriacy conditions. Such conditions can tell us several things about the discourse situation, for example, that a felicitous request for permission can occur only in discourse situations where certain preconditions hold, and conversely, that if a request for permission is deemed to have been performed, the discourse situation must be characterized at least by the propositions expressed in the conditions. For example, if a regards b's utterance as a request for permission, a can know, for the purposes of the discourse situation, that b believes a prohibition exists which a has the power to remove.

In requesting permission the speaker requests that the addressee grant permission. We might be tempted to say that the speaker specifically requests that the addressee perform a speech act GRANT PERMISSION (for γ), i.e., that α (the reply) be such that the following holds:

(53)   GRANT PERMISSION (for γ) $\in \lambda x[SA(x, D_{i+1})] \alpha$,
where $SA(u, D_{i+1})$ gives the set of speech acts that the utterance u can perform in discourse situation D_{i+1}.

But this would too much restrict the possible responses, and misrepresent the speaker's desires: he wants permission from the addressee, not a speech act. In fact, the addressee might grant permission in a variety of ways not involving the use of speech, such as by gesturing, etc.

Nevertheless, there is a reciprocity in form between the speech act types for requesting and granting permission. In granting permission, the speaker says something which has the effect of removing a prohibition applying to the addressee. Furthermore, the speaker expresses his belief that he has authority to remove the prohibition and that it is not the case that the addressee does not want the prohibition removed. This might be given as follows:

$$(54) \quad \text{GRANT PERMISSION (for } \gamma) \ (D_i)$$

1: $d(\underline{permit}, \$, @, \gamma) = 1$
2: $d(\underline{exist}, \beta) = 1$
3: $d(\underline{believe}, \$, \varphi) = 1$
4: $d(\underline{believe}, \$, \psi) = 0$
   where γ is an action or a state,
   and $\beta := [[d(\underline{do}, @, \gamma) = 1]] \gg$
   $\qquad\qquad\qquad d(\underline{suffer\text{-}neg.\text{-}conseq.}, @) = 1]$,
   and $\varphi := d(\underline{be\text{-}able\text{-}to\text{-}do}, \$, \xi) = 1$,
   where $\xi := d(\underline{permit}, \$, @, \gamma) = 1$,
   and $\psi := d(\underline{want}, @, \$, \xi) = 0$,
   and $2 \in D_i, \notin D_{i+1}$,
   and $1, 3, 4 \in D_{i+1}$

Incidentally, we might give the speech act type for (54)'s opposite as follows:

$$(55) \quad \text{DENY PERMISSION (for } \gamma) \ (D_i)$$

1: $d(\underline{permit}, \$, @, \gamma) = 0$
2: $d(\underline{exist}, \beta) = 1$
3: $d(\underline{believe}, \$, \varphi) = 1$
   where γ is an action or a state,
   and $\beta := [[d(\underline{do}, @, \gamma) = 1]] \gg$
   $\qquad\qquad\qquad d(\underline{suffer\text{-}neg.\text{-}conseq.}, @) = 1]$,
   and $\varphi := d(\underline{be\text{-}able\text{-}to\text{-}do}, \$, \xi) = 1$,
   where $\xi := d(\underline{permit}, \$, @, \gamma) = 1$,
   and $2 \in D_i$,
   and $1, 2, 3 \in D_{i+1}$

REQUEST PERMISSION (for γ) and GRANT/DENY PERMISSION (for γ) exhibit the kind of interdependency of types that we find among many discourse pairs. In such cases the first speaker's act introduces or brings into focus a restricted set of facts which form a preferred context for the interpretation of the second speaker's reply. Among the distinguished facts in these permission cases are the identification of the desired act or state, γ, and the prohibition, β, and the explicit constraints on the interpretation of the reply, α.

The last requestive we will consider is a request for action. It is of interest because it is similar to some of the <u>directives</u> (e.g., imperatives which give orders) and introduces the notion of obligation, which, in turn, plays a role in the <u>commissives</u> (e.g., in promises). Requests for action come in a variety of forms. All of the following, for example, could be used as a request for action:

(56)   a. *(Please) Open the door (would you?)*
        b. *Would you mind opening the door?*
        c. *I think you should open the door.*

The difference between a request for action and a directive ordering an action (the difference in status of (56a.) under different conditions of the discourse situation) comes from the relationship between speaker and addressee. The addressee can deny the request with no consequences, but not the directive. Furthermore, the directive makes manifest the unequal relationship between speaker and addressee, encoding an "authority" clause much like the one under the permission cases above.

The speech act type for a request for action might be given as follows:

(57)   REQUEST ACTION (γ) (D_i)
      1: $d(\underline{want},\ \$,\ @,\ \varphi)\ =\ 1$
      2: $d(\underline{request},\ \$,\ @,\ \varphi)\ =\ 1$
      3: $d(\underline{believe},\ \$,\ \psi)\ =\ 0$
          where γ is an action,
          and $\varphi\ :=\ d(\mathbf{do},\ @,\ \gamma)\ =\ 1,$
          and $\psi\ :=\ d(\mathbf{be\text{-}able\text{-}to\text{-}do},\ @,\ \gamma)\ =\ 0,$
          and 1, 2, 3 $\in$ D_{i+1}

In contrast, the speech act type for a directive ordering an action would contain a more complex condition:

(58)   ORDER ACTION (γ) (D_i)
      1: $d(\underline{want},\ \$,\ @,\ \varphi)\ =\ 1$
      2: $d(\underline{order},\ \$,\ @,\ \varphi)\ =\ 1$
      3: $d(\underline{believe},\ \$,\ \psi)\ =\ 0$
      4: $d(\underline{believe},\ \$,\ \xi)\ =\ 1$
      5: $d(\underline{believe},\ \$,\ \zeta)\ =\ 1$

where γ is an action,

and $\varphi := d(\textbf{do}, @, \gamma) = 1$,

and $\psi := d(\textbf{be-able-to-do}, @, \gamma) = 0$,

and $\xi := d(\textbf{have-authority-over}, \$, @, \gamma) = 1$,

and $\zeta := [[d(\textbf{do}, @, \gamma) = 0] \gg$

$d(\textbf{suffer-neg.-conseq.}, @) = 1]$,

and $1, 2, 3, 4, 5 \in D_{i+1}$

In the condition of (58), **have-authority-over** should be understood as "(x) has authority over (y) with respect to some circumstances including (γ)." Just as a person's authority over us cannot legitimately extend to the impossible (*Go fetch the moon!*), neither does it extend to all realms of voluntary action (*Stop thinking about fruit flies!*).

A response to (57) or (58) might only involve compliance with the request (order), that is, no linguistic communication need be involved. But if the addressee does respond verbally then a contract is created. Consider the conditions in the following:

(59)   AGREE TO DO (γ) (D_i)

1:   $d(\underline{\text{say}}, \$, \varphi) = 1$

2:   $d(\underline{\text{believe}}, \$, \varphi) = 1$

3:   $d(\underline{\text{believe}}, @, \varphi) = 1$

4:   $d(\underline{\text{believe}}, \$, \psi) = 1$

5:   $d(\underline{\text{believe}}, @, \psi) = 1$

where $\varphi := d(\textbf{intend}, \$, \xi) = 1$,

where $\xi := d(\textbf{do}, \$, \gamma) = 1$,

and $\psi := [[d(\textbf{do}, \$, \gamma) = 0] \gg$

$d(\textbf{suffer-neg.-conseq.}, \$) = 1]$,

and $1, 2, 3, 4, 5 \in D_{i+1}$

The act of agreeing has the effect, partly, of informing the addressee of an intention, namely the intention to do the desired action. But it also introduces the speaker and adressee in a social contract, the violation of which can affect their relationship and have negative consequences for the speaker.

It would be possible to give speech act types for other responses to (57) or (58), and to give more examples from other families of types (e.g., expressives, commissives, etc.), but for the purposes of illustration, and understanding the applications of the theory developed in Chapters 3 and 4, these few examples should suffice. Where necessary, new types are introduced.

It should be clear that changes in the discourse situation that result from speech acts can be expressed in terms of speech act types. It remains for a complete theory to demonstrate that it is possible to begin with an utterance in a context and arrive at a speech act type that correctly gives the interpretation of the utterance.

CHAPTER 3
A THEORY OF SPEECH ACT INTERPRETATION

3.0.   INTRODUCTION

The problem this chapter addresses is how the use of an utterance in a context (i.) becomes interpreted in a way that is compatible with the form of the speech act types, and (ii.) becomes interpreted as being of some particular speech act type and not others. A theory is developed accounting for speech act interpretation in a four stage process. The first stage involves determining the parts or constituents of an utterance that are capable of being given an interpretation, called the interpretive constituents of the utterance. The second stage utilizes the interpretive constituents in illocutionary mode functions, which convert the unanchored facts of the utterance into candidate propositions relating the speaker and addressee to those facts. It is at this stage that features of the discourse situation first impose themselves on the interpretation process, and at this stage that propositions capable of satisfying the structural requirements of speech act types are produced. The third stage reconciles all candidate propositions produced in stage two with the existing facts of the discourse situation, essentially eliminating redundancies and inconsistencies, and sometimes marking candidate propositions for special treatment. The fourth stage matches all surviving candidate propositions against the inventory of available speech act types, and reserves successful matches for possible implementation, under some criteria of choice. Implementation itself involves nothing more than adding to the discourse situation the propositions associated with the successfully matched speech act type(s), and making appropriate adjustments of facts in the discourse situation to conform to the conditions (if any) on the matched speech act type(s).

Among the central assumptions of the theory are that it is possible to give complete structural (semantic) descriptions to utterances, that there are a relatively small number of primitive modes of using utterances, and that speakers share descriptions of speech act types which are the partial end-states that utterances can achieve. The general process of deriving speech act interpretations involves overgenerating candidate interpretations of utterances, filtering through context, matching speech act types, and choosing some interpretation(s) to implement.

3.1. INTERPRETIVE CONSTITUENTS

Utterances can be given an interpretation only because the subparts of the utterance interact meaningfully with information already present in the discourse situation and also interact meaningfully with one another. Felicitous utterances have constituents whose use effects a desired interpretation relative to the discourse situation.

Now, on the one hand, this can be regarded as observing nothing more than that the meaning of an utterance is compositional. Indeed, in some semantic theories, the interaction of the constituent parts of an utterance is taken to be the sole way that they can contribute to the meaning of the whole. However, as we can see from the effects of speech acts, subparts of utterances can also interact with facts already present in the discourse situation, which are not part of the meaning, *per se*, of anything in the utterance itself. Any semantic theory that fails to account for the contribution of information present in the discourse situation to the interpretation of an utterance occuring in that discourse situation is destined to be incomplete. In terms of speech act theory, this means that the relationship between an utterance's subparts and the units that arise in the interpretive parsing of the utterance must not be based on a strictly rigid compositional semantics.

To take a concrete example, the following two sentences contrast determiners, but it is not the determiner which is in focus, but the whole NP:

(60) *I heard that John saw a man.*

(61) *I heard that John saw the man.*

If we assume that these sentences were uttered with unstressed articles, then it is the final two words as a unit that have an effect on the discourse situation. Using Johnson-Laird's (1980) "mental models" approach to anaphora as a metaphor, we could say that (60) would have the effect of instantiating a token man; (61) would have the effect of directing attention to an already present token man. Whatever semantic representation we might choose, we would want the interpretive component to treat the composed NP as a single entity.

This should not be the case, however, in the following sentences where the determiners are given stress ([eɪ:]/[ði:] respectively):

(62) *I heard that John saw a̱ man.*

(63) *I heard that John saw the̱ man.*

Here, it seems, we do not want to treat the final two words as a unit, but rather wish to isolate the determiner from the noun. The utterance of (62) could be used to assert, among other things, that there was only one man that (the speaker heard that) John saw; the utterance of (63), that the man that (the speaker heard that) John saw was the same as the one being discussed.[1] A semantics which blindly composed the determiner and noun in these cases would be hard pressed to recover the significance of the stressed article.[2]

The point these examples should make is that the interpretation of an utterance will be affected by how the constituents of the utterance are composed. Given numerous possibilities of composition, the interpreter must choose a combination which is meaningful and consistent with the perceived goals of the discourse situation.

We can refer to that part of an utterance that is capable of affecting an interpretation as an <u>interpretive constituent</u>. Interpretive constituents are semantic entities based on or composed of other linguistic constituents, consisting of syntactic, lexical, phonological, and prosodic features.[3] The principal characteristic of an interpretive constituent is that it have a disambiguated semantic interpretation. Thus *the man* in (61) corresponds to some particular individual, which is its interpretation; the use of stress on *the* in (63) corresponds to something like the proposition THIS ITEM IS IN FOCUS (with respect to *the*), which is the interpretation of the use of stress. In short, the interpretive constituents are the significant facts of an utterance, the elements on which an interpretation of the utterance is based.

How one might derive the interpretive constituents of an utterance is clearly a major question for any theory of utterance interpretation. This problem has arisen, for reasons independent of speech acts, in Kamp (1981), where discourse representation structures are discussed. And a suggestion for a means of deriving syntactic structures that would meet Kamp's requirements has come from Klein (1981), where tree-transducers are utilized to generate sentence-like entities based on sub-sentence fragments of an utterance. However, it is beyond the scope of this presentation to explore this question in depth.

For our purposes here, we can assume that interpretive constituents are produced in a two-step process. First, any utterance we might encounter can be input to a "black box" that returns a complete structural description of the utterance. A complete description would include a disambiguated syntactic parsing, disambiguated lexical items, a representation of the prosodic features, and other information related to the performance of the utterance, such as accompanying non-verbal activity.[4] Second, we can assume that there are a series of discourse-level interpretation rules that relate the syntactico-semantic information obtained from the first step to the uses such information can be put to in actual interaction.

Having such a "black box" is quite convenient, since it is very much an open question how some of the features of an utterance should be associated with others, particularly, how prosodic information should combine with syntactic and lexical information, or how non-verbal information should affect interpretation. These are issues of great linguistic interest, and they should not be side-stepped in a theory of language use. Nevertheless, except for suggestions of how such features can combine to affect speech act interpretation, the formal problems of this aspect of interpretive constituent derivation and interaction must be ignored in this dissertation.

The kind of information and rules that the "black box" might need is the kind commonly encountered in syntactic and semantic descriptions of natural language, including a list of categories, with an associated lexicon, and syntactic phrase structure rules and semantic composition rules that utilize the categories and lexical information.[5] For example, this information for a tiny fragment of English might be given as follows:[6]

(64)

Category		Lexicon
CN	(common nouns)	*dog, cat*
PRO	(pronouns)	*I, you, he, she, it*
PN	(proper names)	*Bill, Mary*
DET	(determiners)	*a, the*
IV	(intransitive verbs)	*sleep, think, leave*
TV	(transitive verbs)	*hit, throw*
M	(modals)	*should, shouldn't, does, doesn't*
COMP	(complementizers)	*that*
VP	(verb phrases)	
NP	(noun phrases)	
S'	(clauses)	
S	(sentences)	

Some phrase structure rules based on these categories might be as follows:

55

(65)   Phrase Structure Rules
   (i.)   S → NP VP
   (ii.) S → S *and* S
   (iii.) S → S *or* S
   (iv.) S' → COMP S
   (v.)   NP → {DET CN / PRO / PN}
   (vi.) VP → {(M) IV / (M) TV / (M) IV S'}
   (vii.) VP → VP *and* VP
   (viii.) VP → VP *or* VP

These, in turn, can be rewritten as structural description rules, where individual constituents can be regarded as combining to form other constituents, for example:

(66)   Structural Description Rules
   (i.) $\alpha^{NP}\ \beta^{VP} \rightarrow [\alpha\beta]_S$
   (ii.) $\alpha^{DET}\ \beta^{CN} \rightarrow [\alpha\beta]_{NP}$
   (iii.) $\alpha^{M}\ \beta^{IV}\ \gamma^{S'} \rightarrow [\alpha\beta\gamma]_{VP}$
   (iv.) $\alpha^{S}\ \beta^{S} \rightarrow [\alpha\ and\ \beta]_S$

Finally, we could give, in a situation semantics, a series of rules that convert structural description rules into semantic interpretations. Following Barwise and Perry (1981a:19), for α, a proper name, the interpretation of α, $[[\alpha]]$, should be an individual, $\mathbf{a} \in A$ (the set of individuals); for α, a verb phrase, $[[\alpha]]$ should be a propositional function of individuals; for α, a sentence, $[[\alpha]]$ should be a proposition. Instances of these three cases can be given formally as follows (where "$\leadsto$" in (67ii.) represents a mapping relation):

(67)   (i.) $[[\alpha^{PN}]] = \mathbf{a}$
       (ii.) $[[\ [does\ \alpha^{IV}]_{VP}\ ]] = \mathbf{a} \leadsto \{s \mid s([[\alpha]], \mathbf{a}) = 1\}$
       (iii.) $[[\ [\alpha^{S}\ and\ \beta^{S}]_{S}\ ]] = [[\alpha]] \cup [[\beta]]$

Obviously, the rules presented here do not represent an exhaustive treatment of the fragment introduced in (64), but rather are intended as a sketch of the sort of information that any adequate "black box" would have to utilize in order to provide an analysis of some utterance. One of the strings which could be analyzed by these rules is the string *I think that you should leave*. A possible structural description might be the following:

(68) *I think that you should leave*

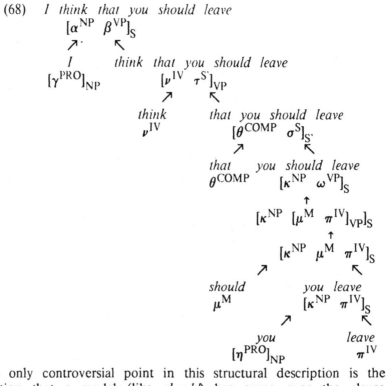

The only controversial point in this structural description is the assumption that a modal (like *should*) has scope over the clause (sentence) in which it appears. In this illustration, the details of that step are omitted, but such an effect can be achieved using λ-abstraction and "Cooper storage" (cf. Cooper (1975, forthcoming)). Here, this is accomplished with an (unmotivated) interpretation rewriting rule:

(69) NP M *V X → M NP *V X

where *V $\in$ {IV, TV}, and X is any string

Operating on (68), a variety of interpretations can be built up. For example, the branch of the tree containing η^{PRO} π^{IV} (*you leave*) could be given a partial interpretation as

(70) {s | s([[π]], [[η]]) = 1}, or
      {s | s(leave, [[η]]) = 1}.

If we assume that μ^M (*should*) is interpretable as a relation on situation-types, we could give a partial interpretation to the branch of the tree represented by μ^M η^{PRO} π^{IV} (*you should leave*), perhaps as follows:[7]

(71) $\{s \mid [s([[\pi]], [[\eta]]) = 0 \Rightarrow$
$$s(\text{suffer-neg.-conseq.}, [[\eta]]) = 1] \}, \text{ or}$$
$\{s \mid [s(\text{leave}, [[\eta]]) = 0 \Rightarrow$
$$s(\text{suffer-neg.-conseq.}, [[\eta]]) = 1] \quad \}.$$

Further, we could give a partial interpretation to the branch of the tree involving the verb ν^{IV} (*think*), specifically, as follows:

(72) $[[\nu^{IV} [\theta^{COMP} \sigma^S]_{S'}]] = a \curvearrowright \{s \mid s([[\nu]], a, [[\tau]]) = 1\},$
$$\text{or}$$
$$= a \curvearrowright \{s \mid s(\text{believe}, a, \varphi) = 1\},$$
where $\varphi := [s(\text{leave}, [[\eta]]) = 0 \Rightarrow$
$s(\text{suffer-neg.-conseq.}, [[\eta]]) = 1].$

Finally, we could give an interpretation to the entire utterance by assuming that the situation being represented is, in fact, the discourse situation, where *I* refers to the speaker (i.e., where $[[\alpha]] = \$$), and *you* refers to the addressee (i.e., where $[[\eta]] = @$):

(73) $\{d \mid d(\text{believe}, \$, \varphi) = 1\},$
where $\varphi := \{d \mid d(\text{leave}, @) = 0 \Rightarrow$
$d(\text{suffer-neg.-conseq.}, @) = 1\}.$

In determining the interpretive constituents of an utterance, we must consider not only the syntactic and semantic information that a structural description of the utterance gives us, but also information we may have about the possible uses of the constituent parts of utterances. This is the second step in the derivation process. While it would be impossible to attempt to present here a complete set of rules that relate syntactic and semantic structural descriptions to their possible uses in a discourse situation, a handful of such rules could be tentatively offered, as follows:

(74) **RULE OF CONSTITUENT USE 1:**
If c is a constituent of an utterance, then one possible interpretation of the use of c in the utterance is that the speaker is calling attention to c.

More formally, the use of c in D_i can always conform to a speech act type:

(75) ISOLATE c (D_i)
1: $d(\underline{\text{want}}, \$, @, \varphi) = 1$
2: $d(\underline{\text{request}}, \$, @, \psi) = 1$
where φ and ψ give states,
$\varphi := d(\text{notice}, @, c) = 1,$

$$\psi \ := \ d(\text{evaluate}, \ @, \ c) \ = \ 0,$$
$$\text{and } 1, \ 2 \ \in \ D_{i+1}$$

This encodes the information that the speaker does not intend the constituent to be given an evaluation, though he does intend the addressee to notice the use of the constituent. This kind of interpretation would be appropriate when practicing elocution or calling attention to a particular phoneme, etc.

(76) **RULE OF CONSTITUENT USE 2:**

If c is a constituent of an utterance of category PN, then one possible interpretation of the use of c in the utterance is that the speaker is referring to the individual designated by c (specifically: $[[c]]$).

This, too, could be given as a speech act type.

(77) REFER TO $[[c]]$ (D_i)
1: $d(\text{be-referring-to}, \ \$, \ [[c]]) \ = \ 1$
2: $d(\text{agree-to}, \ \$, \ @, \ \varphi) \ = \ 1$
where c is of category PN, and $[[c]] \in A$,
and $\varphi \ := \ d(\text{evaluate-as}, \ c, \ [[c]]) \ = \ 1$,
and $1, \ 2 \ \in \ D_{i+1}$

The information encoded here states that the use of c constitutes an act of reference by the speaker, and that that use preempts the future interpretations that c might be given, specifically, by entering into an agreement with the addressee to evaluate c in a consistent manner. One special application this rule has is in the interpretation we give to for-the-nonce "baptisms," as when we dub a clearly understood referent with a name not his own. But this interpretation can be intended in standard acts of reference as well.

(78) **RULE OF CONSTITUENT USE 3:**

If c is a constituent of an utterance of category PRO, then one possible interpretation of the use of c in the utterance is that the speaker is referring to an already present individual in the discourse situation.

As a speech act type, this might be given as follows:

(79) ANAPHORICALLY REFER TO $[[c]]$ (D_i)
1: $d(\text{be-referring-to}, \ \$, \ [[c]]) \ = \ 1$
2: $d(\text{agree-to}, \ \$, \ @, \ \varphi) \ = \ 1$
3: $d(\underline{\text{believe}}, \ \$, \ \psi) \ = \ 1$
where c is of category PRO, and $[[c]] \in A$,

$$\text{and } \varphi := d(\text{evaluate-as, c, [[c]]}) = 1,$$
$$\text{and } \psi := d([[c]] \in D_i) = 1,$$
$$\text{and } 1, 2, 3 \in D_{i+1}$$

This case repeats some of the information in REFER TO [[c]], but adds the clause that the speaker believes that the identity of the referent is part of the factual content of the discourse situation (perhaps in the set of facts representing the mutual knowledge of speaker and addressee). For example, if in December, 1980, someone had rushed up to a normally well-informed American and said *They shot the hostages!*, he would probably have interpreted *they* to refer to Iranian militants, and would have understood the use of the utterance, in part, as introducing information about the speaker's presuppositions regarding their mutual knowledge.

(80) **RULE OF CONSTITUENT USE 4**:
If c is a constituent of an utterance of category DET, then one possible use of c in the utterance is that the speaker is expressing the proposition that the individual or individuals in the scope of the determiner have the number-characteristics associated with the interpretation of c.

As a speech act type:

(81) EXPRESS NUMBER [[c]] (D_i)
1; $d(\textbf{believe}, \$, \varphi) = 1$
2: $d(\textbf{express}, \$, \varphi) = 1$
where c is of category DET,
and [[c]] is a relation, r^1_k, giving the number-characteristics of the individual(s), a_j, in its scope,
and $\varphi := d(r^1_k, a_j) = 1$,
and $1, 2 \in D_{i+1}$

This is designed to capture the information that is imparted by the use of a determiner in characterizing the referent in its scope as having a certain number in the discourse situation. For example, the use of *the* can be interpreted as indicating that the speaker believes that the referent is uniquely identifiable; the use of *a/an*, that the referent is either new in the discourse situation, or non-specific.

(82) **RULE OF CONSTITUENT USE 5**:
If c is a constituent of an utterance of category CN, then one possible interpretation of the use of c is that the

speaker is expressing the proposition that there is a referent in the discourse situation of the equivalence class given by the interpretation of c.

As a speech act type:

(83) EXPRESS CLASS MEMBERSHIP [[c]] (D_i)
1: d(**believe**, $, φ) = 1
2: d(**express**, $, φ) = 1
where c is of category CN, and [[c]] is an equivalence class,
and $\varphi := [(\exists a_j) \text{ s. t. } [a_j \in [[c]] \text{ and } d(a_j \in D_i) = 1]]$,
and 1, 2 $\in D_{i+1}$

The information here is designed to capture the presuppositions that are associated with the designation of something through the use of a common noun. For example, in the use of *the chair*, it might be important to recognize that the speaker intends to characterize the object referred to as being a chair, indeed, that it may be the speaker's principal intention.

Applying these rules to the structural description of *I think that you should leave* (in (68)), new interpretive constituents can be generated. For example, by using *I*, the speaker can be understood to be referring to himself, and indirectly giving evidence of his participation in the discourse situation; by using *you*, the speaker can be understood as referring to the addressee, and indirectly giving evidence of his belief in the addressee's co-participation in the discourse situation (cf. RULE 3).

Applying these rules to an utterance with nearly equivalent structure, *I think that the guy should leave*, we would find, additionally, the information that the speaker is referring to an individual whose identity is part of the discourse situation (cf. RULE 3), that the individual is uniquely determinable (cf. RULE 4), and that the individual is (conventionally) a man (cf. RULE 5).

Without pursuing this discussion further, it should be obvious that the information we extract from an utterance can come from a variety of sources, some conventionally semantic, and some based on discourse-pragmatic aspects of constituent use. In framing a theory of speech acts, we must allow for information of all kinds to affect the final interpretation we give to an utterance's use.

For the balance of Chapters 3 and 4, interpretive constituents, when invoked, will be given as glosses only. Nevertheless, it should be understood that such glosses are based on actual rules that derive interpretive constituents formally.

The utilization of interpretive constituents is essential to the theory of speech acts developed here. In the interpretive parsing of an utterance, as soon as a complete unit of information is available, it can give rise to a speech act. This is especially useful in dealing with utterance fragments. As an example, consider the information that might be extracted from the following:

(84) *I talked to the guy who was here yesterday about...*

Some of the interpretive constituents of (84) might be given as follows:

(85) $ is referring to an individual, x, identifiable in the discourse situation.

(86) x is a man.

(87) x was at the current location one day earlier.

(88) $ talked to x about something.

Each of these constituents could give rise, independently, to a speech act, so each should be able to serve as input to a speech act generation process. While the balance of the utterance (if there is a completion) might add information that would invalidate speech act interpretations based on these interpretive constituents, we would not want to block their interpretation when they are first encountered. Furthermore, when more information about the discourse situation is available, we can see the effects of the interaction of these constituents with other features of context.

As an illustration of the different speech acts that might be associated with some of the interpretive constituents of (84), consider its use in each of the following cases:

(89) a: *So you talked to somebody about our plans?*
      b: *I talked to the guy who was here yesterday about...*

(90) a: *Mary said you spoke to the guy that was here this morning.*
      b: *I talked to the guy who was here yesterday about...*

(91) a: *What did you do with the guy who was here yesterday?*
      b: *I talked to the guy who was here yesterday about...*

The differences in the interpretations we give to (84) in (89), (90), and (91) are not dramatic, but nevertheless substantial.

In (89), (84) seems to function primarily as an answer by providing an identification of the indefinite *somebody* and could perhaps also continue (in the *about...* phrase) to modify the proposition introduced by the question, namely that b talked about the plans he shares with a. In this case, interpretive constituents (85), (86), and (87) are being utilized and constituent (88) is inert.

In (90), (84) functions as a corrective, actually contradicting a's report of Mary's report, and also supplying a slightly more specific account of the activity (*speak to x* is less informative than *talk to x about...*). Here, interpretive constituents (87) and (88), and perhaps also (86), are being exploited.

In (91), (84) again acts as an answer, by providing information about the activity in question, but unlike its role in (89), does nothing to affect the identification of the individual talked about. In this case, only interpretive constituent (88) seems to be relevant.

Clearly, the list of interpretive constituents for fragment (84) could be and would be longer for most cases of the performance of (84) in actual discourse. The sketched interpretations above would be supplemented by information about stress and intonation that might further disambiguate intention. To choose but one example, if *yesterday* in (84) is given contrastive stress in reply to (91), the speaker could be understood as both contradicting the report and asserting that the correct referent should be the guy who was there yesterday; if *yesterday* is given rising (question) intonation, the speaker could be understood as asking for clarification (perhaps of the referent, perhaps of the correctness of the report) as well as suggesting that there is some tentativeness to the proposition he apparently is asserting.

This discussion of the interpretation of (84) is both incomplete and informal. It is precisely here that a theory of speech acts should decide whether the effect of an utterance has speech act status, and if so, it should offer an explanation for the achievement of that effect. Nevertheless, I hope that two aspects of utterance interpretation have been illustrated. First, it should be clear that various parts of an utterance, various interpretive constituents, can be relevant in giving an utterance its force. Second, it should be obvious that the other information that is part of the content of the discourse situation — the context in which the utterance occurs — directly affects what interpretation can be assigned. The component of the theory of speech acts that assigns candidate interpretations to utterances must be sensitive to both the actual interpretive constituents of the utterance and the utterance context.

To return to the formulation of a speech act given in Chapter 1, viz. $D_{i+1} = I(f_u, D_i)$, we can see the role of interpretive constituents more clearly. The constituent subpart of the utterance, f_u, is not just any utterance subpart, but must be an interpretive constituent of the utterance. The speech act itself, $I(f_u, D_i)$, is based on the interpretive constituents and is constrained by other information in the discourse situation.

To illustrate this with another example, consider how the interpretive constituents of an utterance and its context might interact in some simple mode, such as assertion, in the following:

(92) *This is my cap.*

Here, the interpretive constituents would consist of at least the following:

(93) $ is referring to some object, x, identifiable in the discourse situation.

(94) x is a cap.

(95) x is co-present.

(96) x belongs to $.

At the beginning of an interaction, the utterance of (92) could be regarded as asserting all of the facts associated with these interpretive constituents. For example, after uttering (92), the speaker could not deny that he was talking about a cap (an addressee could object: *You said it was a cap*); the speaker could not deny that it belonged to him (*You said it was yours*); the speaker could not deny that it was identifiable in the discourse situation (*You said it was there*).

In terms of speech act types and discourse situation end-states, the assertion of (92) under these circumstances should have the effect of introducing to the discourse situation, for each interpretive constituent, f, of (92), the propositions

(97) $d(\underline{say}, \$, f) = 1$, and
$d(\underline{believe}, \$, f) = 1$.

More specifically, for the interpretive constituents (93) - (96) above, all of the following propositions would be added to the discourse situation:

(98) $d(\underline{say}, \$, (93)) = 1$

$$d(\underline{believe}, \$, (93)) = 1$$
$$d(\underline{say}, \$, (94)) = 1$$
$$d(\underline{believe}, \$, (94)) = 1$$
$$d(\underline{say}, \$, (95)) = 1$$
$$d(\underline{believe}, \$, (95)) = 1$$
$$d(\underline{say}, \$, (96)) = 1$$
$$d(\underline{believe}, \$, (96)) = 1$$

If, however, (92) were uttered not at the beginning of an interaction, but after some other utterance which had added immediately relevant facts to the discourse situation, all of the above propositions might not be introduced. Consider the case where (92) is uttered after (99):

(99)   *Whose cap is this?*

To account fully for the effect of (99) on the discourse situation would require a more complete analysis of questions that can be treated here. Nevertheless, the present example can be understood if two assumptions are made. First, a question like (99) works in part by making its presuppositions part of the currently relevant context, in particular by <u>informing</u> the addressee of the content of its interpretive constituents, where INFORM is taken to be a speech act type (as given before) in which both the speaker and the addressee are represented as believing the content of the interpretive constituents (for the purposes of the discourse). Accepting a question as it is asked means, among other things, accepting the presuppositions of the question. Second, a question identifies the type of response (α) which could satisfy it, as noted before in the discussion of the speech act type, REQUEST INFORMATION. In the case of (99), α is constrained to be something whose interpretation yields an individual. The conditions on this constraint might be given roughly as follows:

(100)   For cap x, ($\exists y$) s. t. x belongs to y, and
for question (99), ($\exists \alpha$) s. t. $[[\alpha]] = y$.

Among the facts of the discourse situation, then, after the utterance of (99) as a question from a to b, are the following:

(101)
$$d(\underline{believe}, a, (93)) = 1$$
$$d(\underline{believe}, b, (93)) = 1$$
$$d(\underline{believe}, a, (94)) = 1$$
$$d(\underline{believe}, b, (94)) = 1$$
$$d(\underline{believe}, a, (95)) = 1$$
$$d(\underline{believe}, b, (95)) = 1$$
$$d(\underline{believe}, a, \varphi) = 1$$

$$d(\underline{believe}, \; b, \; \varphi) \; = \; 1$$
where φ gives the constraints on α.

Other facts will, of course, be present, corresponding to the other effects of the question, but these are the salient facts for this example.

At this point, if b responds with (92) as an answer, we would not want to say that b simply asserted the interpretive constituents (93) - (96) again, introducing the propositions in (98). Much of the information in (98) is redundant after a's question. Given the constraint on possible answers to this question, the only relevant interpretation is that b is asserting that it is his cap. This assertion could be made by exploiting interpretive constituent (96), in short by introducing just the propositions

$$(102) \quad d(\underline{say}, \; \$, \; (96)) \; = \; 1$$
$$d(\underline{believe}, \; \$, \; (96)) \; = \; 1$$

Similarly, if (92) were used after each of the following questions, different interpretive constituents would become relevant.

(103) *Where is your cap?* [relevant constituent: (95)]

(104) *Is this John's cap?* [relevant constituent: (96)]

(105) *Is this your featherduster?* [relevant constituent: (94)]

This is not to say that all the information represented by the propositions in (98) should not be deducible from the use of (92) on any occasion, just that, from the point of view of speech act theory, there will be occasions when only some of those propositions will be the object of speech acts. Any theory of speech acts we might adopt should account for such different effects.

As I indicated before, the analysis of questions and answers to questions is more complex than this example reveals. I have not suggested how the constraints on α are utilized, or how the two propositions of the assertion above are interpreted as an answer (where one constraint on answers is that they conform to INFORM speech act types, not just ASSERT types). Still, this example should provide some sense of how interpretive constituents might interact with the content of the discourse situation to enable some, but not others, to be interpreted as the focus of speech acts.

It remains to be seen explicitly how interpretive constituents become embedded in discourse level propositions, and how the discourse situation constrains illocutionary force.

3.2. ILLOCUTIONARY MODE FUNCTIONS

Up to this point I have described speech acts principally from the point of view of their effects on a discourse situation. Indeed, the assumption I have made is that speech acts are functions that map discourse situations into discourse situations, sometimes with the effect of adding information, sometimes with the effect of deleting it. But the central question for a theory of speech acts is how a particular utterance can come to be interpreted as having a particular force, not signalled overtly by one of its interpretive constituents (as might be the case if one adopted a performative analysis). And furthermore how some speech acts of relatively greater complexity can be built up out of speech acts of lesser complexity. (For example, how retractions can have constituent parts that give assertions, etc.).

To answer these questions it is necessary to formalize the operation that converts the interpretive constituents of an utterance into a form that is compatible with the speech act types. This operation involves the use of <u>illocutionary mode functions</u>.

Illocutionary mode functions convert bare interpretive constituents into propositions that relate the speaker and addressee to the information in the interpretive constituents. Put another way, the illocutionary mode functions generate partial interpretations of utterances that correspond to the use of the interpretive constituents of the utterance with a particular illocutionary force.

More formally, each illocutionary mode function, $L_i \in L$, is defined for certain types of interpretive constituents of an utterance, $f_j \in F_u$, such that if an interpretive constituent, f_j, is accepted by an illocutionary mode function, L_i, a set of candidate propositions, $L_i(f_j)$, is returned, given schematically as follows:

$$(106) \quad \{ \quad d(r^{m+1}_{Li_1}, a_1, \ldots , a_m, f_j) = \delta_1,$$
$$d(r^{k+1}_{Li_2}, a_1, \ldots , a_k, f_j) = \delta_2, \ldots ,$$
$$d(r^{g+1}_{Li_n}, a_1, \ldots , a_g, f_j) = \delta_n \quad \},$$
$$\text{where } \delta_1, \delta_2, \ldots , \delta_n \in \{0, 1\}$$

The predicates in these expressions have superscripts giving the number of argument places and subscripts giving their serial order with respect to the other predicates associated with the illocutionary mode function, L_i. Note that one of the arguments of each predicate is obligatorily the interpretive constituent f_j. The predicates, themselves, and the arguments other than the interpretive constituent, f_j, provide the information that converts the interpretive constituent into a discourse-level, candidate proposition. These are <u>candidate propositions</u> because without reference to context it cannot be determined whether a particular expression in this form should have status as a proposition in the discourse situation.

Intuitively, the illocutionary modes represent the fundamental ways an utterance can be issued. These modes are basic to human discourse, and are constrained by it. One would expect to find a subset of illocutionary modes common to all human languages. These modes have the effect of expressing beliefs or request or directions, and it is only because an utterance is issued in a mode, and in a context, that the utterance can have force as one or another speech act. In one sense, the illocutionary modes correspond directly to the most primitive speech acts, such as asserting. And in each class of speech act types (e.g., constatives, commissives, directives, requestives, etc.) there will probably be one basic type that corresponds directly to an illocutionary mode.

To take a concrete example, we can define an illocutionary mode function, L_1, for constatives in general, capable of accepting interpretive constituents, f_j, that are in the form of propositions, and returning the set

$$(107) \quad \{ \quad d(\underline{say}, \$, f_j) = 1,$$
$$d(\underline{believe}, \$, f_j) = 1 \}.$$

These candidate propositions express the relations that are basic to constatives of all types, namely, *say (that)* and *believe (that)* relations. The discourse level function of constatives is to introduce the speaker and some proposition in these relations.

If we were to apply L_1 to the utterance considered earlier, *This is my cap*, we would derive just the candidate propositions given in (98), where each interpretive constituent is an argument of a **say** or **believe** relation.

In contrast, we might consider the illocutionary mode associated with requests for action, given here as illocutionary mode function L_2. For each interpretive constituent of appropriate type, f_j, L_2 returns the set

$$(108) \quad \{ \quad d(\underline{want}, \$, @, f_j) = 1,$$
$$d(\underline{request}, \$, @, f_j) = 1 \}$$

It should be clear that the interpretive constituents that are accepted by L_1 are not necessarily accepted by L_2, and vice verse. None of the interpretive constituents associated with (92) is an appropriate object of a request for action. What would it mean to generate a candidate proposition such as (109)?

(109) $d(\underline{\text{want}}, \$, @, \varphi) = 1$
where $\varphi := x$ (a cap) belongs to $.

Rather L_2 is sensitive to interpretive constituents that relate the addressee to actions, states, or events. For example,

(110) *Leave!*

might have the interpretive constituent

(111) @ leaves (here).

We would want (111) to be accepted by L_2, giving

(112) $d(\underline{\text{want}}, \$, @, (111)) = 1,$
$d(\underline{\text{request}}, \$, @, (111)) = 1.$

It might appear that (111) is indistinguishable from the kind of interpretive constituent in propositional form that can be the object of assertions, that is, that (111) could be utilized by an illocutionary mode function like L_1 to given an interpretation as a constative. If so, it would seem that the theory could not recognize the obvious difference between (110) and, say, the utterance of

(113) *You leave now.*

This would be the case if the theory could not be made sensitive to the additional information — in the form of syntax and intonation — that (110) conveys. We recognize imperatives largely because of such overt cues, and that knowledge must be represented in our interpretation process. Here, we can treat that information as another interpretive constituent of the utterance, one at a meta-level with respect to the choice of illocutionary mode functions. The interpretive constituent associated with imperative syntax and intonation might be given as follows:

(114) THIS IS A DIRECTIVE.

And the co-presence of (114) during an interpretation process has the effect of blocking all illocutionary mode functions except those which are capable of generating directives, which would include requests for action.

In this instance, (114) would prevent (111) from being input to L_1, so would prevent (111) from being interpreted as the object of an assertion. Note that this is not to say that (111) cannot have a semantic representation that is indistinguishable from the propositions that are, properly, the objects of assertions. In a situation semantics, (111) could be given as

(115) s(**leave**, @, ⟨from here⟩) = 1.

Ignoring the indexical problems, this states, merely, that there is a situation in which the addressee leaves from the current location. In issuing an imperative, however, the speaker does not represent an actual situation but a desired, hence, unrealized one. Questions of truth are irrelevant, while questions of the details of the hypothetical situation may become paramount.

The role of performance features or overt signals is especially important in interpreting a variety of indirect speech act phenomena. Consider, for example, the utterance of (116), below, with an accompanying back-of-the-hand wave away from the speaker, toward the addressee:

(116) *I'm busy.*

Here, we would not want the information associated with the hand gesture to be accepted by an illocutionary mode function that returns asserted propositions. What, after all, is the propositional content of a gesture? Nevertheless, in our culture such a gesture does have a conventional interpretation as a directive to leave or stand away. We certainly would want that information to contribute to the interpretation of (116).

Perhaps it is misleading to think of (116) as performing an indirect speech act; rather, we should regard (116) as having multiple, simultaneous speech act interpretations, some of which create a discourse situation which is recognizable as a type in which a directive has been issued. The overt proposition in (116), one of its interpretive constituents, can be given as

(117) $ is busy.

If this is input to L_1, the candidate propositions

(118) d(**say**, $, (117)) = 1,
d(**believe**, $, (117)) = 1

would be derived. If, in addition, the gesture has a direct interpretation such as

(119) d(**request**, $, @, φ) = 1,
where φ := @ leaves ⟨from here⟩,

then we have a set of candidate propositions which combine to give a discourse situation in which a justified request to leave has been issued.[8]

This might seem like an additional complexity — using direct interpretations of gestures, etc., along with candidate interpretations of utterances to derive candidate discourse situation-types — resulting in a proliferation of interpretations rather than in a disambiguated one; but it is precisely because such situations have multiple, even conflicting interpretations that this complexity is needed. In Sag and Liberman (1975) a variety of indirect speech act situations were investigated in an attempt to relate intonation of utterance to interpretation. It was found that it was possible to force utterances having the syntactic form of questions to be given an interpretation as real questions (not rhetorical ones, or sarcastic comments, etc.) by using a cannonical question intonation; it was not possible, by using other intonation contours, to force interpretations as non-literal questions. This would suggest that conventional cues can have great force in blocking the application of illocutionary modes, and that when such cues are absent, a proliferation of interpretations can result.

Consider another possible indirect speech act situation where a sentence such as (120), below, is uttered.

(120) *I think that you should leave.*

Among the interpretive constituents of this utterance, as derived in section 3.1, we find:

(121) $ believes φ, where φ := @ should leave (here)

(122) @ should leave (here)

(123) @ leaves (here)

All of these are of a type that could be accepted by L_1; but (123) could also be accepted by L_2. We could give the output of L_1 and L_2 operating on (120) as follows:

(124) d(<u>say</u>, $, (121)) = 1
       d(<u>believe</u>, $, (121)) = 1
       d(<u>say</u>, $, (122)) = 1
       d(<u>believe</u>, $, (122)) = 1
       d(<u>say</u>, $, (123)) = 1
       d(<u>believe</u>, $, (123)) = 1
       d(<u>want</u>, $, @, (123)) = 1
       d(<u>request</u>, $, @, (123)) = 1

Assuming that nothing in the discourse situation blocks any of these candidate propositions, the use of (120) could have the effect, simultaneously, of an assertion and a request for action. This corresponds to our intuitions about a sentence like (120) which can have ambiguous interpretations.

It would be possible, as in the case of speech act types, to give many more illocutionary mode functions than the two used in the examples above. However, for expository purposes, no more are needed. We can assume that all illocutionary mode functions conform to the general type given in (126), and that the theory has available a finite subset of the total set to which interpretive constituents are fed. Allowing every illocutionary mode function to apply to every interpretive constituent it can accept, we can generate a large number of candidate propositions for any utterance. Since, in most cases, we would want only some of the candidate propositions to remain as truly plausible interpretations of the utterance, we must consider the other factors that delimit our choices of interpretation. The first of these is the interaction of candidate propositions with the avilable information in the discourse situation, in short, the effect of context.

3.3.   RECONCILIATION WITH CONTEXT

Probably the most elusive aspect of any theory of speech acts, or theory of language use, is the role of context: its effects are ubiquitous, yet unobtrusive. And in any formalization of these effects there is always the danger that too much rigidity, or too little, will be introduced.

The approach taken here is not intended as a complete characterization of context, but only a possible characterization of some limited effects of context. These effects are realized only when information, which would be added if a candidate proposition were implemented, conflicts with or repeats information that is already part of the discourse situation. The actual effects of context in such cases can be regarded as constraints on possible inferences, that is, as rules which either block or enable interpretations. Nevertheless, even in this limited treatment, certain generalizations about complex speech act phenomena can be captured.

In terms of the set of candidate propositions that represents the potentially new information in the discourse situation, these limited effects of context are given via a reconciliation function, X, which either marks or ignores candidate propositions. Schematically, if we let $L_i(f)_k$ stand for the kth (in order) candidate proposition in the set of candidate propositions generated by the application of illocutionary mode function L_i to interpretive constituent f, we could show the effects of X as follows:

$$(125) \quad X(L_i(f)_k) = [L_i(f)_k]^* \text{ or } L_i(f)_k$$

A candidate proposition is returned by X as a "*"-marked candidate proposition when there is information in the discourse situation that is in conflict with or is especially affected by the information of the candidate proposition. A marked candidate proposition can go on to be implemented only under special circumstances. A candidate proposition is returned unmarked (unchanged) when there is no information in the discourse situation that would affect its being implemented.

Before defining the conditions on X that determine which of the two possible fates a candidate proposition will suffer, we might consider a concrete example. Assume we have a discourse situation in which a and b share the common goal of wanting to talk to one another and a initiates the conversation with the utterance

(126) *I am the speaker.*

The relevant information in the discourse situation at the time of the utterance (D_0) is given by the framing facts and some representation of the goals of the participants, a partial interpretation of which might be given as follows:

(127)   d(believe, a, ($=a)) = 1
    d(believe, b, ($=a)) = 1
    d(believe, a, (@=b)) = 1
    d(believe, b, (@=b)) = 1
    d(want, a, b, φ) = 1
    d(want, b, a, φ^{-1}) = 1,
    where φ := s(talk-to, a, b) = 1
    and φ^{-1} := s(talk-to, b, a) = 1

If we further assume the relevant interpretive constituent of (126) is

(128) $ = a,

and that this constituent can be accepted by L_1, the illocutionary mode function for constatives, we can generate the following set of candidate propositions, viz. L_{-1} ((128)):

(129)   d(say, a, ($=a)) = 1,
    d(believe, a, ($=a)) = 1

Ignoring the effects of other illocutionary mode functions which might apply to (128), we can think of (129) as giving the interpretation of (126) as an assertion. That is, if nothing in the context blocks the candidate propositions from being implemented, (129) could match the speech act type for assertions, and both candidate propositions would be added to the discourse situation (actually, would be contained in D_1).

But there is something odd about this example. If (126) is intended literally to apply to the current discourse situation, and not, say, to some other discourse situation which is being reported by the speaker in the current discourse situation, then there is an extreme redundancy involved, the statement of an obvious fact.

As an illustration of when a legitimate assertion of (126) might be meaningful, consider the case where b enters a room filled with people he assumes to be engaged in conversation. At the moment b enters there is silence, hence no obvious speaker, so b softly queries a, the first person he comes upon, as to who is (was) talking. His answer is

(130)   *I am.*

This does not mean "I am the speaker in the discourse situation created by me (a) as speaker and you (b) as addressee." It does mean "with reference to the discourse situation you (b) have entered upon, consisting of me (a) and other people in this room (but not you (b)), I am the speaker." · The differences here reflect differences in the interpretation of (130) ((126)) facilitated by context and forced by the rules of cooperative discourse.

Returning to the first example, then, we can perhaps see that the use of (126) should not count as a mere assertion. It might count as a reiteration, or a demand for attention, or a request for correction or confirmation; but the context in which it is used, specifically the presence of the fact

$$(131) \quad d(\underline{believe}, \ a, \ (\$ = a)) \ = \ 1,$$

repeated in the candidate propositions generated by L_{-1}, seems to block its interpretation as an assertion. The exact interpretation we would give (126) might depend on other factors in its performance, such as whether *I* or *speaker* were stressed, or whether it was issued with question intonation. Without such clues we are left with multiple candidate interpretations.

To repeat, it is not so much that we want to disallow otiose assertions, to prevent (126) from being interpreted as an assertion; rather, we want to enable it to be interpreted as something more complex. One of the roles of the reconciliation function, X, should be to identify circumstances (based on context) which force certain inferences to be drawn.

The desired result — distinguishing special circumstances of interpretation — can be achieved by a straight-forward condition on X and the introduction of a new class of speech act types. The condition can be given as follows:

(132) CONDITION ON X:
> If p is a candidate proposition based on an interpretive constituent derived at time D_i, and $p \in D_i$, then $X(p) = p^*$

In short, (132) provides for marking candidate propositions when they are redundant. The new class of speech act types will be designed to utilize "*"-marked propositions, capturing the complexities of the use of utterances, that, on the surface, appear to repeat obvious information. A logical candidate for inclusion in this class is the speech act type REITERATE, given as follows:

(133) REITERATE φ (D$_i$)
1: $[d(\underline{say}, \$, \varphi) = 1]^*$
2: $[d(\underline{believe}, \$, \varphi) = 1]^*$
where φ is a proposition,
and 1, 2 $\in$ D$_{i+1}$

Another is the speech act type that we might associate with the use of (126) in the first example above.

(134) REAFFIRM φ (D$_i$)
1: $d(\underline{say}, \$, \varphi) = 1$
2: $[d(\underline{believe}, \$, \varphi) = 1]^*$
where φ is a proposition,
and 1, 2 $\in$ D$_{i+1}$

The difference between reiteration and reaffirmation is a difference in antecedent conditions. Reaffirmation is possible in those cases where it is clear, because of shared contextual belief, for example, that the speaker believes φ. If, however, the speaker had previously stated φ, then the speech act type for reiteration would apply.

There is, theoretically, a third speech act type that could be formed using just the **say** and **believe** relations of constatives, and taking "*"-marked propositions, namely, one that would have

(135) $[d(\underline{say}, \$, \varphi) = 1]^*$
$d(\underline{believe}, \$, \varphi) = 1$

in its description. Such a combination would be possible only if there were some way for a speaker to introduce φ without asserting φ, in short, if it were possible to say φ without being understood as committed to a belief in φ. This appears at first glance to be impossible, to be, in fact, a version of Moore's paradox, namely that one can't say φ *but I don't believe* φ. However, though such cases have not been discussed thus far, it should be clear that there are modes of discourse which could have just this effect.

For example, when one speaks ironically he can be understood as achieving, among other things, the addition of the pair

(136) $d(\underline{say}, \$, \varphi) = 1$
$d(\underline{believe}, \$, \varphi) = 0$

to the content of the discourse situation. Furthermore, in recounting stories (indirect reports, or actual narrative discourse) one can state alleged facts without being understood as committed to an attendant belief. Consider the following report by a speaker about someone else's view of his activities:

(137) *According to John I spent Thursday afternoon at Mary's house entertaining her mother. I took them both to dinner at seven, then to a play at nine. Finally, I drove them around the mountain roads until three in the morning. In fact, I drove them around the mountain roads until two in the morning, but I never took them to dinner and a play.*

Much is involved in the interpretation of such a passage that goes beyond the theory as developed to this point. For example, nothing has been said about tense/aspect interpretations, or about the interaction of speech act interpretation with conventional or conversational implicatures. Still, it should be apparent that any complete theory would want to allow

(138) *Finally, I drove them around the mountain roads until three in the morning.*

to introduce

(139) $d(\underline{say}, \$, \varphi) = 1$,
where $\varphi := (\$ \text{ drove Mary and mother around the mountain roads})$

and

(140) $d(\underline{say}, \$, \psi) = 1$, where $\psi := (\varphi \text{ lasted until three in the morning})$

but would not want

(141) $d(\underline{believe}, \$, \varphi) = 1$, or

(142) $d(\underline{believe}, \$, \psi) = 1$

also to be introduced.

If only the **say** propositions were part of the discourse situation at the time that

(143) *In fact, I drove them around the mountain roads until two in the morning...*

were uttered, it would be possible to derive a pair,

(144) $[d(\underline{say}, \$, \varphi) = 1]^*$
$d(\underline{believe}, \$, \varphi) = 1$

which would give the logically possible third type. We could tentatively identify this type as TESTIFY (TO)/CONFIRM.

(145) TESTIFY (TO)/CONFIRM φ (D_i)

1: $[d(\underline{say}, \$, \varphi) = 1]^*$
2: $d(\underline{believe}, \$, \varphi) = 1$
where φ is a proposition,
and $1, 2 \in D_{i+1}$

There is at least one other case — not including simple recitations or instances of "default" (hypothetical) reasoning — where we would want the theory to admit a **say** but not a **believe** proposition as the interpretation of an utterance. Consider speculative answers to questions, as when in response to (146) one says (147):

(146) *Where did John go?*

(147) [shrugging shoulders] *I think he went to his room.*

Here among the usual interpretive constituents of the locutionary act of (147) would be the following:

(148) $\$$ believes φ

(149) $\varphi := $ John$_i$ went to his$_i$ room

But we would also want the information conventionally conveyed by the shrugging of shoulders to be represented, perhaps as follows:

(150) $\$$ does not believe φ

If, among the interpretive constituents of an utterance, there are inconsistencies such as those created by the presence of both (148) and (150), we could achieve coherence in at least three ways.

First, we might require that the interpretive constituents themselves be consistent, so that, before any application of illocutionary mode functions, contradictory facts are cancelled. This would be effective, though not explanatory, but would have one obvious defect. The theory assumes that facts, when available, will be utilized by the illocutionary mode functions, so there is no guarantee that, at any given moment of discourse time, there will ever be a set of interpretive constituents in which a consistency operation might apply.

Second, we could give a hierarchy of preference to interpretive constituents, making, for example, what one <u>does</u> in performing an utterance more important than what one <u>says</u>. This would let us assign a higher priority to the interpretation of the shrug than to the interpretation of the locutionary aspects of the utterance. If we require that speech acts that can be composed of candidate propositions based on interpretive constituents of preferred status are always to be implemented (at the exclusion of others not so composed), we could achieve the introduction of the propositions

$$(151) \quad d(\underline{say}, \$, \varphi) = 1$$
$$d(\underline{believe}, \$, \varphi) = 0$$

Third, we might utilize a procedure like Gazdar's (1979), in which there is an interaction of interpretive constituents based on their type vis-a-vis the discourse, i.e., whether they derive from entailments, implicatures, or presuppositions associated with the utterance. While Gazdar does not consider how his theory would interact with speech acts, and does not consider fragmentary utterances, or gestures, or utterance types other than those which would give assertions, it does not seem unreasonable to extend his treatment to the kinds of cases I have presented. One might make gesture interpretations into preferred entailments that override the contribution of the entailments of the locutionary utterance. This would have the same effect as the second method, above.

There is a great deal to be said about how a theory of speech acts and a theory like Gazdar's should interact. For the present purposes it should suffice to recognize that there is need for some means of handling utterances like (147) and their accompanying gestures and that treating the non-verbal information as a preferred entailment might be satisfactory as a first approximation. For the balance of this presentation I will assume that gestures are given such preferred treatment.

Returning to the case which (146) and (147) were designed to illustrate, if, indeed, the propositions in (151) (repeated below)

$$(151) \quad d(\underline{say}, \$, \varphi) = 1$$
$$d(\underline{believe}, \$, \varphi) = 0$$

are added to the discourse situation by (147), then at a later time the speaker of (147) could say

(152) *John went to his room.*

with the intention not of reiterating his previous remark but of confirming his belief in it. It is just in this case that (152) would give

$$(153) \quad [d(\underline{say}, \$, \varphi) = 1]^*$$
$$d(\underline{believe}, \$, \varphi) = 1.$$

Interestingly, the distinctions among constative types predicted by the theory — given here as distinctions among ASSERT φ, REAFFIRM φ, TESTIFY(TO)/CONFIRM φ — shed some light on Moore's paradox. The apparent impossibility of

(154) φ *but I don't believe* φ

is parasitic on an interpretation of an utterance like (154) as having monolithic structure (i.e., being a single act) involving only one illocutionary mode. If we assume that (154) can only be an assertion, then it does result in inconsistencies. But the theory presented here allows for multiple illocutionary modes and for utterance sub-parts to give rise to individual speech acts. (154) would not be inconsistent if φ were issued in a mode that did not result in its interpretation as an assertion.

Clearly, the role of *but* is important in explaining how we understand (154), for *but* seems to function by signalling and requiring that the second clause contain an explicit contradiction of something that was implicated in the discourse situation created by the interpretation of first clause. In terms of situation semantics, we could say that *but* maps situation-types into situation-types where the condition is that the derived situation-type contain something that · entails the contradiction of something implicated in the first situation-type. Yet, even without a formal definition of *but*, it should be possible to find analyses of (154) that do not result in paradoxical or inconsistent discourse situations.

For example, as we saw in the discussion of (120) (*I think you should leave*), there are at least two interpretations of this utterance that have very different effects on the discourse situation. As a mere assertion, (120) is a statement of the speaker's beliefs; as a request for action (or some other directive), (120) is an indirect imperative, designed to get the addressee to leave. Consider how these two interpretations might interact in a situation in which a statement in the form of Moore's paradox might be given a plausible, coherent interpretation.

Suppose a and b (husband and wife) are attending a reception given by b's colleagues at which a is the only outsider. In representing the situation to b, a says:

(155) *I wonder if I should leave. It seems this is a closed party. If it is, then I should leave. What do you think?*

In response, b could reply:

(156) *I think you should leave, but I <u>don't</u> think you should leave.*

Here, the first clause in b's response answers a's question, accepting the situation as represented by its presuppositions, namely, that if it is a closed party, then a (an outsider) should leave. The implicature is that b wants a to leave. But that conclusion is defeasible as the second clause shows. There, b asserts a preference, revealing a new representation of the situation a described.

This might be given more explicitly in a gloss of (156) as follows:

(157) "Given the situation as you represent it, namely, that the only factors to consider are whether, if you are an outsider in a closed party, you should leave, then I must conclude that you should leave; however, given that you are my spouse and therefore not completely an outsider, I want you to stay."

In terms of speech act types, (156) might be understood as consisting of an evaluation of alternatives (answer) and a request for action. The evaluation depends on the representation of the situation being evaluated. As a speech act type, we could write:

(158) EVALUATE ALTERNATIVES, σ_1, σ_2, σ_3, ... (D_i)
1: $d(\text{choose}, \$, \sigma_i) = 1$
2: $d(\underline{\text{want}}, \$, @, \sigma_i) = 1$
where σ_1, σ_2, σ_3, ... $\in \Sigma$, a set of situation types, and $\sigma_i \in \Sigma$,
and $1, 2 \in D_{i+1}$

Applied to the case at hand, b must choose between two alternatives

(159) $\sigma_1 := d(\text{leave}, a) = 1$, and
$\sigma_2 := d(\text{stay}, a) = 1$

The evaluation is based on a representation of the discourse situation as containing the following facts:

(160) $d(\text{be-attending-party}, a, b, a_1, ... , a_n) = 1$
$d(\text{be-colleagues}, b, a_1, ... , a_n) = 1$
$d(\text{be-colleagues}, a, a_1, ... , a_n) = 0$

To this is added the information derived from the presuppositions in a's question, namely:

(161) $[d(\text{be-closed-party}) = 1 \Rightarrow$
$[d(\text{be-outsider}, a) = 1 \Rightarrow$
$[d(\text{leave}, a) = 0 \gg d(\text{suffer-neg.-conseq.}, a) = 1]]]$, and
$[d(\text{be-colleagues}, a, a_1, ... , a_n) = 0 \Rightarrow$
$$d(\text{be-outsider}, a) = 1].$$

On the basis of this representation of the discourse situation, b chooses σ_1, which conventionally has the implicature

(162) $d(\underline{\text{want}}, \text{b}, \text{a}, \sigma_1) = 1.$

By using *but*, b indicates that this might not be valid, and goes on to deny (162) by requesting a to stay.

More precisely, if we decide that b has evaluated (answered) a's question in uttering the first clause, we will be hard pressed to interpret the second clause as another evaluation. To do so would lead to a contraction. Among the candidate propositions we could generate from this second clause, of course, are propositions associated with requestives, some of which are in the form of **want** relations. Since a **want** relation occurs in the interpretation of the first clause, and since the use of *but* signals an overt violation of expectations, we would be licensed to choose an interpretation that involved a **want** relation of opposite valence. In conclusion, while the discourse situation at the end of the utterance of the first clause contains proposition (162), at the end of the second clause that proposition is removed, and the discourse situation contains its opposite:

(163) $d(\underline{\text{want}}, \text{b}, \text{a}, (\text{NOT } \sigma_1)) = 1$

As this brief discussion of Moore's paradox illustrates, it is important to consider those cases where contextual information is apparently violated in the interpretation of an utterance. As in those cases where contextual information is repeated in the interpretation of an utterance, such instances give rise to special kinds of speech acts. It is worth considering such cases and how the theory might handle them.

First, a definition:

(164) A discourse situation, D_i, is <u>inconsistent</u> (at time i) if it contains propositions φ and ψ such that $\varphi = \text{NOT } \psi$.

Here, we can further define the condition ($\varphi = \text{NOT } \psi$) as follows:

(165) $\varphi = \text{NOT } \psi$ iff
φ is of the form $d(r^{k+1}_n, a_1, \dots, a_k, \xi) = \delta$, and
ψ is of the form $d(r^{k+1}_n, a_1, \dots, a_k, \xi) = 1-\delta$; or
φ is of the form $d(r^{k+1}_n, a_1, \dots, a_k, \xi) = \delta$, and
ψ is of the form $d(r^{k+1}_n, a_1, \dots, a_k, (\text{NOT } \xi)) = \delta$,
where ξ is a proposition, and $\delta \in \{0, 1\}$.

A stronger version of (164) would be:

(166) A discourse situation, D_i, is <u>inconsistent</u> (at time i) if it contains propositions φ and ψ such that $\varphi \models \text{NOT } \psi$.

(166) is stronger in the sense that explicit contradictions need not be present to give rise to inconsistency. Rather, a contradiction might be derived as a result of a chain of inferences, as given in the following:

(167) $\varphi \models \psi$ iff

$\exists(\xi_1, \dots, \xi_n)$ s. t.

$\varphi \Rightarrow \xi_1$, and $\xi_1 \Rightarrow \xi_2$, ... , and $\xi_{n-1} \Rightarrow \xi_n$, and

$$\xi_n \Rightarrow \psi,$$

where $\xi_1, \dots, \xi_n$ are propositions.[9]

Actually, these definitions are unnecessary since the propositions φ and ψ are in the form of discourse situation-types, and the (partial) function, d, which gives the type of the discourse situation, cannot have two values, e.g., both 1 and 0, at the same time, without ceasing to be a function. In short, it is impossible for a situation-type to be inconsistent in the way suggested above.

However, what we are concerned. with here is offering some guidelines to be used in evaluating candidate propositions vis-a-vis an existing discourse situation. So, while discourse situation-types cannot be inconsistent, certain operations on discourse situations can lead to a situation in which d is no longer a function. Such an operation would be the addition to the discourse situation of any proposition that exhibited a value of opposite valence from an existing proposition. This is what must be avoided. So we might rewrite (164) as follows:

(168) A candidate proposition, p, is inconsistent with a discourse situation (of type given by d), if the addition of p to the discourse situation results in d ceasing to be a function.

Now, one obvious principle for a theory of speech act interpretation would be to avoid the derivation of inconsistent discourse situations. This might be accomplished by deleting any candidate propositions that conflict with existing propositions in the discourse situation, as in the following condition on X:

(169) CONDITION ON X

If p is a candidate proposition based on an interpretive constituent derived at time D_i, and $\exists q \in D_i$ s. t. $p = $ NOT q (or $p \models$ NOT q), then $X(p) = \emptyset$.

The effect of this condition would be to block interpretations that lead to contradictions.[10] For example, if a and b are in a discourse situation and it is understood that a thinks that Mary is beautiful, then when a utters

(170) *Mary is not beautiful*

he will not be interpreted as literally asserting the proposition that Mary is not beautiful. In terms of the theory, the candidate proposition

$$(171) \quad d(\underline{believe}, a, (NOT \ \varphi)) = 1,$$
$$\text{where} \ \varphi := d(\underline{be\text{-}beautiful}, Mary) = 1$$

which would be generated, along with

$$(172) \quad d(\underline{say}, a, (NOT \ \varphi)) = 1, \ \varphi \text{ as before,}$$

as the result of the application of illocutionary mode function L_1 to the interpretive constituent

(173) It is not the case that Mary is beautiful,

would be deleted by the reconciliation function, X, since the proposition

$$(174) \quad d(\underline{believe}, a, \varphi) = 1, \ \varphi \text{ as before,}$$

is already contained in the discourse situation. Specifically, since (171) = NOT (174), $X((171)) = \varnothing$.

Without (171), the speech act type for assertions could not be matched, so, according to the theory, (170) could not be interpreted as an assertion. But is a mechanism that deletes propositions the best means of preventing (171) from being so interpreted? Perhaps, as in the case with repeated information, we should not so much want to block certain interpretations but to enable certain other, more complex ones.

One problem with (169) as it now stands is that it would prevent utterances from being interpreted as retractions or (self-) contradictions as defined earlier. Furthermore, it is not clear that a gross reduction in the number of candidate propositions would necessarily result in a set of surviving propositions that conform to more complex speech act types

Before modifying or removing (169), we should consider wh information would be included in a complex speech act type for (1 Under the circumstances outlined above, we would probably inte (170) as an instance of irony or sarcasm.

More precisely, sarcasm occurs when the discourse situation c the proposition

$$(175) \quad d(\underline{believe}, \$, \varphi) = 1,$$

and the speaker produces an utterance with candidate pro

$$(176) \quad d(\underline{believe}, \$, \psi) = 1, \text{ where } \psi \vDash NOT$$

with the intention of strongly asserting (REAFFIRMING)

84

belief (viz. (175)).

As a speech act type we might write:

(177) SARCASTICALLY ASSERT φ (D_i)
    1: $d(\underline{say},\ \$,\ \varphi) = 1$
    2: $d(\underline{believe},\ \$,\ \psi) = 1$
    where $\varphi,\ \psi$ are propositions
    such that $\varphi \models NOT\ \psi$,
    and $2 \in D_i$,
    and $1,\ 2 \in D_{i+1}$

Irony, as suggested before, also involves saying the opposite of what is intended, but with a subtle difference. The best irony occurs when the speaker and addressee apparently share a set of beliefs that support a series of assertions by the speaker, say $\varphi_1,\ ...\ ,\ \varphi_n$, which have the cumulative effect of undermining one or more of the shared beliefs, thereby revealing the speaker's actual position. This involves the speaker in a deliberate violation of the cooperative principle, where the discourse situation itself is the object of misrepresentation. Put another way, while the speaker appears to be participating in discourse situation, D_i, and appears to share with the addressee a set of beliefs, including the role of sincerity and cooperation, in fact the speaker is issuing utterances in clandestine discourse situation D_i', where one of the central assumptions is that the speaker is neither sincere nor cooperative. The irony has its effect only if the addressee can discover D_i' (in which the role of the addressee might be that of a fool).

To render all this in a speech act type is not easy, but a first attempt might be given as follows:

IRONICALLY ASSERT φ (D_i)
    1: $d(\underline{say},\ \$,\ \psi) = 1$
    2: $d(\underline{believe},\ \$,\ \psi) = 0$
    $d(\underline{believe},\ \$,\ \varphi) = 1$
    $d(\underline{believe},\ \$,\ \xi) = 1$
    $d(\underline{believe},\ \$,\ \zeta) = 1$
    where $\varphi,\ \psi,\ \xi,\ \zeta$ are propositions,
    such that $\psi \models NOT\ \varphi$,
    $\xi := [\exists s\ s.\ t.\ [s(\underline{say},\ \$,\ \psi) = 1 \Rightarrow$
    $s(\underline{believe},\ \$,\ \psi) = 0\ \text{and}\ s(\underline{believe},\ \$,\ \varphi) = 1]]$
    $\wedge\ [s(\underline{believe},\ @,\ \psi) = 1 \Rightarrow s(\underline{be\text{-}fool},\ @) = 1]]$
    $\zeta := (s=d)$
    $\zeta \in D_i$

3: $d(\underline{\text{believe}}, \$, \varphi) = 1$
4: $d(\underline{\text{believe}}, \$, \xi) = 1$
5: $d(\underline{\text{believe}}, \$, \zeta) = 1$
where φ, ψ, ξ, and ζ are propositions
such that $\psi \models \text{NOT } \varphi$,
and $\xi := [\exists s \text{ s. t. } [s(\underline{\text{say}}, \$, \psi) = 1 \Rightarrow$
$[s(\underline{\text{believe}}, \$. \psi) = 0 \text{ and } s(\underline{\text{believe}}, \$, \varphi) = 1]]$
and $[s(\underline{\text{believe}}, @, \psi) = 1 \Rightarrow s(\underline{\text{be-fool}}, @ = 1]]$
and $\zeta := (s=d)$
and 3, 4, 5 $\in D_i$,
and 1, 2, 3, 4, 5 $\in D_{i+1}$

An example of how the conditions on IRONIC ASSERTION come into play in other types of ironic situations is found in the following ironic joke, explicitly involving a discourse situation:[11]

(183)   a: *I know a great "knock-knock" joke.. Want to hear it?*
        b: *Yeah.*
        a: *O.K.   You begin.*

The joke might end at this point; if it continues the situation becomes hopeless for b, for example:

(184)   (continuation of (183))
        b: *"Knock-knock."*
        a: *"Who's there?"*
        b: [silence]

There is no response that b can make, for the role b plays in the "knock-knock" dialogue — that of initiator — is the role played by the joke-teller, the one with the punch line.   But it is a who apparently claimed to know the joke, hence who should be the joke-teller.   The joke, it turns out, is on b who has been unwittingly lead into a role reversal.

This is an ironic joke because the addressee is made the fool and because there is a parallel discourse situation, to the one b participates in, in which the assumptions that produce the joke situation are clearly manifested.   By offering to tell a joke, a tacitly agrees to derive a situation which is humorous.   Typically, that situation is a fiction, involving some imaginary participants, for example, the mock interlocutors of a "knock-knock" dialogue.   In this case, however, the humorous situation is the actual discourse situation itself.

In terms of situation types we could characterize this as follows:

$$\text{and } 1, 2, 3, 4, 5 \in D_{i+1}$$

Note that in terms of speech act types it is not, strictly speaking, necessary to represent the discourse situation as it stood before the addressee recognized the irony. For the addressee, that discourse situation was dramatically impoverished, reflecting a naive presumption of literalness. Recognition of the irony has the effect of adding a great deal of information to the discourse situation at one stroke, bringing the addressee's and speaker's understanding into congruence.

A step toward correcting the condition on X (viz. (169)), and simplifying the speech act types for sarcastic and ironic assertion, can be taken by, first replacing the deletion of the candidate proposition by rewriting as its negation with "*"-marking, and second, making the condition optional. The new version would read:

(179) CONDITION ON X (OPTIONAL)
If p is a candidate proposition based on an interpretive constituent derived at time D_i, and $q \in D_i$ s. t. $p \models$ NOT q, then $X(p) = p^*$.

Now, when (150) is uttered, the candidate proposition (151) is converted to

(180) $[d(\underline{believe}, a, (NOT \ \varphi)) = 0]^*$
where $\varphi := d(be\text{-}beautiful, Mary) = 1$

The set of surviving candidate propositions then includes (180) along with (172), which can not match the speech act type associated with simple assertions.

We can now rewrite the speech act types for SARCASTICALLY ASSERT φ ((177)) and IRONICALLY ASSERT φ ((178)), taking advantage of the new marking convention, as follows:

(181) SARCASTICALLY ASSERT φ (D_i)
1: $d(\underline{say}, \$, \psi) = 1$
2: $[d(\underline{believe}, \$, \psi) = 0]^*$
3: $d(\underline{believe}, \$, \varphi) = 1$
where φ, ψ are propositions
such that $\psi \models$ NOT φ,
and $3 \in D_i$,
and $1, 2, 3 \in D_{i+1}$

(182) IRONICALLY ASSERT φ (D_i)
1: $d(\underline{say}, \$, \psi) = 1$
2: $[d(\underline{believe}, \$, \psi) = 0]^*$

(185) a offers to tell a "knock-knock" joke:
d(**derive**, **a**, **s**) $= 1$
s. t. s(**be-humorous**) $= 1$
and s(**be-"knock-knock"-joke**) $= 1$

(186) a operates under several crucial assumptions, viz:
s $=$ d, and
[d(<u>say</u>, **a**, φ) $= 1 \Rightarrow$
[d(<u>believe</u>, **a**, φ) $= 0$ and d(<u>believe</u>, **a**, ψ) $= 1$]]
where $\varphi := $ s(**be-"knock-knock"-joke**) $= 1$
and $\psi := $ s(**be-joke-on-b**) $= 1$
and [d(<u>believe</u>, **b**, φ) $= 1 \Rightarrow$ d(**be-fool**, **b**) $= 1$]

(187) The remaining assumption might be shared by b:
[d(**be-fool**, **b**) $= 1 \Rightarrow$ d(**be-humorous**) $= 1$]

The above example and the earlier ones in this section have been designed to illustrate the role of contextual information in the interpretation of speech acts. While there are many ways that context and interpretation can interact, only two aspects of that interaction have been focused on here, namely, those cases where contextual information is repeated or violated in candidate propositions. The theory handles these cases via simple conditions on the reconciliation of candidate propositions with discourse situation content, and the definition of a new class of speech act types designed to capture the complexities of such discourse situations. But there is another feature of context that affects speech act interpretation, which has only been alluded to in the previous examples. Given several candidate speech act interpretations, what in the discourse situation influences an addressee to make specific choices? To answer this question we should consider the final stage in the derivation of speech act interpretation, where candidate propositions are matched against speech act types and successfully matched types are chosen for implementation.

3.4. MATCHING TYPES AND IMPLEMENTING CHOICES

After candidate propositions have been reconciled with context, giving a set containing possibly modified versions of the original candidate propositions, it must be decided whether any of the available speech act types has been matched, and, if so, whether to implement a matched type.

One way of deciding whether a speech act type is matched by a set of candidate propositions would be to generate the power set of the set of candidate propositions, then systematically compare each subset of candidate propositions with each speech act type. This would be effective, of course, since the power set would give all the possible combinations of candidate propositions, and any match would involve some combination of candidate propositions. However, this would result in a computational nightmare, since, for even a small number of candidate propositions, the distinct combinations will be quite large, and many will be impossible.

For example, just the four candidate propositions derived from the application of L_1 and L_2 to interpretive constituent (123) (reflecting the ambiguity in the interpretation of *I think that you should leave*), have $(2^4 - 1)$ or 15 combinations. Yet, among these 15, only a few could possibly match speech act types.

A more judicious approach would be to consider each speech act type in order, then determine whether the requisite candidate propositions are available, along with the conditions on context that the speech act type demands. One by one, the inventory of speech act types would be exhausted and all possible (candidate) interpretations of an utterance would be found. It should be clear that an effective algorithm for giving matches could be written for any finite set of candidate propositions and any finite set of speech act types.

A much more interesting problem arises when we consider the factors that affect choices for implementation. In the theory developed here, all matches have equal status as candidates for implementation, reflecting the ambiguity of interpretation associated with natural language utterances. In actual discourse, however, multiple ambiguity cannot be tolerated and choices are made, giving some interpretations, in effect, higher status than others.

Several factors could determine which of more than one matched speech act type is to be chosen. First, we might consider a hierarchy of "preferred" types, corresponding to the unmarked conditions on utterance situations. For example, if the preconditions for both simple assertion and ironic assertion are met, we might decide to choose the simple assertion interpretation on the grounds that we impute less to the speaker by such a choice. This operating principle corresponds to Bach and Harnish's "Presumption of Literalness" (1979:12) to the extent that the default condition here as well as there is to assume that the most direct interpretation has a higher value than any other type. Of course, in a theory utilizing speech act types, many of which might be matched simultaneously, "direct" interpretation must be defined explicitly in terms of speech act type ranking. Here, ranking reflects the amount of inferencing required to produce a match: in general, the less inferencing, the more direct the interpretation. An incomplete ranking of some of the constatives discussed in previous sections might be given as follows:

(188)   assertion < reiteration < contradiction < retraction < ironic
                                                                   assertion

On this scale, assertions are the least marked types; ironic assertions the most marked. The arrows indicate an implicational valence: all types to the left require fewer steps of inferencing. For example, an ASSERT speech act type has no conditions on the context, D_i, and the propositions that compose it are directly generated by the illocutionary mode function, L_1. In contrast, a REITERATE speech act type requires that existing facts of the context be matched, in addition to the adding of the asserted propositions to the content of the discourse situation. A CONTRADICT speech act type requires further that a chain of inferencing leading to the negation of existing facts of the context be found (in the stronger sense of CONTRADICT), or at least an overt negation of existing facts (in the weaker sense). A RETRACT speech act type requires that an assumption be made that the speaker intentionally is changing his position (and not merely misspeaking, or forgetting his earlier stand). Finally, in IRONIC ASSERTION, the addressee must decide, based on an unspecified chain of inferencing, that despite all appearances to the contrary, the speaker intends just the opposite of what he says. In this case, the addressee must not only make inferences based on actual facts of the context, but must impute to the speaker a motive unsupportable in terms of the overt semantics of the utterance.

The scale above leaves open the question of whether there might be other speech act types that fall between the given ones; or whether there are other types that are more "complex" than ironic assertion. Indeed, the scale as presented here serves only an expository purpose. The theory does not depend on its absoluteness, and in fact considers the presence or absence of types to be an empirical, language- (or dialect-) specific matter.

A second factor affecting choice among several candidate speech act types might be discourse genre or type. While the problem of characterization of discourse genre is orthogonal to that of a theory of speech acts, it seems altogether reasonable that discourse genres should make reference to speech act types.[12] For example, if we believe that the speaker is engaging in narration, we might assign a high priority to interpreting utterances as constatives in general, and a low priority to interpreting them as requestives. On the other hand, if we believe the speaker to be engaged in instruction, we might assign a higher priority to requestives (as when the speaker gives us the directions for baking a cake).

Another way of viewing this factor is in terms of how our perception of speaker-addressee goals affects our decision to implement a particular speech act type. Given that a particular utterance can be interpreted in many ways (reflecting many possible types of speaker-addressee relationships), it seems wise to choose just those interpretations that are consonant with achieving the kinds of relationships that contribute to the goals of the discourse situation. *Ceterus paribus*, if someone is telling a story, we should tend to interpret a statement such as *John wants to go home* not as an indirect request for the addressee to open the door (for John), but as a stage-setting fact uttered in "historical present" tense; if someone is giving us directions on how to assemble an air compressor, we should tend to interpret a statement such as *The screwdriver is in the top drawer* not as an assertion of fact but as a request to get the screwdriver (cf. Grosz (1978)).

This interaction of apparent goals and speech act interpretations is the source of the association of speaker intention with illocutionary force. (Recall the earlier paraphrase of Searle in which speech acts were defined at every level as involving speaker intention.) The speech act is just that discourse event that brings about the changes that the speaker intends in order to achieve the effect desired.

Perhaps in a solely production oriented, or speaker-based theory of speech acts such a perspective is justified. But in a more general theory, and certainly, in any theory that is neutral with respect to point of view (encoding/decoding), it is an unnecessary complication to introduce speaker intention directly.

It is precisely at this point that a theory of speech acts manifests its limitations as a theory of discourse. Discourse involves more than the construction of utterances or connected series of utterances. It involves an encounter with a special kind of beginning, middle, and end (cf. Schiffrin (1977)), in which information is exchanged and relationships between interlocutors are created. The problems of navigating through a discourse cannot be solved by a knowledge of speech act types and illocutionary mode functions alone. Much more general planning mechanisms are needed — the same as would be required for almost any non-reflex driven task — but sensitive to the specific kinds of choices that are associated with speech acts.

It is as a result of a general planning mechanism that we can formulate our own goals, models of others' goals, and models of what has been achieved (and remains to be achieved) in some planning space involving (possibly multiple) agents.[13] It is only because of our ability to view the discourse situation as goal directed that we can resolve the ambiguity of utterances, and in particular, make speech act assignments.

The theory of speech acts should not include a general planning mechanism; rather, it should tell us how an utterance can come to be given one or many interpretations. But it should not tell us which of many interpretations, ultimately, to choose.[14] The theory of discourse, however, should make and explain such choices.

Speaker intentionality is a function of the goals the speaker seeks to achieve in the discourse, not directly a function of the speech act. Whenever a choice among competing speech act types must be made, the theory should appeal to the planning mechanism for a resolution.

It might be that our knowledge of discourse genres reflects, merely, the canonical "scripts" (cf. Shank and Abelson (1977)) associated with the interaction of speakers who engage in such discourse. Alternatively, in terms of conventionalized plans, someone telling a story has long-range and immediate goals, best achieved by "constating;" someone engaged in giving instructions or directions, requiring our participation and designed to effect concrete physical changes as well as abstract ones, has goals best achieved by "requesting."

It goes without saying that our ability to engage in conversation is general enough so that, even without scripts guiding us, we should be able to decide what is being attempted or achieved by a particular utterance. To the extent that our general planning and problem solving mechanisms share a significant amount of data, an utterance's use can be deduced. However, the computational complexity of disambiguating an utterance's use can be greatly reduced if it is known or suspected that the utterance's use conforms to a well-specified set of shared rules. Some of those rules may take the form of illocutionary mode functions and speech act types, and some may take the form of scripted behavior. We could reasonably think of preference hierarchies as generalizations about the interaction of speech act theory and discourse genre, derived, ultimately, from empirical experience and deduced in the course of general problem solving in discourse.

In the final analysis, the theory of speech acts may offer nothing better than the direction *make a choice*, when confronted with competing candidate speech act types. Here there could be three possible outcomes.

First, one could choose all the candidate speech act types, by keeping, in effect, separate models of the discourse situation for each candidate. This corresponds to implementing all interpretations. This, of course, is the least attractive computationally and theoretically, since it leaves the interesting question of discriminatory interpretation unresolved. Presumably this would work only if one required that later contradictions would be used to guide pruning of the non-viable branches of the model. But the problem of multiple interpretations of a single utterance could not be accommodated, unless all the combinations of the candidate speech act types were admitted.

Second, one could choose a single speech act type, say, at random, and continue until the model of the discourse situation became non-viable, at which point backtracking and a second choice would be effected. This is not an unreasonable solution, since really bad choices would manifest their inappropriateness in a relatively short amount of time. So bookkeeping and backtracking might not be too expensive. However, this task absolutely rules out the possibility that an utterance might be given more than one speech act interpretation.

Third, one could choose several speech act types, in combination or alone, for some limited branching models. In this case, of course, multiple acts could be accommodated, and the number of alternative models of the discourse situation could be restricted. This does nothing to solve the problem of what to chose, but, in theory, it gives an upper limit on the number of distinct choices to be made.

Implementation of a choice involves nothing more than first, adding the propositions that match the speech act type being implemented to the set of propositions that give the content of the discourse situation, and second, performing all operations specified by the conditions on the speech act type. In the case of the implementation of a retraction, say, having the form below (repeating the information given in (46)), this amounts to adding propositions 2, 3, and 5 to the set of propositions which hold of the discourse situation, and removing the propositions that correspond to 1 and 4.

(189) 1: $d(\text{\underline{say}}, \$, \varphi) = 1$
2: $d(\text{\underline{say}}, \$, \psi) = 1$
3: $d(\text{\underline{believe}}, \$, \psi) = 1$
4: $d(\text{\underline{believe}}, \$, \varphi) = 1$
5: $d(\text{\underline{believe}}, \$, \varphi) = 0$
where φ, ψ are propositions
such that $\psi := d(\text{\underline{believe}}, \$, \varphi) = 0$

Put another way, if 1 and 4 were true of the old discourse situation, then 2, 3, and 5 would be true of the new discourse situation, but not 1 and 4

Implementation of multiple choices is possible only to the extent that the conditions on the speech act types being implemented are mutually satisfiable. It would be non-problematic to implement both the speech act type ASSERT and the speech act type REQUEST ACTION (derived, say, for (130) as before) since nothing in the conditions of one conflicts with the conditions of the other. All the following could be added compatibly to the content of the discourse situation:

(190) $d(\text{\underline{say}}, \$, \varphi) = 1$
$d(\text{\underline{believe}}, \$, \varphi) = 1$
$d(\text{\underline{want}}, \$, @, \varphi) = 1$
$d(\text{\underline{request}}, \$, @, \varphi) = 1,$
where $\varphi := @$ leaves ⟨from here⟩

However, it would be impossible to implement both a RETRACT and REITERATE since the conditions are not compatible. (Indeed, it would be impossible for both to be candidates for implementation at the same point in the discourse.)

While implementation presents no special problems for the theory, deciding what to do with unutilized candidate speech act types does, for it seems that in actual discourse there is an interpretive paradox. Once a particular speech act type is chosen for implementation, competing candidate types no longer interfere, that is, they seem to be disposed of. Yet, later, it is often possible to reinterpret individual utterances or even whole discourses by resurrecting competing candidate types. The paradox, computationally, is that these unutilized interpretations are apparently buried but not forgotten.

This phenomenon could be accounted for in several ways. First, it might be possible to retain an accurate memory of the literal performance of the utterances in any discourse, and to reenact portions, utilizing different representations of the content, based perhaps on hindsight, to generate new choices (corresponding at some points to the earlier unused candidate speech act types). This is not implausible, but seems to conflict with the observation that, in terms of longer term memory, what is retained has the form of interpreted rather than literal information. Second, more plausibly, it might be that only problematic choice-alternatives, and even the literal performance factors that lead to the choice problems, are retained, and serve as a focus for later analysis. This would mean that an individual's model of the discourse situation would include not only a set of propositions that held for the discourse, but also a set of propositions' reflecting degrees of indecision and alternative interpretations. Only after more information about the context of the utterances is deduced (later) can indecision be resolved.

A related issue that goes to the heart of the present theory, and is woefully ignored in previous theories, is the problem of supra-utterance acts. Recall that the supra-utterance acts can be achieved only after a series of steps or accrued effects have occurred. In the most interesting cases one might not know at the outset that a particular supra-utterance act is being attempted, but recognizes the achievement of the type only after the last step. Where the type is defined in terms of complex conditions on context, each of which can be established by non-problematic simple acts, the supra-utterance phenomena are readily explanable. But where the type is defined in terms of special interpretations that must be made across the board (from first step to last), it seems that we must simultaneously retain many candidate representations of the discourse situation in order to derive the intended type.

More concretely, consider two supra-utterance effects briefly discussed in preceding sections, a refutation and an ironic joke. Even without committing ourselves to detailed speech act types[15] some generalizations are possible.

The conditions on a refutation are such that, almost without any sense of the speaker's goals, if the addressee has been able to interpret the speaker's utterances leading up to the refutation in the most straightforward way — taking assertions to be literal assertions, even questions to be literal questions — by the time the "punch line" of the refutation is reached, the context will contain all the propositions necessary to satisfy the refutation. In short, if REFUTATION is part of the addressee's repertoire of speech act types, at the point at which the ultimate, completing utterance is being interpreted, according to this theory, the speech act type REFUTATION will be matched (among, no doubt, others). At least the addressee will have the option of recognizing the utterance as achieving a refutation, even if he doesn't exercise the option of implementing that interpretation.

However, in the case of an ironic joke, a straight-forward interpretation of the utterances preceding the "punch line" will not suffice to establish the preconditions needed.[16] Here it is necessary for the addressee to recognize that the speaker does not believe some of the propositions he is stating, etc., though he may deliver them in the same fashion as if he were making true assertions. In order to derive the correct type as the interpretation of the punch line, an addressee must either have alternative (indeed, contradictory) models of the discourse situation covering the stretch of interaction preceding the punch line, or initiate a reanalysis of the preceding text based on the raw data of the interaction which he has stored in memory.

The problem is, simply, that this latter case seems to defy the determinism which underlies the theory presented here. We wish to have real choices made which affect the form of the resulting discourse situation, and have alternatives (ambiguities) resolved away. At the same time, we wish to remain flexible enough to allow for radical reinterpretations of indeterminately long stretches of discourse.

I would suggest that this problem is illusory, and stems from a misunderstanding of what utterances achieve in discourse. It has traditionally been assumed in speech act theory that speaker and addressee share context. But, clearly, this is an idealization. Speaker and addressee may share many assumptions about the context, but still have unique models of the discourse situation. And what is achieved by an utterance may vary greatly in absolute terms without affecting the perception of either speaker or addressee that their representations of the effects differ markedly.

An ironic joke as intended by a speaker reflects a systematic issuing of false statements all of which are reflected in his model of the discourse situation. The addressee might regard the statements as assertions and thereby create a model of the discourse situation that diverges significantly from that of the speaker. At the point of the punch line the speaker's model is complete, the effect is achieved, and the discourse is rounded. If we were to write a theory of speech acts that took only the speaker's point of view, we could say that the effect of the punch line was just what the speaker intended. But from the addressee's point of view the situation is gravely different. If the punch line proves anomalous, he must either dismiss it or seek a repair. If it proves interpretable, non-ironically, he can go on as if nothing special had happened (indeed, for him, nothing special had). Regardless of the course the interpretation takes, including one in which a reanalysis is initiated and the ironic flavor captured, it will be a different effect for the addressee than for the speaker.

For example, the speaker's utterance might have the (perlocutionary) effect of convincing the addressee that his model of the discourse situation is faulty, and of initiating a reanalysis of the preceding stretch of conversation. If it is recognized that the utterance is delivered in the fashion of a punch line — a summary type statement, perhaps, followed by a phonemic pause during which the speaker makes eye contact with the addressee — the addressee might short-circuit the reanalysis process by changing the value of the propositions thematically related to the punch line. For example, one could change some the propositions of the form

$$d(\underline{\text{believe}}, \$, \varphi) = 1$$

to propositions of the form

$$d(\underline{\text{believe}}, \$, \varphi) = 0$$

and thereby create some of the preconditions for an IRONIC JOKE interpretation.

Here, the processes for the speaker and addressee are very different: the speaker arrives at the discourse situation D_{i+1} (giving the effect of the utterance) in a step-by-step fashion; the addressee, by radical reconstruction of a moribund representation. If we equate the ultimate meaning of the act with the procedure which derives it, then this joke-telling will have a different meaning for the addressee than for the speaker. The acts will not be the same.

This is a problem for speech act theory only if we are bent upon maintaining an <u>equivalence</u> of representation for each act, as opposed to an <u>equipotentiality</u>, in which not the intended act type, but an act type compatible with the current most informed representation of discourse situation content, is found. In the case of the ironic joke, the addressee can derive a representation of the content that is compatible with that of the speaker by an operation on selected propositions (a case of repair-driven, backwards inferencing); a speech act type match can be made. But while the speaker's intention might be discovered in the successful match, the effects of the earlier, contributing utterances leading up to the punch line will have been lost.

It is a strength of the present theory that absolute equivalence of representation is not required, and that it is the content of speech act types, as matched, that determines what is added to the discourse situation. If we are the misunderstood speaker who tells an ironic joke, we can be glad that a type match can occur which brings our addressee's representation of the discourse situation more into line with our own, even if we are sad that the style of delivery and the practiced subtlety of our telling must go unappreciated.[17]

When it is decided that a particular speech act type is matched, even if such matching can occur only after the content of the discourse situation is reanalyzed, just those propositions that correspond to the matched type are added, and the content is made current and brought into conformity with the conditions on the matched type. It is not necessary to return to misanalyzed segments of earlier discourse and reexamine the speech act types chosen. Our concern always should be that current content of speaker and addressee be in congruence as much as possible, not that the paths taken to a particular point be identical.

Excess or unused candidate propositions can be dropped, once a match or matches are chosen; they serve no purpose in future reanalysis, since they can be regenerated on the basis of what is remembered of the literal text. To a certain extent they may be retained in the form of the propositions that alternative, candidate speech acts contain, whenever such alternatives are represented. At branching points, then, some unutilized candidate propositions will be carried along. In these cases, too, we can assume that once a branch becomes non-viable all the propositions associated with it are discarded.

All of the operations discussed in this section, representing the final stage of a speech act interpretation process, can be summarized formally with the aid of the following conventions:

> (191) Let P be a finite set of candidate propositions derived from the application of illocutionary mode functions $L_i \in L$, to the interpretive constituents of the utterance (or utterance fragment) under consideration.

> (192) Let D_i be the set of propositions which hold of the discourse situation at time i.

(193) Let T be a finite set of speech act types, with each individual speech act type, t_i, composed of one or more propositions in general form (i.e., with variables unevaluated) and one or more conditions on the discourse situation and the variables.

In addition we can define the following operations based on these conventions:

(194) A speech act type, t_i, is matched by a set of propositions, $P' = \{ p_j, \dots, p_n \}$, in a discourse situation, D_i, if each $p_m \in P'$ is also $\in P \cup D_i$, and there is an evaluation of the variables in the speech act type such that each proposition under t_i is in P', and no proposition not under t_i is also in P', and all the conditions under t_i are met.

(195) A match function, $\dot{M}$, returns matched speech act types given a finite set of speech act types, T, a finite set of candidate propositions, P, and a discourse situation, D_i:
$$M(T, P, D_i) = T^*,$$
where T^* is a set of matched speech act types, such that each $t_i^* \in T^*$ is matched, relative to P and D_i, and all propositions under t_i^* are evaluated (i.e., variable-free).

After application of M there is a set of candidate speech acts (i.e., evaluated speech act types) which represent the potential speech act interpretation of the utterance (or fragment) under consideration. One or more of these candidates (t_i^*) must be chosen for implementation. As mentioned above, a variety of factors can influence choice, including considerations of perceived speaker-addressee goals, and discourse genre. The effects of this last factor might be incorporated as follows:

(196) Let G be a finite set of discourse genre types, with each individual genre type, g_i, consisting of a partially ordered subset of speech act types and an assignment function, h_i. To any candidate speech act, $t_j^* \in T^*$, h_i assigns a number corresponding to the rank of the speech act type represented by t_j^* in the subset under g_i (with no assignment if there is no corresponding speech act type).

Then we can define a choice function as follows:

(197) A choice function, C, returns a partially ordered set of matched speech act types, T^{**}, given a set of matched speech act types, T^*, a set of genre types, $G' \subseteq G$, and a

discourse situation, D_i:
$$C(T^*, \ G', \ D_i) \ = \ T^{**},$$
where each $t_j^* \in T^{**}$ bears a rank number derived as a result of the application of every $g_j \in G'$ to T^*, and each $g_j \in G'$ is compatible with D_i.[18]

The last operation involves the derivation of the new discourse situation, given by the implementation of one or more speech acts. Depending on whether we allow branching models of the discourse situation, this can be simple or complex. For example, we might define an implementation function for non-branching models as follows:

(198)   An implementation function, I, returns a new discourse situation upon being presented with an ordered set of candidate speech acts, T^{**}, and a discourse situation, D_i:
$$I(T^{**}, \ D_i) \ = \ D_{i+1},$$
where D_{i+1} represents the addition of the highest ranking candidate speech act in T^{**}, t_j^*, to D_i, such that all the conditions in t_j^* are met in D_{i+1}.

Alternatively, of course, more than one candidate speech act or even all could be implemented, depending on compatibility. If branching models are allowed, I could be redefined to return a <u>set</u> of new discourse situations, perhaps along the following lines:

(199)   An implementation function, I, returns a set of new discourse situations upon being presented with an ordered set of candidate speech acts, T^{**}, and a discourse situation, D_i:
$$I(T^{**}, \ D_i) \ = \ \mathbf{D}_{i+1}$$
where each $D_{i+1, \ j} \in \mathbf{D}_{i+1}$ represents the addition of one or more candidate speech acts in T^{**}, to D_i, such that all the conditions on the speech acts are met in $D_{i+1, \ j}$.

Again, individual choices of one or more candidate speech acts would depend on mutual compatibility and on some criteria of choice.

The entire speech act interpretation process is presented schematically in Figure 2. It remains for us to consider some concrete discourse situations and the kinds of interpretations that this theory would generate. To that enterprise we turn in Chapter 4.

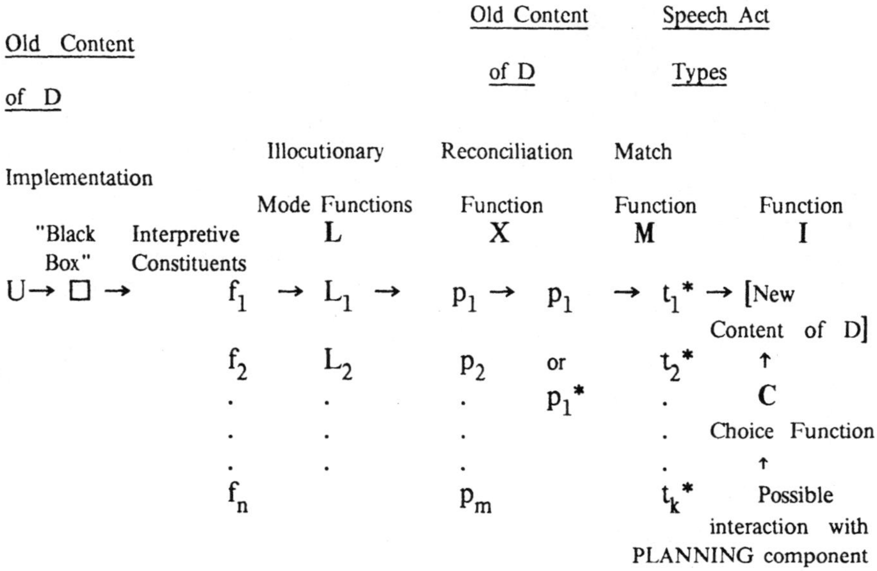

Old Content
of D

Old Content
of D

Speech Act
Types

		Illocutionary	Reconciliation	Match	
Implementation					
		Mode Functions	Function	Function	Function
"Black	Interpretive	L	X	M	I
Box"	Constituents				

$U \rightarrow \square \rightarrow$ $f_1 \rightarrow L_1 \rightarrow p_1 \rightarrow p_1 \rightarrow t_1^* \rightarrow$ [New Content of D]

$f_2 \qquad L_2 \qquad p_2 \qquad \text{or} \qquad t_2^* \qquad \uparrow$

$. \qquad . \qquad . \qquad p_1^* \qquad . \qquad C$

$. \qquad . \qquad . \qquad\qquad\qquad . \qquad \text{Choice Function}$

$. \qquad . \qquad . \qquad\qquad\qquad . \qquad \uparrow$

$f_n \qquad\qquad\qquad p_m \qquad\qquad t_k^* \qquad \text{Possible}$

interaction with
PLANNING component

An Overview of the Speech Act Interpretation Process

Figure 2.

CHAPTER 4 SPEECH ACTS, MEANING, AND TRUTH

4.0. INTRODUCTION

It is the goal of this chapter to explicate and test some central aspects of the theory presented in Chapter 3, and the framework in which it is set. This is accomplished in two ways: first, by offering an interpretation of what roles meaning and truth play in a discourse setting; and second, by examining in detail several kinds of discourse situations and the interaction of speech act interpretation and context of utterance. The first of these approaches is preliminary to the second, and serves as a general discussion of the semantics of discourse situations, where the problem of truth is redefined as a problem of orientation in a discourse situation and the evaluation of interpretive constituents. The second approach proceeds through the discussion of three cases, each successively more complex and more complete as an arena for testing speech act theory.

The first of these cases is based on Stalnaker (1978), where the speech act *assertion* is discussed. Stalnaker considers the problem of specifying the propositional content of an assertion, then evaluating it relative to some context. The examples he uses are repeated and applied to the present theory which offers a more detailed analysis of the situations he discusses. In particular, it is argued that Stalnaker fails to distinguish among a variety of constatives that figure in his discussion, collecting all under the single term, "assertion." The important difference between essential speech act effects and contingent discourse-pragmatic effects is emphasized.

The second of the cases is based on Goffman (1976), and focuses on the hypertactic functions of speech acts, as well as their more usual interpretations. Goffman considers the class of responses that could be made to the utterance, *Do you have the time?*, which depend both on factors of context and on interlocutor knowledge of speech act types, including knowledge of possible moves in a discourse situation. The subclass of responses involving real questions is examined in detail, and the effect of question presupposition on answer interpretation is probed.

The final case is based on Coleman and Kay (1981) where the semantics of the word (speech act) *lie* is discussed. Of interest to us is the difference between the prototype definition of lying, which they offer, and the speech act type definition which we could formulate. Their data is reexamined and the question is raised whether the judgments of degrees of lying their subjects reported could not better be accounted for by introducing other parameters (e.g., degree of cooperation) at the level of the discourse situation. In general, the Coleman and Kay test cases represent the most complex discourse situations for constatives, and the most interesting proving-ground for the theory of speech acts developed here, because aspects of the world (truth), the speaker's knowledge (representation of beliefs), and the discourse situation event (involving perceived intentions), all interact.

The program for this chapter, then, consists of a general introduction to the conception of truth that the theory presupposes, and an investigation of a number of concrete cases where distinctions between the discourse situation and the world are critical. For the most part, the types of speech acts in focus in these cases are constatives (though others play a role); and the cases proceed from the relatively more simple to the relatively more complex. In all instances, the theory accounts for the phenomena presented at least as well as the proposals made by the original investigators; and at some points, is more natural and more explanatory.

4.1. ORIENTATION IN THE WORLD

While the term *meaning* has largely been dropped from the technical vocabulary of formal semantics, it is, nevertheless, the meaning of utterances that concerns anyone who deals with the problem of representing and explaining the effects of natural language; and it is that which concerns us in a theory of speech acts. Traditionally, two rather different, though equally formal, approaches have been taken to the issue of meaning representation, broadly divisible, along academic lines, into the philosophical and psychological camps.

The philosophical camp includes both philosophers and logicians, and takes as its object the explication of meaning in terms of truth-conditions, specifically, in terms of relationships between expressions of the language and states of affairs in a model (typically intended to represent the actual world). Proceeding from the classical tradition in logic, this approach was seminally influenced in the 19th century by the work of Frege[1], though in this century it has bifurcated somewhat. In a relatively narrower conception of the enterprise, one finds, for example, the work of Tarski, Quine, and most recently Montague; in a relatively broader conception, one finds the work of Russell, Strawson, and Davidson.[2] The general concern of both groups has been to develop models of the world that admit of ready mapping into linguistic structure. The kinds of linguistic objects studied are principally (though not exclusively) sentences in indicative mood, under a limited range of modalities. The difference between the two groups is basically one of style: the first group takes linguistic objects to be special kinds of mathematical entities that have determinate values in the world; the second group, in a more "common sense" analysis of natural language, stresses the conditions on the use of linguistic objects that affect their value. Neither group deals with discourse situations in great detail.

The psychological camp includes linguists, psychologists, and, recently, computer scientists, who see the goal of formal semantics as a specification of the representation constructs that are produced in the comprehension of an utterance. Eclectic in origin, this tradition has roots in the work of von Humboldt, Piaget, and Whorf, but has become more focused in linguistic work on semantics, including that of Katz and Jackendoff, and the generative semanticists. Recently it has flowered in the discipline of Cognitive Science, among whose practitioners we find Johnson-Laird, H. Clark, Schank, and Winograd. There is in this approach nothing like the consensus of direction or focus of goals that one finds in the philosophical tradition. Rather, there is a strong sense that a complete semantics must involve a variety of aspects of cognition, including some means of representing human memory, perception, and thought processing. The meaning of a word or utterance, it is held, might best be given in terms of the procedures that are involved in comprehending it, and less solipsistically, in terms of how the representation process models the world. There is a greater tendency in this approach to view discourse situations as the framework in which to develop semantics, though there is no standard notion of what discourse should be understood as including, or of the formal apparatus to be used in representing discourse situations.

While I have characterized these two groups, the philosophical and the psychological, as wholly distinct, most modern work on semantics, especially among linguists, is informed by both traditions; and even those authors who strongly identify themselves as belonging to one group are not insensible to the assumptions and methods of the other. The theory presented here is not meant to bridge any gaps, or to demonstrate the superiority of a particular approach, rather to suggest formal means of dealing with one of the phenomena of discourse. And it should be understood as borrowing from both traditions.

Necessarily, we should be concerned with the rules that translate linguistic structure into propositions that reflect relationships in the world, hence, have truth-conditions. But we should also recognize that much of the information we derive from discourse is not stateable in terms of truth-conditions alone, and is not intended to represent the actual world. Instead, much of the purpose of interactive communication is to affect an interlocutor in a certain way, possibly by expressing one's views on a matter (involving revelation of one's beliefs, which may or may not be anchored in the actual world[3]), possibly by changing the discourse situation (hence, changing the actual world) so that an interlocutor must react.[4] With this in mind, we might adumbrate the assumptions that form the basis of the approach to semantics taken in this thesis. Broadly speaking, the assumptions are designed to characterize the role of language in mediating between the private world of cognition ("mind") and the actual world ("reality").

To recapitulate the position taken by situation semantics, it is assumed that the actual world consists of primitive objects having primitive properties, and standing in primitive relationships. It is further assumed that any model of the world requires constructs which represent, to some arbitrary degree of fine-grainedness, such objects, properties, and relationships. Any information about some state of the world, relative to such a model, can be reduced to information about the objects, properties, and relations that obtain in that state; and any information about some event in the world can be induced from information about a series of successive states. The construct that is employed here to capture the information in a state of the world, of course, is the situation-type.

It is assumed, further, that cognitive states are states in the world, with the Gödelian wrinkle that some cognitive states are self-referential. Nevertheless, the objects, properties, and relations that are represented in cognitive states are the objects, properties and relations of the actual world. So a perception of the world — which might be represented in a cognitive state — is accurate to the extent that the objects, properties and relations exhibited in the cognitive state are isomorphic to the actual objects, properties, and relations that obtain in the world. If S is the set of situations as determined by the perception, and W is the set of situations in the actual world, 'the question of truth is the question whether S is contained in W:

(200) S $\subseteq$ W

Note, this is trivially true if we believe that the question is merely whether the cognitive state is part of the world — it is. The relevant question is whether the representation of the world as encoded in the cognitive state is accurate. That will be the case only if the set of situation-types that give the perception also characterize the situation perceived.

There are certainly many times when it is just this question that interests us; when we want to know if a given representation of the world is precise. But there are also many other times when the actual world need not enter the picture; when we are only interested in knowing what someone thinks. In such cases we are concerned with the details of the perception, not its veracity. More generally, we could say that mental representations of situations (perceptions) are not truth-functional, but claims about the relationship between mental representations and the world are.

Discourse situations are characterized by having interlocutors engage in information exchange. The information is necessarily mediated by perceptions that give rise to belief-states. If someone asserts

(201) *It's raining*

we have information about a belief-state of the speaker (assuming we have no reason to doubt his sincerity). Depending on other factors, we may have information about some situation in the actual world as well.

As in the case discussed in section 2.3 (with reference to the utterance *It's hot*), if the speaker intends to state a fact of the current situation (the discourse situation) the problem can be represented as one of deciding whether the situation in which it is raining (S) contains the discourse situation (d), and is contained in the actual world (**W**):

(202) $d \subseteq S \subseteq \mathbf{W}$.

If the speaker merely intends to reveal his perception of some situation, as might be the case if (201) were uttered in a narrative told in "historical present"[5], we are concerned immediately only with S, not d or **W**.

If the speaker intends to involve us in a fiction, where we are to accept asserted facts as real, then we are concerned that the discourse situation conform to the situation created by the asserted facts; specifically, we are concerned with the conditions that result in the discourse situation being embedded in S:

(203) $d \subseteq S$

One function of the truth conditions, thus, is to provide us with a means of determining coherence relationships. If we understand the discourse situation to be of a type given by

(204) $d(\mathbf{be\text{-}raining}) = 1$

(where, as before, we take all "meterological" predicates to be 0-place), then a statement by an interlocutor in that discourse situation such as

(205) *It's hot and dry,*

which might translate as

(206) $d(\mathbf{be\text{-}hot}) = 1$, and
$d(\mathbf{be\text{-}dry}) = 1$,

has to be regarded as incoherent (or, at least, contradictory) vis-a-vis the prior constraints on the type of the discourse situation.[6] In all of this, the actual conditions of the world may play no part, though it may indeed be hot and dry.

Another function of the truth conditions is to allow for "selective inferencing"[7] to fill out the "facts" of the discourse situation. If the discourse situation is accepted to be of the type given by (204), then additional information about the discourse situation can be deduced, which might affect the interpretation of utterances. *Ceterus paribus*, in the situation given by (204), an interlocutor's admonition

(207) *Be careful!*

might be understood as a warning about dangers associated with wet weather, for example, catching cold, slippery driving conditions, or poor visibility. In the situation given by (206), in contrast, the same admonition could have none of those interpretations, but might be a warning about sunburn or dehydration.

The position taken by the theory presented here is that speech acts are not themselves truth functional; rather, the interpretation of an utterance as performing a particular speech act necessitates that the discourse situation relative to which the speech act is interpreted manifest certain relationships (especially among the interlocutors) with certain truth values. If it is impossible for such relationships to obtain, then the utterance must be given another interpretation; if such relationships can obtain, then the decision to give the utterance that particular speech act interpretation is a decision to recognize that the relevant relationships have become part of the discourse situation. Again, the relationships have a truth value, but only relative to the discourse situation. In understanding discourse, we must first understand the rules which determine discourse situation-internal relationships (and truth values) before we can determine relationships of scope outside the discourse situation.

The problem we face in moving from the "null-context"[8] interpretation of an utterance to its interpretation in a particular discourse situation is one of orientation. We must decide whether to interpret it as factual (or fictional); as of present (or remote) discourse situation relevence; as expressive (or neutral). If it is interpreted as factual, then the truth conditions on the relations of objects as characterized by the utterance must be intended to represent some situation in the actual world. If it is interpreted as of present discourse situation relevance, then the truth conditions given by the utterance must be part of the present discourse situation. If it is interpreted as expressive, then the truth conditions must accord with the speaker's actual feelings and beliefs. These orientations can combine to give the relevant dependency relations on truth conditions, schematically presented as follows:

(208)

			+expressive	(i.)	$d \subseteq W$
	+present $<$				
+factual $<$			−expressive	(ii.)	$d \subseteq S \subseteq W$
	−present $<$		+expressive	(iii.)	$S \subseteq d \subseteq W$
			−expressive	(iv.)	$S \subseteq W$
	+present $<$.		+expressive	(v.)	d
−factual $<$			−expressive	(vi.)	$d \subseteq S$
	−present $<$		+expressive	(vii.)	$S \subseteq d$
			−expressive	(viii.)	S

What (208) shows is that if an utterance is to be understood as factual, then, ultimately, the conditions in the actual world determine the truth values; if it is to be understood as non-factual,- then the actual world plays no role. Further, if the utterance represents some situation, that situation may have some relationship to the discourse situation, principally as being subordinate to or superordinate to the discourse situation in scope of truth value.

The truth condition hierarchies given by (208) are designed to apply to sets of relationships among the situations **W**, **S**, and **d** that can be established by the effect of any speech acts, but for purposes of illustration we can confine ourselves to the effects of constatives. Consider each of the eight cases in turn.

(208i.) represents those cases in which a speaker sincerely reports his current feelings or beliefs, as he might in uttering any of the following:

(209) *I'm hot.*
I'm unhappy.
I think that daughters are delightful.

The interpretation of such utterances as constatives (e.g., as assertions) establishes certain facts in the discourse situation, for example, in the use of *I'm hot*, that the speaker says and believes that he is hot. That much is true with respect to the discourse situation regardless of the speaker's actual feelings. But the fact of the matter depends on the state of the world, i.e., whether or not the speaker actually does feel hot. So, in the final analysis, if we wish to establish the truth of the proposition in the discourse situation, we must appeal to the set of facts that obtain in the actual world.

(208ii.) gives those cases where the speaker makes objective statements about conditions affecting the discourse situation, as in the following:

(210) *It's hot (here).*
It's three o'clock.
There's a doughnut on your head.

The interpretation of such utterances involves a proposition (of which the speaker is not overtly a part) in which certain elements of the discourse situation are represented as manifesting certain properties or standing in certain relationships. In asserting *It's hot (here)*, the speaker introduces himself in an assert relationship to the proposition, but the truth of the proposition depends on empirical factors outside the speaker's judgment. In particular, as noted before, the proposition is true just in case there is a set of situations in the actual world which are hot, which include the discourse situation.

(208iii.) includes cases where the speaker relates past experiences (feelings and beliefs) which are not immediately relevant to the discourse situation, but which become part of the factual content of the discourse situation through the speaker's telling of them. For example, in uttering the following, the speaker represents a (past) situation which does not directly involve the discourse situation:

(211) *I was a boy scout until I was thirteen.*
I spent a summer in Paris.
My favorite high school teacher taught biology.

The status of the propositions in these cases depends on the actual (past) experiences of the speaker which in turn depend on who the speaker is, where personal identity is understood as some function of an individual's past experience and present predisposition. Ultimately, statements such as those in (211) are true only if the speaker had the experiences they represent.

(208iv.) gives cases where the speaker relates factual events, not involving himself. This occurs in non-autobiographical, factual narrative, an instance of which any of the following might represent:

(212) *Abe Lincoln authored the Emancipation Proclamation.*
The Japanese bombed Pearl Harbor on December 7, 1941.
Henry Kissinger authorized illegal wiretaps on his aides.

The propositions expressed by these sentences represent (historical) individuals, properties, and relations whose factual status depends solely on their truth value in the actual world. If we wish to know the veracity of a claim, say that Henry Kissinger authorized wiretaps, we must determine whether the set of situations in which Henry Kissinger authorized wiretaps is contained in the set of situations giving actual events (e.g., wiretap-authorizations) in the world.

All four of the preceding cases involve representations intended to be factual, hence all necessarily involve the actual world, **W**. But there are many instances where the truth conditions on utterances need not be subordinate to the truth conditions that obtain in the actual world. Such cases involve fictions of various kinds.

(208v.), for example, involves those cases where the effect of an utterance on the discourse situation gives all the truth conditions of relevance. Indeed, a whole class of speech acts, the <u>expressives</u> (including salutations, congratulations, condolences, etc.), has just this function. All of the following are common examples:

> (213) [after: *How are you?*] *I'm fine, thanks.*
> [after a *faux pas*] *I'm terribly sorry.*
> [at a party, to host] *I'm having a wonderful time!*

Each of these, if successful as expressives, affects only the discourse situation by establishing socially conventional relationships between speaker and addressee. Whether the speaker of the above sentences is, respectively, fine, sorry, or having a wonderful time, is irrelevant. Using, say, *I'm fine*, in response to *How are you?*, commits neither speaker nor addressee to a belief in the apparent proposition; rather, it establishes a fact of the discourse situation that allows the interaction between speaker and addressee to proceed, by acknowledging a conventional greeting in a way which indicates that there are no immediate barriers to further communication.[9]

(208vi.) represents the use encountered most frequently in play-acting, but found also in some kinds of irony and sarcasm. Consider the utterance of the following in the context of a play:

> (214) *I hate you, Black Jack.*
> *The king is dead!*
> *Mary has found out that we're in love.*

In each utterance, a state of affairs is represented, by one speaker to an addressee, which is true, vis-a-vis the play, only if there are circumstances in the play that conform to those representations. If an actress, playing Little Nell, utters *I hate you, Black Jack* to an actor

111

playing Black Jack, when according to other facts in the play it is clear that Little Nell loves Black Jack, we can determine that the literal proposition expressed is false. If nothing blocks a literal interpretation, we can take the proposition as true. In either case there is no actual Little Nell, Black Jack, or set of circumstances relating them to which we can appeal, outside the context of the play itself.

The same conditions attend the performance of certain kinds of jokes, for example, the ironic joke discussed in section 3.3. The joke succeeds only if the discourse situation is made funny, in short, if the set of humorous situations contains the discourse situation.

(208vii.) gives the cases that are the fictional analogue of those under (208iii.). Here, the speaker exaggerates his views, hyperbolizes his feelings, and generally, misrepresents himself. The archetypal example is provided by the stand-up comic who weaves a monologue out of incredible experiences, but elements are found throughout natural discourse. Though the stories related may contain selected facts, they serve to represent fictional situations in which the speaker plays a role, and to characterize the speaker as having certain attributes. The stand-up comic must be funny (in the discourse situation in which we are addressees) to be successful; he is funny to the extent that we accept his characterization of himself as inherited from the humorous situations he recounts. In any case, the question of truth depends not on the actual status of events in the world, but on our willingness to accept the speaker as he characterizes himself. If Phyllis Diller were to say to us

(215) *I was so ugly as a teenager that we had to give the dog tranquilizers to keep it from crying.*

we might agree to view her as "ugly" for the purposes of the discourse situation and to understand future utterances with this in mind. The situation would be very different if the speaker were not someone who was trying to be humorous, say, but someone who was indeed physically unattractive.

(208viii.) is perhaps the least complicated of the fictional cases and is typified by non-personal fictional narration. Examples could be taken from fictional literature of all kinds. Neither the facts of the discourse situation nor the facts of the actual world play a role: the truth values on the constellations of objects, properties, and relations evoked are just as given. If a speaker says

(216) *Huck Finn ran away from home.*

we are free to understand the situation portrayed as involving someone (given by *Huck Finn*) who ran away from home, and any future references to that same character must be in contexts that are consistent with his having run away from home.

The eight classes of truth condition dependency relations explicated here are designed to illustrate the need for flexibility in assigning semantic interpretations to utterances. In order to decide the truth value of a proposition it is necessary to know its intended scope. It makes no sense to say that the proposition given by (216) is false because there is (was) no individual, Huck Finn, unless one understands (216) to be intended as fact.

The problem of determining the meaning of an utterance is only partly affected by the relationships of scope given here. These focus on the need for a proper orientation of d, S, and W, before truth value can be assessed. The other, co-determining factors in deriving utterance meaning — to repeat points made in previous sections — include the discourse-pragmatic function of the utterance (its hypertactic function, or the "move" it represents); the speech act it performs (with the attendant constraints on context and interpretation); and, of course, the "null-context" semantic structure it manifests. All of these affect the interpretation of every utterance produced in human discourse. In the analysis of specific discourse situations, all play a role.

4.2. ASSERTION AND TRUTH

One of the most universal and most basic uses of language seems to be in making assertions. This deceptively simple act apparently involves nothing more than the statement of a proposition — the representation of a state of affairs by the speaker. Yet, there are many problems associated with deciding, first, what the proposition being stated actually consists of, and second, what purpose the proposition is to serve (including its scope of validity) in the discourse situation where it is stated. So, in exploring the effects of context on speech act interpretation, we are well advised to begin with a consideration of this most fundamental of semiotic effects.

While there have been many interpretations in the literature of what phenomena the term "assertion" should cover, for our purposes here, we can confine ourselves to just one well-reasoned and generally accepted version, that detailed in Stalnaker (1978). To that end, we might briefly review the assumptions Stalnaker makes, and the theoretical constructs he proposes to deal with some of the phenomena of assertions.[10]

Stalnaker begins with an informal statement of "some truisms about assertions" (1978:315) which merit repeating here because they clarify the notion of assertion that he employs, and they overlap to a certain extent with the notion of assertion that is developed in this thesis.

> (217) First, assertions have content; an act of assertion is, among other things, the expression of a proposition — something that represents the world as being a certain way. Second, assertions are made in a context — a situation that includes a speaker with certain beliefs and intentions, and some people with their own beliefs and intentions to whom the assertion is addressed. Third, sometimes the content of an assertion is dependent on the context in which it is made, for example, on who is speaking or when the act of assertion takes place. Fourth, acts of assertion affect, and are intended to affect, the context, in particular the attitudes of the participants in the situation; how the assertion affects the context will depend on its content. (Stalnaker (1978:315))

These points cover a variety of aspects of the use of constatives,[11] in general, that have been explicated in previous sections. All constatives contain an embedded proposition (φ) that represents some situation (but not necessarily the world (W)) as being of a certain type. All constatives are speech acts, hence occur only in discourse situations, which requires that they be issued by a speaker to at least one addressee; and further, that the identity of speaker and addressee(s), and some subset of their beliefs and intentions, be part of the framing facts and other content of the discourse situation at the time of utterance. All constatives *qua* speech acts affect the discourse situation by introducing changes in the set of propositions that characterize the discourse situation, therefore change the discourse situation. And finally, all constatives *qua* constatives express propositional attitudes of the speaker, which can be interpreted only relative to the existing set of propositions that characterize the discourse situation, and which become part of the content of the discourse situation.

The point in (217) which is least readily incorporated into the theory of speech acts developed here is the final one, given as "how the assertion affects the context will depend on its content". On one interpretation, this is trivially true: according to the theory, an assertion (a constative; any speech act) has a content (in the form of speaker-addressee propositions) which uniquely determine its effect, which in turn is realized via the addition of that content to the discourse situation (context), and the enforcement of the conditions on the speech act (which, in some cases, might lead to the removal of propositions which characterize the discourse situation). However, on another interpretation, the theory and Stalnaker would take very different positions. If by "content" we understand "the (embedded) proposition" expressed by the assertion, then Stalnaker would seem to be claiming that the effect of the assertion is related to the proposition expressed, while the theory would claim that the effect of the assertion is independent of the proposition expressed. In short, at issue is whether it is possible to describe the effects of an assertion independently of the embedded proposition; and this in turn focuses on the relationship between embedded propositions and the kinds of constatives that can be performed in a particular discourse situation.

If by "assertion" Stalnaker means "constatives, in general," then the theory would agree: the distinctions among the many constatives defined in previous sections depend on such factors as whether or not a particular (embedded) proposition is present (in some form) in the discourse situation at the time of utterance. This condition is exploited in the difference between an act of reiteration, say, and simple assertion (as defined by the theory). But if Stalnaker means "assertion as distinct from other constatives" then the theory obviously disagrees. To resolve this question we must consider the uses which Stalnaker attributes to assertions.

In developing his views, Stalnaker utilizes three concepts: proposition, propositional concept, and speaker presupposition (1978:315). These are defined in a "possible worlds" semantic framework. Lest there be some objection that a direct comparison between Stalnaker's notion of assertion and that of the theory is impossible because of the difference in semantic systems supporting each — possible worlds, on the one hand, situations, on the other — we might offer a few generalizations about their expressive compatibility.[12]

In both possible worlds semantics and situation semantics, a proposition represents a constraint on the set of all the possible situations that could obtain. In a possible worlds semantics, a proposition is a function from possible worlds to truth values; so the set of possible worlds in which the proposition is true represents all the possible situations characterized by the proposition. In a situation semantics, a proposition determines a situation-type, which in turn determines the set of situations which are characterized by the proposition. In both cases a proposition effects, in part, a reduction in the number[13] and the value of the situations that must be considered.

For example, in a possible worlds semantics, the proposition given by the statement *It is hot (here)*, is a function, say, F, which takes possible worlds as arguments and returns truth values. For any possible world in a set of possible worlds, $z_i \in Z$, we would write, typically,

(218) $F(z_i) = 1$ iff the proposition represented by F is true in z_i;
 $F(z_i) = 0$ iff the proposition represented by F is false in z_i; and
 $F(z_i) = $ undefined otherwise.

The set of possible worlds for which F gives value 1 (true),

(219) $Z' = F^{-1}(1)$,

is just the set of situations which the proposition represents. Similarly, in a situation semantics, the proposition determines the situation-type

(220) s(**be-hot**) $= 1$,

which determines the set of situations, say, S', in which it is hot, which in turn is distinguished from the set of all possible situations (S). Whether in terms of possible worlds or situations, the proposition represents a restriction on the set of all possible alternatives.[14]

Stalnaker takes propositions to be functions from possible worlds to truth values, as is customary in a possible worlds semantics, but he introduces a further notion, <u>propositional concept</u>, to deal with problems that arise when it is not the truth value of the proposition but its content that is in question. Formally, a propositional concept is "a function from an ordered pair of possible worlds into a truth value" (1978:318). The utility of the notion can be illustrated in the following example, a modified version of an example Stalnaker uses.[15]

Suppose there are three individuals a, b, and c, each wearing a hat. Suppose, further, that a's hat is black, b's hat is red, and c's hat is white, but that there is some confusion as to these facts. Specifically, a and c both believe their hats are, respectively, black and white; but b (falsely) believes that his hat is green, since he intended to wear his green hat but mistakenly and unknowingly grabbed his red one; and b also (falsely) believes that c's hat is red, since c is inadvertently standing under a red light, obscured from b's view, which creates the illusion that his hat is red. Suppose, finally, that a says to b *You are wearing a red hat*, which c misunderstands as directed to him.

Stalnaker characterizes the resulting situation as follows:[16]

(221) Both b and c thought a said something false; b understood what a said, but disagrees with a about the facts; c, on the other hand, agrees with a about the fact (he knows that b is wearing a red hat), but misunderstood what a said.

To illustrate the difference between proposition and propositional content, using this example, Stalnaker identifies three possible worlds, i, j, and k, where i is the world as it is, j is the world as b thinks it is, and k is the world as c thinks it is. Then, according to Stalnaker, the <u>proposition</u> can be represented by the following matrix:

(222)

i	j	k
T	F	T

The <u>propositional concept</u>, however, is represented by a more complex matrix:

(223)

	i	j	k
i	T	F	T
j	T	F	T
k	F	T	F

In (222), the proposition that b is wearing a red hat is evaluated from three points of view — true in the actual world, i; false as b understands the world to be, j; and true as c understands the world to be, k. That is, it is consistent with both the actual world and c's understanding of the world that b is wearing a red hat, but it is inconsistent with b's understanding that he is wearing a green hat.

But in the situation described there is a further misunderstanding concerning what a actually said. From c's point of view, a was not talking about b but about c, and c would not accept the proposition that he is wearing a red hat, since he thinks it is a white hat. This additional interpretation is reflected in (223). As Stalnaker puts it:

> (224) The vertical axis represents possible worlds in their role as context — as what determines what is said. The horizontal axis represents possible worlds in their role as the arguments of the functions which are the propositions expressed. Thus the different horizontal lines represent WHAT IS SAID in the utterance in various different possible contexts. Notice that the horizontal line following i is the same as the one following j. This represents the fact that [b] and [a] agree about what was said. Notice also that the vertical column under i is the same as the one under k. This represents the fact that [c] and [a] agree about the truth values of both the proposition [a] in fact expressed and the one [c] thought [a] expressed. (Stalnaker (1978:318))

We can recast this in a situation semantics, and capture the distinctions among the various possible worlds, in their role both as context and content, with the aid of the following situation-types:

$$(225) \quad s(\text{be-wearing, } a, x) = 1$$

$$(226) \quad s(\text{be-wearing, } b, y) = 1$$

$$(227) \quad s(\text{be-wearing, } c, z) = 1$$

$$(228) \quad s(\text{be-hat, } x) = 1$$

$$(229) \quad s(\text{be-hat, } y) = 1$$

$$(230) \quad s(\text{be-hat, } z) = 1$$

$$(231) \quad s(\text{be-black, } x) = 1$$

$$(232) \quad s(\text{be-red, } y) = 1$$

$$(233) \quad s(\text{be-white, } z) = 1$$

$$(234) \quad s(\text{be-green, } y) = 0$$

$$(235) \quad s(\text{be-green, } y) = 1$$

$$(236) \quad s(\text{be-red}, \ y) \ = \ 0$$
$$(237) \quad s(\text{be-red}, \ z) \ = \ 1$$
$$(238) \quad s(\text{be-red}, \ z) \ = \ 0$$
$$(239) \quad s(\text{be-white}, \ z) \ = \ 0$$

Everyone involved in the hypothetical situation believes that the situation he is in is given by (225) - (230). This represents everyone's agreement that a, b, and c are the individuals involved, and that each is wearing an article of clothing, respectively x, y, and z, that is a hat. The disagreements, of course, concern which of (231) - (239) are believed also to characterize the situation. From a's and c's point of view, (231) - (233) are types of the actual situation; from b's point of view, (231), (235), and (237) are the correct types. Presumably, also, a and c would accept (234) and (238); and b would accept (236) and (239).

To represent what happens in a's utterance of

(240) *You are wearing a red hat,*

we must consider not only the set of facts which characterize the context in which truth is determined, but also the set of facts that determine the proposition expressed, viz. the constraints on the discourse situation that affect the interpretation of *you*. Specifically, in the discourse situation created by a and b, the following framing facts obtain:

$$(241) \quad d(\$=\mathbf{a}) \ = \ 1$$
$$(242) \quad d(@=\mathbf{b}) \ = \ 1.$$

This, in turn, determines the proposition expressed: in d,

$$(243) \quad [[\text{you}]] \ = \ @ \ = \ \mathbf{b},[17]$$

so a can be understood as representing the discourse situation as given by the following:

$$(244) \quad d(\text{be-wearing}, \ \mathbf{b}, \ \mathbf{y}) \ = \ 1,$$
$$(245) \quad d(\text{be-hat}, \ \mathbf{y}) \ = \ 1,$$
$$(246) \quad d(\text{be-red}, \ \mathbf{y}) \ = \ 1.$$

However, in the discourse situation created by a and c, a different set of framing facts obtain, namely:

$$(247) \quad d'(\$=\mathbf{a}) \ = \ 1,$$
$$(248) \quad d'(@=\mathbf{c}) \ = \ 1.$$

Thus, in this discourse situation, the proposition expressed is different: in d',

(249) $[[you]] = @ = c,$

so a can be understood as representing the discourse situation as given by the following:

(250) $d'(be\text{-}wearng, c, z) = 1,$

(251) $d'(be\text{-}hat, z) = 1,$

(252) $d'(be\text{-}red, z) = 1.$

In Stalnaker's matrix (given in (222)), the left-hand side possible worlds i, j, and k represent these different interpretations of a's utterance. In the actual world, i, a is addressing b, so states the proposition given by (244) - (246). In the world as b understands it, a also is addressing b, and also states the proposition given by (244) - (246). In the world as c understands it, a is addressing c, so states the proposition given by (250) - (252). This much represents just *what was said*, in Stalnaker's phrase.

The validity of what was said depends on the "facts" in the different worlds, captured in the matrix as the top row of possible worlds, i, j, and k. In the actual world, i, the facts are given by (225) - (232) (and (234) and (238)), so the claim represented by (244) - (246) is true relative to i, but the claim represented by (250) - (252) is false. In the world as b understands it, the facts are given by (225) - (230), (231), (235), and (237) (and (236) and (239)), so the claim represented by (244) - (246) is false relative to j, but the claim represented by (250) - (252) is true. Similarly, in the world as c understands it, k, the facts are as in i, and the claim represented by (244) - (246) is true, relative to k, but the claim represented by (250) - (252) is false.

All of this together — the different interpretations of what was said and the different contexts of evaluation — gives the propositional concept of (240). We find no important differences in expressing the propositional concept in a possible worlds framework or a situation semantics framework at this level of description, and we clearly agree with Stalnaker's judgments, at least as long as we interpret the scope of evaluation to be

$d \subseteq S \subseteq W$ (i.e., factual, of present relevance, and non-expressive). But nothing has been said about how assertions affect the discourse situations in which they occur, and it is that issue that interests us in a theory of speech acts.

Stalnaker's remarks to that point are prefaced by an explication of the third concept he introduces, <u>speaker</u> <u>presupposition</u>:

(253) This, I want to suggest, is the central concept needed to characterize speech contexts. Roughly speaking, the presuppositions of a speaker are the propositions whose truth he takes for granted as part of the background of the conversation. A proposition is presupposed if the speaker is disposed to act as if he assumes or believes that the proposition is true, and as if he assumes or believes that his audience assumes or believes that it is true as well. Presuppositions are what is taken by the speaker to be the COMMON GROUND of the participants in the conversation, what is treated as their COMMON KNOWLEDGE or MUTUAL KNOWLEDGE. [Footnote omitted, D.A.E.] The propositions presupposed in the intended sense need not really be common or mutual knowledge; the speaker need not even believe them. He may presuppose any proposition that he finds it convenient to assume for the purpose of the conversation, provided he is prepared to assume that his audience will assume it along with him. (Stalnaker (1978:321))

In fact, Stalnaker does not talk of the speaker presuppositions as a set of propositions, "but rather as a set of possible worlds, the possible worlds compatible with what is presupposed...the CONTEXT SET" (Stalnaker (1978:321)), but this does not affect the comparison to the theory presented in this thesis, where this same concept is given by D_i, the content of the discourse situation at time i, which is a set of propositions. Stalnaker also stresses the importance of speaker and addressee(s) mutual knowledge of the context set in order to insure effective communication:

(254) We may define a NONDEFECTIVE CONTEXT as one in which the presuppositions of the various participants in the conversation are all the same. A DEFECTIVE CONTEXT will have a kind of instability, and will tend to adjust to the equilibrium position of a nondefective context....A context is CLOSE ENOUGH to being nondefective if the divergences do not affect the issues that actually arise in the course of the conversation. (Stalnaker (1978:322))

This repeats the constraint of congruence that underlies the theory of speech acts presented here, and reminds us that in any actual discourse situation there can be important differences between the speaker's and addressee's views of the discourse situation (which can affect differences in encoding utterances, on the one hand, and evaluating and interpreting utterances, on the other); and the actual status of the discourse situation (in some abstract sense).

With this background, Stalnaker suggests that an assertion changes the context in two ways. The first way captures the effects which I have called "hypertactic," as related to the move the act represents and the information introduced to the discourse situation as a result of that move:

> (255) The fact that a speaker is speaking, saying the words he is saying in the way he is saying them, is a fact that is usually accessible to everyone present. Such observed facts can be expected to change the presumed common background knowledge of the speaker and his audience in the same way that any obviously observable change in the physical surroundings of the conversation will change the presumed common knowledge. (Stalnaker (1978:323))

The second way captures the essential condition, namely, how the content of an assertion alters context:

> (256) To make an assertion is to reduce the context set in a particular way, provided that there are no objections from the other participants in the conversation. The particular way in which the context set is reduced is that all of the possible situations incompatible with what is said are eliminated. To put it a slightly different way, the essential effect of an assertion is to change the presuppositions of the participants in the conversation by adding the content of what is asserted to what is presupposed. This effect is avoided only if the assertion is rejected. (Stalnaker (1978:323))

Stalnaker explicitly states that he does not intend (256) to be a definition of assertion, but merely one essential effect of assertions. He elaborates:

> (257) There are several reasons why one cannot define assertion in terms of this effect alone. One reason is that other speech acts, like making suppositions, have and are intended to have the same effect. A second reason is that there may be various indirect, even non-linguistic, means of accomplishing the same effect which I would not want

to call assertions. A third reason is that the proposed essential effect makes reference to another speech act — the rejection of an assertion [footnote omitted, D.A.E.], which presumably cannot be explained independently of assertion. (Stalnaker (1978:323-4))

It should be clear from (256) and (257) that Stalnaker's understanding of assertion and the concept of assertion developed in previous sections of this thesis are divergent. But more: it should be clear that Stalnaker has subsumed under "assertion" a variety of phenomena that do, indeed, attend the use of speech acts, but that are better understood as being independent discourse processes and effects. Consider some of Stalnaker's claims point by point.

First, an effect of an assertion is "to reduce the context set in a particular way...[viz.] all of the possible situations incompatible with what was said are eliminated." Given that the context set is characterized as a set of possible worlds, any new information (any act) can reduce the context set, since new information introduces further constraints on possible worlds compatible with the propositions that constitute the discourse situation. In the theory presented here, the discourse situation — given by a set of situation-types — is expanded by new information, which results in further constraints on the kind of situation that the discourse situation can be. This, then, is an effect of speech acts in general, and of the way in which discourse situations are known.

Second, the essential effect is "to change the presuppositions of the participants in the conversation by adding the content of what is asserted to what is presupposed." On this point the theory both agrees and disagrees, depending on how we understand *content*. In one sense, the content of the speech act is the set of propositions (and attendant conditions) given schematically in the speech act type. The theory assumes that it is precisely this which is added to the set of propositions giving the discourse situation. In another sense, the one Stalnaker intends, the content is the representation made by the assertion, the embedded proposition mentioned in the speech act type. Here, the theory states that — in terms of the immediate effects of the speech act — the proposition itself, the representation encoded in the assertion, is not made directly a part of the discourse situation; rather it is present in the discourse situation to the extent that it is a subpart of the propositions that are directly introduced.

Returning to a concrete example, the case of a, b, and c and the three hats, we can focus on the problem of what changes in the discourse situation when a says to b *You are wearing a red hat*. Suppressing possible speech act interpretations other than assertion, we could say that a has changed the discourse situation by making certain information available to b. That information does involve b and his hat in some sense, but the representation of b in a certain relationship to a certain hat is not the essential fact of the speech act. That is, the information one extracts from the speech act itself — the information that is absolute and reliable, independent of the facts concerning b and his hat — is that a is stating a proposition (φ) and a purports to believe the proposition. This does change the context set. Regardless of b's beliefs, once a has gone on record as stating and believing φ, anything b might say to a about φ is constrained by the discourse situation fact that a has taken a certain position on φ; but φ alone is not a part of the discourse situation at this stage.

On this point, Stalnaker seems confused about the difference between the direct effects of the speech act and the meta-effects that obtain in cooperative discourse. An instance of a metarule that captures the effect Stalnaker describes might be given as follows:

(258) METARULE OF COOPERATIVE DISCOURSE:
If d(believe, $, φ) = 1, then d(φ) = 1,
unless d(believe, @, (NOT φ)) = 1,
or d(believe, @, φ) = 0.

This metarule makes the representation embedded in an assertion part of the discourse situation (i.e., a fact, for the purposes of the discourse situation) unless the addressee has a contradictory view on the matter. Stalnaker seems to be thinking of just this phenomenon in his third point, the caveat he states twice in (256), namely, that the "effect is avoided only if the assertion is rejected." But this, surely, cannot be intended to refer to the effect of the speech act. What can it mean to reject a speech act?

If a asserts that b is wearing a red hat, nothing b does can change the fact of the assertion, that is, that a has made such and such an assertion. If b is cooperating with a, but sincerely disagrees with a about the proposition embedded in the assertion, then b might object to that proposition. The effect would be to block the application of the metarule. But b's objection cannot change a's views regarding the proposition, which are an important part of the discourse situation and which b must acknowledge if he is to engage in successful communication with a on any matter touched on by the proposition.[18]

Consider how the theory developed in this thesis would represent the event of a's utterance. The discourse situation containing a and b has the framing facts given in (241) and (242). The other facts of the world, represented by (225) - (234) and (238) are not a part of the discourse situation, though they are potentially accessible; similarly, a's and b's individual beliefs regarding (225) - (239), etc., are not a part of the discourse situation at this stage. Choosing to interpret a's utterance as an assertion, in the language of the theory, is to decide that applying the illocutionary mode for constatives (L_1) to the interpretive constituents of the utterance results in no conflicts with existing discourse situation content, so that the speech act type ASSERT can be matched (in each case), and implemented. More concretely, the interpretive constituents of (240) (*You are wearing a red hat.*) can be glossed as

(259) b is wearing y.

(260) y is a hat.

(261) y is red.

Alternatively, these might be given as:

(262) φ_1 := s(be-wearing, b, y) = 1

(263) φ_2 := s(be-hat, y) = 1

(264) φ_3 := s(be-red, y) = 1

Under the operation of L_1, these are converted to candidate propositions:

(265) d(**say**, a, φ_1) = 1

(266) d(**believe**, a, φ_1) = 1

(267) d(**say**, a, φ_2) = 1

(268) d(**believe**, a, φ_2) = 1

(269) d(**say**, a, φ_3) = 1

(270) d(**believe**, a, φ_3) = 1

Each pair can match the speech act type ASSERT, so each pair can give rise to a speech act of assertion. The decision to regard (240) as an assertion is simply the decision to implement the matched speech act types.

Actually, it is not φ_1 - φ_3 which are the embedded propositions, but an oriented version of them. Specifically, the interpretive constituents of the utterance, (259) - (261), can be understood as determining a set of situation-types, given by φ_1 - φ_3; but the relevant claim in this act of assertion is that the situation characterized by $\varphi_1 - \varphi_3$ is the discourse situation, and that this characterization is factual. So the oriented versions of $\varphi_1 - \varphi_3$,

(271) $\varphi_1{'} := d(be\text{-}wearing, b, y) = 1,$

(272) $\varphi_2{'} := d(be\text{-}hat, y) = 1,$ and

(273) $\varphi_3{'} := d(be\text{-}red, y) = 1,$

are the propositions that are actually embedded in the speech act; and the scope of truth conditions is as given before, $d \subseteq S \subseteq W$.

If the act took place at time i, then the discourse situation at time $i+1$ would contain (among the framing facts, etc.) the propositions represented by correctly oriented versions of (265) - (270). Since there are propositions of the form $d(\text{believe}, \$, \varphi) = 1$ in this set, in a cooperative discourse situation we could add propositions of the form $d(\varphi) = 1$. Here, that would mean adding

(274) $d(\varphi_1{'}) = 1,$

(275) $d(\varphi_2{'}) = 1,$ and

(276) $d(\varphi_3{'}) = 1.$

At this point the addressee has a choice. Either he can accept the discourse situation as represented, or he can make an objection. Proceeding without objection amounts to a tacit acceptance of the characterization of the discourse situation, and any utterances he makes will be constrained by the set of propositions that then obtains. Making an objection does change the discourse situation, but not quite as Stalnaker suggests.

For example, if at time $i+1$, b says

(277) *That's not true,*

the theory offers the following analysis. Under one interpretation[19] of (277) we have the interpretive constituent

(278) $\varphi_3{'}$ is not true (i.e., NOT $\varphi_3{'}$),

which might be given as

(279) $\psi := s(\text{NOT } \varphi_3{'}) = 1.$

Through the action of the illocutionary mode function for constatives (L_1) we generate

(280) $d(\underline{\text{say}}, b, \psi) = 1,$ and

(281) $d(\underline{\text{believe}}, b, \psi) = 1.$

126

Assuming nothing blocks the match with the ASSERT speech act type,[20] these propositions will be added to the discourse situation. Actually, again, a question of orientation arises. We might assume that b is making the claim that the situation given by (279) is, in fact, the discourse situation. Then, the oriented proposition is

$$(282) \quad \psi': \quad d(NOT \; \varphi_3') = 1,$$

and it is this proposition that is embedded in the assertion. At discourse time $i+2$, the discourse situation will contain all of (265) - (270) and (280) - (281). It will also contain (274) and (275), since the metarule generating these propositions can apply at time $i+2$; but it cannot contain (276) since (281) is in a form that blocks the metarule.

Stalnaker would argue that, at this point $(i+2)$, φ_3' is not part of the discourse situation. But he would attribute its absence to the rejection of an assertion, where we are to understand "assertion" to mean "the speech act of asserting." He would not claim that the fact of the speaker's having said something could be rejected, we might suppose, since that aspect of an assertion is part of the hypertactic effect (represented, in part, by the say relations in the speech act type). But he would claim that the essential effect — "to change the presuppositions of the participants in the conversation by adding the content of what is asserted to what is presupposed" — is rejected. And if this is so, he would seem to be identifying the essential effect with the effect of the metarule ((258)).

While such an effect is an important aspect of the use of assertions, we should question whether it is the essential effect of the speech act of assertion. As has been shown in the example above, a great deal of information is added to the discourse situation at each move. By the end of the exchange (at time $i+2$), we know about a's view of the matter, and b's contradictory view, and about how their views were expressed. In the adapted example,[21] some of the information introduced by the metarule is not rejected, and so remains a part of the discourse situation. All of this contributes to the reduction in the context set, since all of the information serves to constrain the type of the discourse situation. And all of this has come about by "adding the content of what is asserted to what is presupposed."

Stalnaker specifically rejects the characterization of an asertion as "trying to get the audience to accept THAT THE SPEAKER ACCEPTS the content of the assertion" (Stalnaker (1978:324)), but any interpretation of the rejection of an asserted proposition that is not directed at the speaker's attitude but merely to the embedded proposition leaves us with a context in which the addressee has accepted that the speaker accepts the proposition. In terms of the example, unless b's *That's not true* refers to a's purported belief, that purported belief remains part of the context set. Though b may not agree with a, he would certainly be an incompetent interlocutor if he did not accept that a had expressed a belief.

Stalnaker seems to have failed to distinguish (i.) among speech act effects and other pragmatic effects such as given by the metarule ((258)), and (ii.) among kinds of constatives which all involve embedded propositions but which will have different "essential effects."

On this last point, Stalnaker's characterization of assertion seems closer to the speech act given in the theory and as INFORM φ type, than the one given as an ASSERT φ type. Recall that under certain circumstances, the effect of a constative might be to introduce (or make part of the context set) two propositions, of the form

$$(283) \quad d(\underline{believe}, \$, \varphi) = 1, \text{ and}$$
$$(284) \quad d(\underline{believe}, @, \varphi) = 1.$$

At such times, the effect of the metarule is guaranteed, so φ can be made directly a part of the discourse situation as well. This occurs (in cooperative discourse) when the speaker is telling a (fictional) story, or revealing personal history, or framing an hypothesis — all of which activities are not subject to contradiction by an addressee. Further, this occurs (in cooperative discourse) when the speaker is responding to a request for information made by the addressee. These cases are different from the action of an ASSERT type act since they are marked for cooperation and the application of the metarule. In assertion, something much simpler happens, involving the addressee's cooperation not at all.

Applied to the example above, the theory would seem to be both more descriptive of what occurs and more explanatory. If one of the goals of an explanation is to validate inferences, then the inferences we would make based on the discourse situation at the end of the exchange (at time $i+2$) must include inferences about the specific content of a's and b's beliefs, and inferences about how remarks on the question of b's hat will be interpreted. The context set as derived by the theory (the set of propositions giving the discourse situation) contains explicit information about a's and b's beliefs, and about the other facts (via the metarule) that are relevant to those beliefs.

In sum, it would appear that in treating the example, the theory can account for all aspects of truth condition and propositional content that Stalnaker describes, and goes beyond Stalnaker in giving a more detailed analysis of the effects of an assertion — both contingent and essential — and of the state of the discourse situation at various points of interaction. The theory distinguishes among varieties of constatives, where Stalnaker appears to consider only one; and the theory distinguishes speech act effects from other pragmatic effects based on speech act effects, where Stalnaker regards all as speech act effects.

Whether or not one wishes to see in this discussion a potential validation of the theory, it should be obvious that the action of even the simplest kinds of speech acts, such as assertion, involves a great deal of complexity reflecting a number of discourse phenomena, including decisions concerning the scope of truth conditions and the pragmatics of cooperative interaction. A theory of speech acts should endeavor to distinguish between what is essentially an effect of speech acts and what is an effect of other discourse processes.

4.3. QUESTIONS AND RESPONSES

The discussion of assertion in the preceding section was based on an example involving a minimal exchange: a said something and b replied. Yet, even in this limited case, the interpretation of b's action and the effects that action had on the discourse situation are highly constrained by what a had done.

In any response we find information about the former addressee's perception of the discourse situation. Since we are able to communicate only to the extent that our (speaker's) understanding of the relevant set of propositions in the discourse situation and our addressee's are congruent, we must constantly monitor our addressee's remarks for indications of divergent views or misapprehensions, and we must strive to bring about corrections and changes to maintain congruence. But the kind of information we get from our addressee about the state of the discourse situation can be classified along a relatively small number of parameters. And in examining such parameters we sharpen our understanding of the role of speech acts in discourse.

An especially interesting analysis of the effects of responses is found in Goffman (1976). While we need not be concerned with the theoretical assumptions Goffman brings to his task, or with the precise definition of the discourse parameters he utilizes, it is interesting to consider one "metaschema" (Goffman (1976:306ff)) he presents.[22]

> (285) Start, then, with a conventionalized, perfunctory social litany, one that begins with A's
>
> (a.)   *Do you have the time?*
>
> and restricting ourselves to B's verbal response, consider the following unfoldings:
>
> **I. Consensual**
>
> 1. The "standard" response, comprising variants of a more or less functionally equivalent kind:
>
> (b.)   *Five o'clock.*
>
> (c.)   *Yes I do. It's five o'clock.*
>
> (d.)   *Sorry, my watch isn't working.*
>
> (e.)   *There it is.* [pointing to big wall clock].
>
> 2. A standard schema of interpretation fundamentally

different from the one pertaining to clocks proves to be the one that both participants are applying:

(f.) *No, but I still have the Newsweek.*

(g.) *Sure. Anyway, what you want won't take but a minute.*

(h.) *No, I left it with the basil.*

3. A mutually and openly sustained full transformation of the original (a "keying") proves to prevail:

(i.) Director to actress: *No, Natasha. Turn your head or you'll never reach beyond the footlights.*

(j.) Librarian: *No, that wasn't the title, but it was something like that.* [Footnote omitted, D.A.E.]

(k.) Language teacher: *That's just fine, Johann. A few more times and you'll have the "t" right.*

4. Indirect meaning given direct reply:

(l.) *Stop worrying. They'll be here.*

(m.) *All right, all right, so I did lose your present.*

(n.) Prospective john: *How much for the whole night?*

II. Procedural problems holding off illocutionary concerns

1. System constraints not satisfied:

(o.) *What did you say?*

(p.) *Bitte, ich kann nur Deutsch sprechen.*

(q.) *What dime?*

2. Ritual constraints not satisfied:

(r.) *I'm sorry, we are not allowed to give out the time. Please phone T16-6666.*

(s.) *Nurse, can't you see I'm trying to tie off this bleeder?*

(t.) *Shh, that mike carries.*

III. Addressing ritual presuppositions so that the illocutionary point of the initial statement is denied at least temporarily, and a side sequence is established in

which the erstwhile respondent becomes the initiator:

(u.) *Why the formality, love?"*

(v.) *Could I ask where you learned your English?*

(w.) *Don't you remember me?*

IV. Warranted or unwarranted treatment of asker's move as trickery — in this particular case the assumption being that once a claim is established for initiating talk, it will come to be exploited:

(x.) *No.* [Not meeting the asker's eyes and hurrying away from him on the assumption that the question might be an instance of the now standard ploy to ready a robbery]

(y.) *Say, are you trying to pick me up?*

(z.) *Never mind the time, Peterkins, you know you're supposed to be in bed.*

V. Jointly sustained fabrication relative to passers-by; e.g.,

(aa.) [Spy recognition signal] *Yes. Do you happen to have a match?*

VI. Unilateral use of features of interaction for the open purpose of play or derision:

1. Failure to perform anticipated ellipsis:

(ab.) *Yes, I do...*

2. Use of unanticipated scheme of interpretation:

(ac.) *Yes, do you have the inclination?*

(ad.) [In mock Scots accent] *And may I ask what you want it for?*

3. Anything covered in I. through V. but reframed for playful use, e.g.,:

(ae.) [Huge, tough-looking black in black neighborhood, on being asked the time by a slight middle-class, white

youth, looks into youth's eyes while reaching for
watch] *You ain' fixin' to rob me, is you?*

In reviewing this long outline of classes of responses, we can see some of the many features of language use that interact with speech act interpretation. Let us consider the extent to which these features are accommodated in the theory of speech acts presented in this thesis.

We might begin by briefly recapitulating the notion of (two-person) discourse that the theory employs. First, there is the assumption that no discourse can occur outside a discourse situation which is given by certain framing facts (including the identification of a speaker and an addressee), and which is constrained by a set of propositions that represent the mutual knowledge of the interlocutors (cf. sec. 1.2). Second, there are specific "moves" that interlocutors can make which directly affect the framing facts and conventionally determine some of the relationships between the interlocutors (cf. sec. 2.2). Third, there are specific ways that utterance constituents can be used that affect the discourse situation by introducing the proposition that the speaker is referring to the object denoted by the constituent or expressing some relation inherent in the constituent, and which might be called "para-speech act" phenomena (cf. sec. 3.1). Fourth, there is the assumption that speech act interpretation derives from knowledge of (i.) the kinds of illocutionary modes that can be applied to utterance constituents (cf. sec. 3.2), (ii.) the rules that govern consistency relations in the set of propositions that determine the discourse situation (cf. sec. 3.3), (iii.) the possible end-states, given as speech act types, that the use of an utterance can achieve (cf. sec. 2.3), and finally, (iv.) the discourse-level rules (including rules of genre, knowledge of plans and scripts, etc.) that affect the choices of interpretation available (cf. sec. 3.4).

Furthermore, the notion of speech act, itself, is based on the informal characterization of "constitutive rule" in Searle (1969:36), paraphrased as

(286) Saying X in context Y counts as doing Z.

This, in turn, is represented in the theory as the cause which effects the determination of a new discourse situation (to repeat (23)):

(287) $D_{i+1} = I(f_u, D_i)$.

And, finally, the notion of truth in a discourse situation must be relativized to the notion of evaluation of a specific proposition under some orientation, whose scope may include the discourse situation.

Now, in uttering the words of (285a) (*Do you have the time?*), A

133

initiates an interaction in which it is clear that A is the speaker, someone (B) is the addressee, and a response is called for.[23] This establishes a discourse situation with, at least, the following facts (say, at time i):

(288) $d(\$ = A) = 1$
$d(@ = B) = 1$
$d(\underline{request}, A, B, \varphi) = 1$
where φ includes the information that B should assume the turn and otherwise respond.

All the pairs in (285) have this much in common. And this reflects the information that is available at the hypertactic level of the interaction. The differences we see in the pairs, in other respects, come from additional features of context or from differences in speech act interpretation.

Of the six major divisions Goffman identifies, the responses under I. ("consensual") represent completions of the kind most typically discussed in speech act theories. The so-called "standard" responses all involve the interpretation of (285a) as a literal question. In terms of the theory, this means deciding that (285a) is either a literal polar question or is a request for information. This latter interpretation is available to those interlocutors who regard (285a) as wholly conventional, having a direct interpretation as given by:

(289) THIS IS A REQUEST FOR THE CURRENT TIME.[24]

As a speech act type, REQUEST INFORMATION (cf. (51) in section 2.3), we would have the following propositions added to the discourse situation at D_i:

(290) $d(\underline{want}, A, B, \langle\alpha, q(x)\rangle) = 1$

(291) $d(\underline{request}, A, B, \langle\alpha, q(x)\rangle) = 1$

(292) $d(know, A, \langle\alpha, q(x)\rangle) = 0$

(293) $d(\underline{believe}, A, \varphi) = 0$
where α is a reply s. t. $\lambda x[d(t=x) = 1]$ $[[\alpha]]$
is well-formed and complete,
where t gives the current time;
and $\varphi := d(know, B, \langle\alpha, q(x)\rangle) = 0$

Note that α itself is not the time, but is an answer to the question, where the significant constraint on the answer is that it be interpretable as establishing a particular proposition in the discourse situation, namely, one giving the current time. Response (285b) supplies α directly. The act that (285b) represents is an act of giving information, or, as a speech

134

act type, an INFORM φ. It adds the following propositions to the discourse situation:

(294) $d(\underline{say}, B, \psi) = 1$

(295) $d(\underline{believe}, B, \psi) = 1$

(296) $d(\underline{believe}, A, \psi) = 1$
where $\psi := [d(t=5 \text{ o'clock}) = 1]$

The responses in (285d) and (285e) can be interpreted as acts which supply information that invalidates the request (i.e., changes propositions in the discourse situation so that the preconditions on the request for information no longer hold). For example, (285d) provides information that, under reasonable Gricean corstraints, would lead us to conclude that

(297) $d(\underline{know}, B, \langle\alpha, q(x)\rangle) = 0$

and hence, that (293) cannot be maintained. On the other hand, (285e) might be regarded as supplying information that leads to the invalidation of (292), since the mutually recognized presence of a clock undermines A's position of ignorance.

The response in (285c) reflects multiple interpretations of (285a), one of which is as a polar question. While polar questions have not been discussed previously, they can be analyzed as special cases of requests for information, where the information ($[[\alpha]]$) is restricted to the value (0 or 1) of a proposition. As a speech act type, we might write:

(298) REQUEST POLARITY OF φ (D_i)
1: $d(\underline{want}, \$, @, \langle\alpha, \varphi\rangle) = 1$
2: $d(\underline{request}, \$, @, \langle\alpha, \varphi\rangle) = 1$
3: $d(\underline{know}, \$, \langle\alpha, \varphi\rangle) = 0$
4: $d(\underline{believe}, \$, \psi) = 0$
where φ is a proposition of the form
$d(r^n, a_1, \dots, a_n) = \delta$,
with $\delta \in \{0, 1\}$,
and α is a reply s. t. $[[\alpha]] = \delta$,
and $\psi := [d(\underline{know}, @, \langle\alpha, \varphi\rangle) = 0]$,
and 1, 2, 3, 4 $\in D_{i+1}$

If (285a) is regarded as having the interpretive constituents:

(299) THIS IS A POLAR QUESTION,

(300) B knows the current time,

then (under suitable translation) the discourse situation can be regarded as having the following propositions after the utterance of (285a):

(301) $d(\text{want}, A, B, \langle\alpha, \varphi\rangle) = 1$

(302) $d(\text{request}, A, B, \langle\alpha, \varphi\rangle) = 1$

(303) $d(\text{know}, A, \langle\alpha, \varphi\rangle) = 0$

(304) $d(\text{believe}, A, \psi) = 0$
where $\varphi := [d(\text{know}, B, t) = \delta]$,
and t is the current time, and $\delta \in \{0, 1\}$,
and α is such that $[[\alpha]] = \delta$,
and $\psi := [d(\text{know}, B, \langle\alpha, \varphi\rangle) = 0]$.

B's response ((285c)) can be analyzed as satisfying both the polar question interpretation and the request for information interpretation.

In the responses given under (285f–h), none of the above interpretations are acceptable. We are reminded that what occurs in the utterance of (285a) is not *time* but |talm|, which can have numerous interpretations unrelated to clock-time. Still, all the interpretations of the question are as requests for information, so the same kinds of propositions are involved, as before, with slightly different constraints.

In (285i–k) no actual request for information is involved. Instead (285a) is performed (in i and k) or quoted (in j), with this last instance being a fragment of a larger than simple pair sequence — (285a), apparently, is a tentative response to a question, and (285j) addresses the implicit uncertainty.

The examples in (285l–n) underscore the importance of mutual knowledge in the discourse situation, and the great freedom of choice of interpretation that almost any utterance in any situation affords. To examine one example in detail, consider the discourse situation in which (285n) might occur. The framing facts include the information under (288), but also include information about the role identities of speaker and addressee. Specifically,

(305) $d(\text{be-prostitute}, A) = 1$

(306) $d(\text{be-john}, B) = 1$

are part of the discourse situation, along with the knowledge of associated scripts, which can radically affect interpretation.

For example, assume that a "solicitation" script[25] exists with the following content:

(307) The SOLICITATION script:

Players: one or more "prostitutes;" one or more "johns"

Setting: an area for pick-ups (bar, street corner, hotel lobby, etc.)

Props: ?

Events:
1. Prostitute approaches john or vice versa.
2. An offer is made involving any of the following:
   a. statement of intention
   b. statement of time
   c. statement of cost
   d. statement of location
   e. statement of style
   f. any question mentioning any of the above key points
3. An agreement is reached and both parties proceed to a
   location together or individually; or
4. No agreement is reached and both parties separate.

Possible interpolations:
1. During offer enter a NEGOTIATE script

Pre-conditions (presuppositions):
1. The activity behind the offer is sexual
2. The activity is limited to relatively brief contact after
   which both parties go their separate ways
3. The activity costs the john money
4. The activity involves risk (statutory; health; etc.)

Expected consequences:
1. Sexual satisfaction of john
2. Financial satisfaction of prostitute

Exceptional situations:
1. The setting is insecure
RESULT: suspend solicitation activity or relocate
2. One or more preconditions are not met
RESULT: suspend solicitation activity or work to rectify defective precondition

The information that a script such as this contains can be included in the discourse situation as a set of inference rules and a set of distinguished entities. Thus, intention, time, cost, etc. can be related to a specific kind of activity, in focus in the script; and the plans the interlocutors utilize to achieve various steps can be governed by conventional procedures. All of these aspects of the script will affect utterance interpretation and will help set parameters at the discourse level that determine speech act implementation choices.

Now, in a discourse situation where the facts under (288), (305), (306), and (307) obtain, and (285n) has been spoken, the addressee has several interpretation paths open. Consider the schematic representation of four such paths, based on two alternative interpretations of *the time*:

(308)   (i.)   REQ. FOR INFO.
            "current time" <
                          ↑
    Do you have the time ?   (ii.)   REQ. FOR POLAR.
                          ↓
            "enough time <
            (for some activity)"   (iii.)   REQ. FOR ACT.

The path leading to (308i.) is as discussed before, under the interpretation presented in (289). The paths leading to (308ii.) are also as discussed before, under the interpretation presented in (299), though, of course, in the case of the "enough time (for some activity)" reading of *the time*, the relevant proposition, whose polarity is being queried, would be as follows:

(309) $d(\text{have-sufficient-time-for}, \mathbf{B}, \alpha) = \delta$
where α is some activity,
and $\delta \in \{1, 0\}$

Finally, the path leading to (308iii.) is based on the interpretive constituents:

(310) THIS IS A REQUESTIVE

138

(311) B has enough time for α (some activity)[26]

(312) α (some activity)

Here, the presence of (310), based on overt syntax (and perhaps intonation), insures that the illocutionary mode function for requestives in general (L_2) will be applied. Since L_2 is defined for interpretive constituents that related the addressee to action, states, or events, candidate propositions based on both (311) and (312) can be generated, giving, respectively:

(313) $d(\underline{want}, A, B, \varphi) = 1$

(314) $d(\underline{request}, A, B, \varphi) = 1$
where $\varphi := [d(\text{have-sufficient-time-for}, B, \alpha) = 1]$
and α is some activity,

and

(315) $d(\underline{want}, A, B, \alpha) = 1$

(316) $d(\underline{request}, A, B, \alpha) = 1$
where α is some activity.

A speech act type for REQUEST STATE and REQUEST ACTIVITY, which could accept these candidate propositions, might be given as follows (based on, and similar to, the REQUEST ACTION speech act type, (57), presented in section 2.3):

(317) REQUEST STATE (α) (D_i)
1: $d(\underline{want}, \$, @, \alpha) = 1$
2: $d(\underline{request}, \$, @, \alpha) = 1$
3: $d(\underline{believe}, \$, \varphi) = 1$
where α is a state,
and $\varphi := [d(\text{be-able-to-be-in}, @, \alpha) = 1]$,
and 1, 2, 3 $\in D_{i+1}$

(318) REQUEST ACTIVITY (α) (D_i)
1: $d(\underline{want}, \$, @, \alpha) = 1$
2: $d(\underline{request}, \$, @, \alpha) = 1$
3: $d(\underline{believe}, \$, \varphi) = 1$
where α is an activity,
and $\varphi := [d(\text{be-able-to-do}, @, \alpha) = 1]$
and 1, 2, 3 $\in D_{i+1}$

Deciding that one or both sets of candidate propositions could match these speech act types would result in the introduction to the discourse situation of the **want**, **request**, and **believe** propositions above (under proper substitution of variables). The interpretation of A's question, then, would be as a request to B to bring about the activity, directly. Coupled with the solicitation script — a list of inference rules in the discourse situation — this is tantamount to engaging in "Event 2," making an offer.

The choice which the addressee (B) has to make is which of (308i.) - (308iii.) to implement. The kinds of responses available to him (the time — yes/no — some comment, etc.) are appropriate for only some combinations of interpretations, so how he responds determines what the discourse situation will be, that is, what propositions will be part of the context set. There is great latitude here, and ambiguous responses are possible (e.g., *yes*).

Even if B accepts his role as john, and identifies A as a prostitute, he may not wish to acknowledge that the solicitation script is being played. His goal may be to frustrate A's attempts to engage him in conversation; or to make A identify her intentions more overtly; so he might choose to respond to the literal question (REQUEST FOR POLARITY), or to an innocent conventional interpretation (REQUEST FOR INFORMATION = THE CURRENT TIME). If B wishes to acknowledge the solicitation he can implement the request-for-activity interpretation by responding in a way that focuses on the activity or some aspect of the script.

Suppose B does wish to interpret A's query as an offer, and wishes to continue the interaction. From B's point of view, the discourse situation at D_{i+1} (after A has spoken) contains not only the framing facts, the set of inference rules giving the solicitation script, and the propositions introduced by the interpretation of (285a) as a request-for-activity speech act, but also the <u>derived</u> propositions that A and B are in a solicitation script, that A has made an offer to B, and that they must next either agree, negotiate, or part. At this point B's *How much for the whole night?* — which focuses on a presupposition of the offer — can be understood as initiating a negotiation side sequence and continuing the solicitation script.

It might be noted that a number of responses that Goffman identifies as subsumed under different classes actually can be accounted for in the same way as the different responses above. For example, (285x) and (285ab) simply address the literal polar question, which as we have seen, even in a case where there are inference schemata at work, introduces little information outside the specific content of the speech act. Similarly, (285y) and (285ac) indicate that a solicitation script is being used (justifiably or not).

In fact, most (if not all) of Goffman's examples seem amenable to inclusion under a simple schema, whose major divisions reflect differences in levels of interpretation in interactive discourse. An illustration is given in Figures 3 and 4.

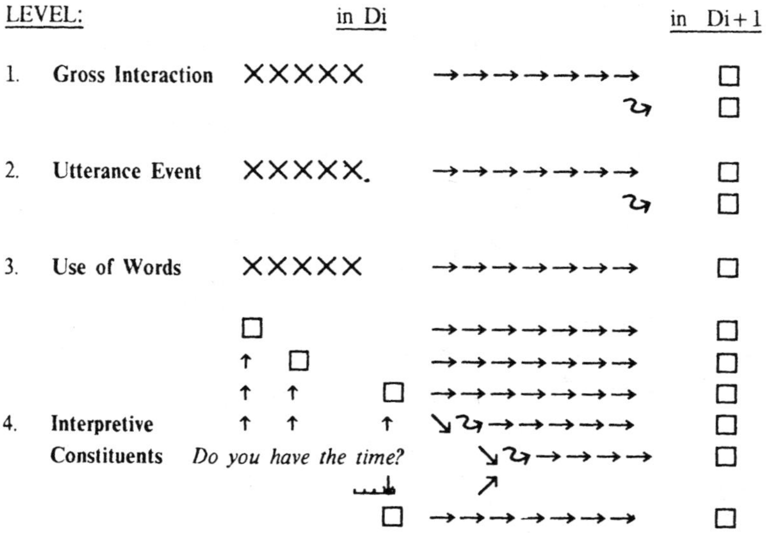

LEVEL:		in Di		in Di+1
1.	Gross Interaction	✕✕✕✕✕	→→→→→→→	□
			⤳	□
2.	Utterance Event	✕✕✕✕✕.	→→→→→→→	□
			⤳	□
3.	Use of Words	✕✕✕✕✕	→→→→→→→	□
		□	→→→→→→→	□
		↑ □	→→→→→→→	□
		↑ ↑ □	→→→→→→→	□
4.	Interpretive	↑ ↑ ↑	↘⤳→→→→→	□
	Constituents	*Do you have the time?*	↘⤳→→→→	□
		⌐⌐↓	↗	
		□	→→→→→→→	□

An Overview of Levels of Interpretation

Figure 3.

141

Figure 3 presents in skeletal form the various effects that the utterance of (285a) has on a discourse situation. Four levels are identified, corresponding to the type of information that serves as a basis for interpretation of utterance meaning. The first level accessible to any interlocutors is the level of gross interaction, which includes information about who is speaking to whom, where the interaction is taking place, what the interlocutors are (say, visibly) doing during the interaction, etc., as typically given in the framing facts of the discourse situation. (For this particular case, some of those facts are given by (288).) The second level is that of the utterance event, itself, which provides information about the phonetic and prosodic features of the utterance, including accent, pronunciation, tone of voice, etc. The third level involves the identification and use of words *qua* constituents of the utterance, which characterizes the utterance as being, for example, in a certain language (or code). The fourth level, the level we have examined in greatest detail in this and other sections, is the level of the interpretive constituents, or, put another way, the level of the semantics of the utterance — "what the words mean." All the levels contribute information to the discourse situation; and any information from any level might contribute to the identification of the speech act effects of the utterance. In the response we find an indication of what interpretation was made and what level of information is being focused on.

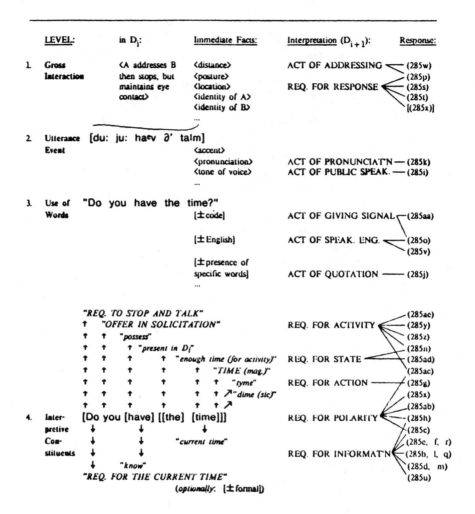

A Schematization for the Interpretation of *Do you have the time?*

Figure 4.

Figure 4 presents this relationship between interpretation levels and response focus in greater detail.[27] Here, some of the features of the utterance and its content, which contribute immediately accessible facts to the discourse situation, are given, along with the kind of interpretation that can be made for each of the four levels. Each possible interpretation can be thought of as a speech act, though not necessarily one generated by the application of illocutionary mode functions. As a speech act, each will introduce a finite number of propositions to the discourse situation, and each will be sensitive to conditions on the context. The principal division is between those acts that preempt illocutionary modes — the acts that derive from the pragmatics of interaction and issuing an utterance — and so can directly match speech act types, and those acts — based on the interpretive constituents of the utterance — which derive from the application of illocutionary modes and give rise to multiple interpretations. In this schematization, that difference is represented as the difference between interpretations in levels 1, 2 and 3, and interpretations in level 4.

The interpretations shown in level 4 both repeat information that was presented in earlier discussions in this section and incorporate some new material. At the level of the whole utterance, several interpretations are possible. These are based on the identification of the whole utterance as having a conventional meaning (given in capitals), such as a request for the time, or an offer to engage in sexual activity, or as a means of initiating an interaction (possibly with some ulterior motive). At the level of the constituents, there are numerous alternative interpretations possible, based on different readings (evaluations) of the constituents. Clearly, only some of those are represented in Figure 4. Under the action of the illocutionary mode function for requestives (L_2), and depending on what propositions are regarded as currently present in the discourse situation, different speech act interpretations are possible, as indicated.

The responses that B makes can be reanalyzed as directed to propositions introduced on different levels, which, in turn, focus on the parameters or interpretive constituents that give rise to the propositions. By far, the greatest number of responses are directed to an interpretation of the utterance as some kind of request. Within that group, most are directed to a request for information, with differences related to the different senses of *time* and *have* that combine to give individual propositions. Some of these, as well, address the polar question (e.g., (285h) and (285c)). The next largest sub-group is directed to an interpretation as a request for action, state, or activity, again, with some responding to the polar question, as well (e.g., (285g) and (285ac)). All of the responses directed to interpretations at level 4 are made in a discourse situation (D_{i+1}) among whose propositions are propositions introduced as a direct result of a speech act interpretation process, as illustrated earlier in this section. The balance of the responses, on levels 1, 2, and 3, are addressed to propositions introduced as a result of speech act type matches that utilize some of the immediate facts (pragmatic features) of the utterance and its context. For example, (285p) qualifies as a response in a highly impoverished discourse situation, where the only information available to both interlocutors (the limits of congruence) is that an act of addressing B has occurred, and a response is called for. In this discourse situation, B might not even recognize that A was speaking English, but, assuming that the rules of discourse interaction are similar for individuals from both English and German speaking communities, would be able to recognize that a response was called for.[28] Another possible analysis of (285x) is that it is addressed to just this level, where it functions to signal B's refusal to engage in "interactive response." Other responses, at levels 2 and 3 might also have multiple interpretations not indicated in Figure 4. Response (285v), for example, might address an act of pronunciation as well as the act of speaking English it is linked to in the figure.

The point of this exercise in reclassification is simply to demonstrate that the notion of discourse situation and speech act that the theory employs is sufficiently rich to provide a basis for explicating the wide variety of interpretations and responses given in Goffman's example. That basis for explication is, of course, the set of propositions in the discourse situation, introduced by the utterance, that the response addresses. It is not my intention to dispute the classification schema that Goffman offers, or to question his approach to discourse: his observations and assumptions are supplementary to those underlying the theory presented in this thesis. Rather, I wish to suggest that the features he identifies as parameters for classification can be incorporated into the speech act theory and rendered, perhaps, more objective, at least to the extent that the information he offers about speaker-addressee intentions or manipulations can be made a reflex of the interpretation process.

An important question that reemerges here is what counts as a speech act. The best answer seems to be — as before — that, though many aspects of an utterance can introduce propositions to a discourse situation, just those effects leading to propositions, which combine with propositions already present in the discourse situation to match speech act types, are speech acts. The speech act types, themselves, describe the partial states of the discourse situation achieved by the utterance. In this section, speech acts based on propositions introduced via the pragmatics of discourse interaction; on direct or conventional interpretations of an utterance; and on propositions generated via application of illocutionary mode functions, were considered. In the following section, the question of speech act definition is examined in greater detail.

4.4. LIES

An interestng test for a theory of speech acts that strives to account for the truth conditions that arise in discourse situations is found in the problem of lies. Lying seems to involve aspects of language use that are properly the domain of speech act theory, but also involves aspects of interlocutors' beliefs and truth in the world. In approaching this problem it is useful to consider the discussion of lying presented in Coleman and Kay (1981).

Coleman and Kay address the problem of representing the meaning of a complex concept, *lie*, and, in particular, contrast the "semantic features" or "checklist" approach to representing meaning with what they term a "prototype view of word meaning" (Coleman and Kay (1981:27)). While a discussion of lexical semantics and the issue they pursue is outside the focus of this thesis, a number of points they raise have a direct bearing.

One assumption in their discussion is that lying is a speech act. Since the present theory utilizes speech act types to represent the effects of speech acts, we might well ask to what extent semantic prototypes and speech act types overlap in function. Further, we might question whether lying — which involves evaluation of truth, a process we have characterized as outside the scope of speech act effect, *per se* — actually can be regarded as a speech act phenomenon; or whether it should be viewed as an effect of proposition evaluation.

Another assumption they make is that judgments about lying in reported interactions — that is, judgments about the speech act *lie* — will reveal something about the constituent properties of the concept *lie*. On the one hand, this is unexceptionable, since our only source of information about word meaning is, ultimately, native speaker judgment. But, on the other hand, we must ask what phenomena are being evaluated in judgments of discourse situations. Are our judgments limited to the effects of speech acts, or do other parameters of discourse interaction also contribute to our evaluations? And, in this latter case, we must wonder whether their attempt to validate their proposed prototype experimentally actually succeeds.

We might begin by considering the prototype for *lie* that Coleman and Kay propose (Coleman and Kay (1981:28)):

> (319) When we try to define *lie*, the first thing that comes to mind is probably the idea of saying something untrue. This, however, is not adequate, since people frequently say

things that are not true but which nonetheless are not called lies — e.g. when the speaker is sincerely trying to convey what he believes to be true information. Honest mistakes and innocent misrepresentations occur frequently, and are not labeled lies. Thus we need a second element in the definition of *lie*, which is that the speaker believes that what he is saying is false.

This, however, still leaves a large number of utterances which we would not want to call lies, even though they are not true. For example, cases of metaphoric speech (*He's a pig*), sarcasm (*You're a real genius, all right!*), and hyperbole (*It's so hot out there, you could fry an egg on the sidewalk*) differ from cases of lying in that the speaker is not trying to induce the hearer to believe something which is not true. Hence the third property of the definition of lying is that the speaker intends to deceive the hearer.

This gives us the following definition of a "good" lie, where the speaker (S) asserts some proposition (P) to an addressee (A):

    a. P is false.
    b. S believes P to be false.
    c. In uttering P, S intends to deceive A.

The prototypical lie, then, is characterized by (a) falsehood, which is (b) deliberate and (c) intended to deceive. [Footnote omitted — D.A.E.]

Several points in this definition are worth noting. First, only lies that arise from assertions of some kind are being considered. This means that the use of speech act types that conventionally introduce propositions based on presuppositions is not (for the purposes of this definition) to be considered lying, even if there is an intention to deceive. For example, if a wishes to know whether c and d have secretly gotten married, he might ask b (who certainly knows):

    (320) *Did you know that c and d are married?*

or, more subtly:

    (321) *Do you know where c and d have decided to go on their honeymoon?*

In asking these questions, a's strategy is to introduce the factive presupposition that c and d are married (in the case of (320)), or the inferred presupposition that they are married based on the factive presupposition that c and d are going on a honeymoon (in the case of (321)), in order to deceive b into believing that a is party to the secret and to stimulate b to respond in a way that reveals the true state of affairs. This kind of situation is outside the scope of Coleman and Kay's definition.

Second, there are no constraints on the kinds of discourse situations in which lies might occur. So, according to (319), if a, a known schizophrenic, who believes that he is Napolean, says to his physician, b:

(322) *I am actually the Duke of Wellington.*

with the intention of misleading b, he would be lying, despite the fact that b knows a's actual identity and is predisposed not to believe any statements a makes. So situations in which deception is *a priori* impossible are to be considered within the scope of lying.

Finally, unless we want to extend the caveat in (319) covering metaphoric speech, sarcasm, and hyperbole, instances of ironic assertion would have to be considered lies. Thus, most of what Socrates says to his three sophistic interlocutors in Plato's *Apology*[29] would be termed lying. For example, at the beginning of the dialogue, Socrates states that he was puzzled by the Delphic oracle's pronouncement that he was the wisest of men. He continues by recounting his attempts to get at the truth of the matter by querying all the great wise men of Greece, only to discover that their knowledge was replete with contradiction. His interlocutors, themselves celebrated "wise men," take Socrates' problem to heart and attempt to help him understand the oracle, thereby revealing their own ignorance, and discovering Socrates' wisdom. It is clear that Socrates did not believe his representation of himself as "puzzled," that he did understand the meaning of the oracle's words,[30] and that he intended to deceive his interlocutors on this point. Still, we might not wish to describe what Socrates did as lying. Since he created a situation in which his true position was discoverable, hence gave evidence that he wanted not so much to deceive as to instruct by elaborate example. So this kind of situation might be regarded as only incompletely covered by Coleman and Kay's definition.

It should be clear that (319) cannot be translated into a speech act type. In the first place, it is outside the province of the conditions on speech act types to encode truth conditions of the actual world, as would be necessary to translate (319a). Indeed, as Coleman and Kay

149

acknowledge, that is one aspect of lying that is even outside the realm of speaker control: we might think that some proposition is false and taking that assumption as a basis tell a lie, but in fact be telling the truth. In the second place, the notion of speech act on which the speech act types are based is intention-free, making the encoding of (319c) a violation of the spirit, if not the formal conditions, of speech act typology. Indeed, the only element that seems to rest squarely in the domain of the propositions that speech act types utilize is (319b), concerning the speaker's beliefs.

However, if we were to suspend these objections, we might attempt to give a speech act type that is faithful to Coleman and Kay's definition as follows:

(323)   *LIE (D_i)
   1: $d(\underline{say}, \$, \varphi) = 1$
   2: $d(\underline{believe}, \$, \varphi) = 0$
   3: $d(\underline{believe}, \$, \psi) = 1$
     where φ and ψ are propositions such that φ is
     actually false,
     and $\psi := [d(\underline{say}, \$, \varphi) = 1) \Rightarrow$
     $[(d(\underline{believe}, @, \varphi) = 1)$ and $(d(\underline{deceive}, \$, @ = 1)]]$;
     and 1, 2, 3 $\in D_{i+1}$

This speech act type states that to lie (perform the speech act *lie*) is to state a proposition (φ), which one doesn't believe, in the belief that by so doing the addressee will believe the proposition and the addressee will be deceived. The paradox, from the point of view of the theory of speech acts developed in this thesis, is that, in order for the speech act lie to be performed, the addressee must match the speech act type *LIE, that is, interpret the utterance as a lie, thereby making the speaker's belief in one of the critical conditions, namely that the addressee be deceived, untenable.

In a sense, this criticism overstates the case and misrepresents the role of speech act types. When a speaker utters something that can be interpreted as having interpretive constituent φ, and if that interpretive constituent can be regarded as issued in the illocutionary mode for constatives (L_1), then the addressee may have numerous choices from among his inventory of speech act types for matching and implementing propositions. He might choose to regard the act as an assertion, or an ironic assertion, or even as a lie. All that his choice does is add specified propositions to the discourse situation. If he views the act as a lie, then he adds the relevant propositions, among which is the proposition that —

for the purposes of the discourse situation — the speaker believes that stating φ will deceive the addressee. Surely, when we do interpret an utterance as a lie, we understand that the speaker has manifested this belief. So, ignoring the programmatic objections to the translation of the prototype (319) into the speech act type (323), perhaps we should accept the speech act type *LIE for the time being and consider other aspects of the problem.

One way in which *lie* seems not to pattern with other constatives is in its inability to take *that*-complements. For example, consider the following:

> (324) a. *John asserted that he would go.*
> b. ? *John lied that he would go.*
> c. * *John asserted when he said that he would go.*
> d. *John lied when he said that he would go.*

It would be possible to list numerous "illocutionary/performative" verbs that pattern with *assert* (such as *acknowledge, accuse, add, admit,* etc., as given in Fraser (1974:6ff)), but only relatively few that pattern with *lie* (such as *overstate, joke, jest,* and verbs reflecting addressee evaluations of the act, including *surprise (us), inspire (us),* and *deceive (us)*). The contrast in (324c) and (324d) seems to show that there are aspects of manner and addressee-judgment involved in lying that do not appear in asserting. This is reminiscent of the difference between *threat* and *scare* discussed in section 2.1, where a distinction was drawn between immediate utterance effects (such as those when uttering x in discourse situation D constitutes a threat), and mediated utterance effects (such as deciding that a speaker's threat should be grounds for being frightened).

If there are factors of judgment involved, where might they come from? The theory offers two possible explanations. The first involves discourse-level parameters, rules governing the interaction in the discourse situation; the second involves truth-condition scoping relations and problems of evaluation.

At the level of discourse interaction, the principle that has the single greatest affect on the interpretation of utterances is the principle of cooperation (ala Grice (1975:45) or, alternatively, Bach and Harnish (1979:166ff)). If speaker and addressee cannot trust each other to "play by the rules" of normal discourse — including the linguistic and social conventions that govern the use of a particular language in a particular situation — then communication collapses. These rules extend to speech act interpretation, of course, so speaker and addressee must not only share, to a significant extent, an inventory of illocutionary mode functions, rules governing consistency relations in context, speech act types, and axioms of genre and choice, but they must agree to apply them to the discourse situation at hand, and, further, work jointly to correct any defects or misapprehensions that might arise. Thus, one source of lies is in the violation of the cooperative principle, where one interlocutor unilaterally decides to stop cooperating and thereby allows a defective discourse situation to develop.

At the level of truth-conditions and scope of evaluation, a major problem for any kind of discourse situation — not just one in which someone is lying — is to decide how to evaluate propositions that are apparently introduced by an utterance. Recall that the propositions that are typically introduced in speech acts give conditions on the discourse situation only; it is another matter whether or not they should be regarded as representing some remote situation, or the actual world. For example, if I tell you the story of Diogenes and say that after interviewing twenty-three men he found one that was honest, you might object saying, *That's not true; he never found an honest man.* I could rejoin, however, that my Diogenes did find an honest man, and that I was telling a story which you falsely inferred to represent either some historical event or a well-known account of Diogenes. We might consider it to be a lie if I intended you to think that my version of the story was the cannonical version; but would it be a lie if I merely wished to offer another, fictional account of the incident? In story telling it is often the case that we believe and know something to be false, and by our performance in telling the story do participate in an intentional deception (especially obvious if we consider the ways adults tell stories of all kinds — fictional and factual — to children), but we would probably not call the activity "lying" without reference to the scope of truth-conditions.

The signature of a lie seems to be the deliberate misrepresentation of a fact of the actual world in situations where one's interlocutor is interested in the details of the fact of the actual world. If we were to include this condition in the speech act type, we could rewrite (323) as follows:

(325) *LIE (D_i)
      1: $d(\underline{say},\ \$,\ \varphi)\ =\ 1$
      2: $d(\underline{believe},\ \$,\ \varphi)\ =\ 1$
      3: $d(\underline{believe},\ \$,\ \psi)\ =\ 1$
      4: $d(\underline{believe},\ @,\ \xi)\ =\ 1$

where φ, ψ, and ξ are propositions such that φ is actually false,

and $\psi := [(d(\underline{say}, \$, \varphi) = 1) \Rightarrow (d(\underline{believe}, @, \varphi) = 1)];$

and $\xi := (d \subseteq W);$

and 1, 2, 3, 4 $\in D_{i+1}$

The new condition requires that the addressee regard the representation made for the purposes of the discourse situation as actually true of the world. In a sense, this specifies the kind of deception that the lie perpetrates. An example of a situation in which the condition does not hold, and, hence, a situation in which one might not be regarded as lying, though the other conditions apply, is found in expressives where the speaker misrepresents his own state for the sake of social convention. In response to *How are you?* the speaker says, *I'm fine, thanks*, almost regardless of his actual condition. As discussed earlier, the truth-value scoping of this kind of expressive is strictly limited (cf. (213), sec. 4.1), and though there might be an actual deception, there is usually no danger that the addressee believe that the speaker's response has validity outside the scope of the discourse situation.[31]

To test their version of the prototype *lie*, Coleman and Kay devised eight stories, which manifested various possible combinations (±) of the three criterial features they identified, and asked subjects to judge whether or not a lie had been told in each story.[32] The stories are repeated here for reference (Coleman and Kay (1981:31)):

(326) I. Moe has eaten the cake Juliet was intending to serve to company. Juliet asks Moe, *Did you eat the cake?* Moe says, *No.* Did Moe lie?

II. Dick, John, and H.R. are playing golf. H.R. steps on Dick's ball. When Dick arrives and sees his ball mashed into the turf, he says, *John, did you step on my ball?* John replies, *No, H.R. did it.* Did John lie?

III. Pigfat believes he has to pass the candy store to get to the pool hall, but he is wrong about this because the candy store has moved. Pigfat's mother doesn't approve of pool. As he is going out the door intending to go to the pool hall, Pigfat's mother asks him where he is going. He says, *I'm going by the candy store.* Did Pigfat lie?

IV. One morning Katerina has an arithmetic test she hasn't studied for, so she doesn't want to go to school. She says to her mother, *I'm sick*. Her mother takes her temperature, and it turns out to Katerina's surprise that she really is sick, later that day developing the measles. Did Katerina lie?

V. Schmallowitz is invited to dinner at his boss's house. After a dismal evening enjoyed by no one, Schmallowitz says to his hostess, *Thanks, it was a terrific party.* Schmallowitz doesn't believe it was a terrific party, and he really isn't trying to convince anyone he had a good time, but is just concerned to say something nice to his boss's wife, regardless of the fact that he doesn't expect her to believe it. Did ·Schmallowitz lie?

VI. John and Mary have recently started going together. Valentino is Mary's ex-boyfriend. One evening John asks Mary, *Have you seen Valentino this week?* Mary answers, *Valentino's been sick with mononucleosis for the past two weeks.* Valentino has in fact been sick with mononucleosis for the past two weeks, but it is also the case that Mary had a date with Valentino the night before. Did Mary lie?

VII. Two patients are waiting to be wheeled into the operating room. The doctor points to one and says, *Is Jones here the appendectomy or the tonsillectomy?* Nurse Braine has just read the charts. Although she is anxious to keep her job, she has nevertheless confused the charts in her mind and replies, *The appendectomy*, when in fact poor Jones is the one scheduled for tonsillectomy. Did Nurse Braine lie?

VIII. Superfan has got two tickets for the championship game and is very proud of them. He shows them to his boss, who says, *Listen, Superfan, any day you don't come to work, you better have a better excuse than that.* Superfan says, *I will.* On the day of the game, Superfan calls in and says, *I can't come to work today, Boss, because I'm sick.* Ironically, Superfan doesn't get to go to the game because the slight stomach ache he felt on arising

154

turns out to be ptomaine poisoning. So Superfan was really sick when he said he was. Did Superfan lie?

The stories manifest the elements of the prototype according to the following chart, reproduced from Coleman and Kay (1981:32):

(327)		P IS FALSE	S BELIEVES P IS FALSE	S INTENDS TO DECEIVE
STORY				
I	(Moe)	+	+	+
II	(John)	−	−	−
III	(Pigfat)	+	−	+
IV	(Katerina)	−	+	+
V	(Schmallowitz)	+	+	−
VI	(Mary)	−	−	+
VII	(Nurse Braine)	+	−	−
VIII	(Superfan)	−	+	−

The subjects responded on a seven point scale where 7 represented the most certain judgment that a lie had been told, and 1 the least certain judgment (i.e., the judgment that a lie had not been told). The following chart[33] gives the mean score and rank (as a lie) for each story, based on responses for 67 subjects:

(328)	STORY	ELEMENTS			MEAN SCALE SCORE
I	(Moe)	+	+	+	6.96
IV	(Katerina)	−	+	+	5.16
V	(Schmallowitz)	+	+	−	4.70
VIII	(Superfan)	−	+	−	4.61
III	(Pigfat)	+	−	+	3.66
VI	(Mary)	−	−	+	3.48
VII	(Nurse Braine)	+	−	−	2.97
II	(John)	−	−	−	1.06

Furthermore, based on a pairwise comparison of stories that differed from each other in exactly two elements it was determined that "[element b] (believe false) is the most important element of the prototype; [element c] (intent to deceive) is the next most important; and [element a] (false in fact) is the least important" (Coleman and Kay (1981:35)).

While we should not want to argue with the conclusion that Coleman and Kay reach — that the meaning of a word like *lie* is "not a list of necessary and sufficient conditions that a thing or event must satisfy to count as a member of the category denoted by the word, but rather a psychological object or process which we have called a PROTOTYPE" (Coleman and Kay (1981:43)) — we should nevertheless ask whether the meaning being explicated in the prototype is the meaning of a speech act. More precisely, we should ask whether the meaning of the word *lie* is based on a speech act, *lie*, or whether it is based on a particular, complex configuration of a discourse situation, including states which could be produced by a variety of speech acts and discourse phenomena.

An example of such a distinction (in a parallel phenomenon) is the difference between telling a joke and saying something funny (i.e., saying something which results in a funny situation). In telling a joke, one tacitly promises to derive a funny situation; if the derived situation is not funny, one has failed to tell a successful joke. However, when one says something (not understood as a joke) which results in a situation that is funny, one has not told a joke, but merely said something funny. In this case, there is no tacit promise, and no criterion of success. A good joke will work by itself, regardless, almost, who tells it. But the words that are judged humorous in one context might be ordinary in another. If a grown man goes to a cocktail party and orders *whiskey on the rocks*, nothing unusual results; if a 4-year old child does the same thing, it might be very amusing.

In the cases presented in (326), there are a variety of speech acts performed. For example, in stories I, II, III, VI, and VIII the statement that we are to judge is a response that answers a question. In story IV, the statement appears as a simple assertion. In story V, it appears as either an expressive or an assertion. The one thing that all the statements have in common is that as a result of the statement in each case a proposition of the form

(329) $d(\underline{\text{believe}}, \$, \varphi) = 1$, for some φ,

is part of the discourse situation. In every case where that misrepresents the speaker's actual beliefs, the subjects judged the situation to be relatively more lie-like.

In terms of the theory of speech acts presented here, a proposition like (329) has a variety of consequences for the discourse situation in which it appears. In cooperative discourse, where metarule (258) would apply, the presence of (329) has the effect of introducing

(330) $d(\varphi) = 1$,

unless the addressee believes otherwise. The one case where this caveat might apply is in V, where Schmallowitz' statement under the metarule would give rise to a proposition that contradicts what seems to be a fact of the discourse situation (viz. that it has been "a dismal evening enjoyed by no one"). This might be regarded as evidence of uncooperative behavior on Schmallowitz' part: he creates a situation in which it is impossible for the metarule to apply, where he must be understood as professing a false belief.

Indeed, in all the cases where (329) is a misrepresentation of the speaker's actual beliefs (I, IV, V, and VIII) a defective discourse situation results if metarule (258) applies; and if the addressee is cooperative, it would apply. So here is the seed of deception that is planted in each of these stories: the addressee is being deceived as to the cooperation of the speaker, regardless of the other intentions the speaker might have.

In the case of III and VI the addressee is again being manipulated, this time along Gricean lines. If Pigfat and Mary are cooperating with their respective addressees, they will obey the rules of cooperative interaction including the Maxim of Quantity: "1. Make your contribution as informative as is required (for the current purposes of the exchange). 2. Do not make your contribution more informative than is required." (Grice (1975:45)) In answering the questions they are asked, Pigfat and Mary fail to obey this maxim, but calculate that their interlocutors will assume that it applies. If so, their incomplete answers will be regarded as complete, or at least sufficient to permit an inference that does complete the answer.

For example, as discussed in sec. 4.3, a question like John's to Mary (in VII) can be interpreted as a polar question or as a request for information. If Mary is cooperating, she will answer in a way that removes any ambiguity as to her interpretation of the question. She provides information that — under the Gricean maxim — can be regarded as an answer to the polar question as well. Her cooperative interlocutor does draw the inference that since Valentino has been sick, Mary has not seen him.

If anything, the kind of analysis that the present theory of speech acts brings to these cases supports the claim that the meaning of *lie* is a complex collection of perhaps gradable elements. But the theory would be hard-pressed to characterize the effects of a lie as a speech act. Rather, the theory would regard lying as a condition on the discourse situation (or an evaluation of the discourse situation) that was independent of the particular speech act which gave rise to the lie-state.

An interesting case for the speech act theory is that of the Liar's Paradox (of Eubulides). In its simplest form we have a discourse situation with a speaker saying

(331) *I am lying.*

The question, of course, is whether the speaker is telling the truth. Now, there is the possibility of confusion on several levels which should be clarified. One question is whether lying is performative in the sense of, say, promising in

(332) *I am promising.* (Better: *I promise.*)

Recall that *promise*, and constatives like *assert, agree, aver,* etc., can take *that*-complements, so expressions like

(333) *I promise that* φ,

or

(334) *I assert that* φ,

can have the interpretation that φ is, respectively, promised or asserted; while expressions like

(335) * *I lie that* φ

are impossible. But note also that the appearance of performative verbs in expressions of the form of (331) and (332) does not necessarily entail that a speech act of the type conventionally associated with the performative verb is being performed by the expression. For example, in the following cases the speech act interpretation of the second sentence is not given by the surface performative verb:

(336) *Are you going out? I'm asking you a question!*

(337) *I want you to buy Dysan. I'm agreeing with you!*

Here, the second sentence functions in part as a constative (probably, as an assertion) which, among other things,[34] clarifies the speaker's interpretation of what speech act the first sentence has performed. Similarly, there is a very natural role for an expression such as (331) in an analogous context:

(338) *Bob ate the cake. I'm lying.*

The natural interpretation is to regard *I'm lying* as a statement about the truth-value of the preceding sentence, specifically, about the speaker's beliefs concerning Bob and the cake. Under this kind of interpretation (331) is not a paradox, but merely incomplete or out of context.

But suppose we take (331) to be as Eubulides intended, totally self-referential. According to Coleman and Kay's prototype (319) three conditions must hold if (331) is a consummate lie:

(339) i. The proposition *I am lying* must be false (where *I* = the speaker).
ii. The speaker must believe that the proposition *I am lying* is false.

iii. The speaker must intend to deceive the addressee (on the value of the proposition).

In this formulation, the paradox is manifest. First, the "lying" of the proposition is not primitive but encompasses the same three points given in (339), which leads to an infinite regress. Second, the speaker's intention to deceive is self-cancelling: one can't deceive by making the deception known.

According to the theory of speech acts, an expression such as (331) can be used in numerous ways. It might occur as a question (meaning: "Are you accusing me of lying?"), as a self-reprimand (meaning: "What I have just said is false."), as a quotation, or as a recitation. How it can be used is constrained by the available illocutionary mode functions, the conditions of the discourse situation (context), the available speech act types, and the discourse-level parameters that influence choices for implementation. The only time that (331) might be a problem is when it is used as a constative, specifically as an assertion. If we let φ represent the proposition expressed by (331) (i.e., the relevant interpretive constituent of (331)), then the illocutionary mode function L_1 generates the following candidate propositions:

(340) $d(\underline{\text{say}}, \$, \varphi) = 1$

(341) $d(\underline{\text{believe}}, \$, \varphi) = 1$

Now, if they were to match the speech act type for assertions (if nothing in the discourse situation were to prevent the match), and if they were implemented, and if the metarule of cooperation were to apply, not only (340) and (341) would be added to the discourse situation, but

(342) $d(\varphi) = 1$

would be added as well. But if φ were of the form

(343) $d(\underline{\text{believe}}, \$, \varphi) = 0,$

then the type of the discourse situation would explode, i.e., would no longer be a function since it would give contradictory values in (341) and (342).

Since this interpretation is not possible, then, other interpretations must be sought. The two directions the alternative interpretations take are just the directions mentioned earlier in this section: an interpretation at the level of discourse interaction, and an interpretation at the level of scope of truth-values.

At the level of discourse interaction, (331) is interpreted as a violation of the cooperative principle. Since applying the metarule of cooperation leads to an impossible discourse situation, the speaker must be regarded as suspending the principle. On this level, the utterance of (331) means, simply,

(344) I am not cooperating.

At the level of scope of truth-values, the question becomes whether φ (the interpretive constituent) can be interpreted as giving a type of the discourse situation, or whether it gives the type of a remote situation. Since interpreting it as characterizing the discourse situation leads to the explosion of the function, we are forced to consider it as a characterization of a remote situation. Making this more explicit, we could write:

(345) $\varphi := s(\underline{believe}, \$, \varphi) = 0$

Thus, the assertion which introduces (340) and (341) does not lead to contradictions in the discourse situation, itself; rather, it introduces the speaker as having a bizarre belief, namely, that there is a situation in which φ has the value given by (345).

I do not wish to suggest that the interpretations offered of the Liar's Paradox by the theory of speech acts presented here should supplant the classic (e.g., Russellian) solutions to the problem. Rather, I wish to suggest only that there are avenues of interpretation offered by the theory that defuse the paradox and provide a means for understanding the way lies work in discourse situations. Like Coleman and Kay, we can regard the concept *lie* as multi-faceted, with components that derive from various aspects of discourse interaction; unlike them, we do not regard lying as a speech act but as a violation of conditions that hold for normal speech acts.

CHAPTER 5   SUMMARY AND EVALUATION

5.0.   INTRODUCTION

This chapter summarizes and evaluates the theory developed in Chapters 1 through 4, and outlines directions for future research. In recapitulating the thesis, the crucial assumptions the theory makes and the important components the theory utilizes are reidentified and briefly explained.

As a step toward evaluating the theory, the desiderata given in section 1.4 are reviewed. The theory satisfies most, though not all, of the points presented there. The noteworthy successes of the theory include its ability to deal with subutterance and suprautterance speech acts, and its natural treatment of one class of indirect speech acts, namely those where there is a divergence in proposition expressed and overt syntactic form. A principal deficiency of the theory is the absence of a set of well-specified inferencing rules to account for other classes of indirect speech acts. More fundamental problems stem from the choice of primitives and the ontological commitment that represents, and the absence of a detailed account of the derivation of interpretive constituents.

Among the goals of future work based on this theory should be a more complete development of inferencing schemata that link the components that are invoked during the speech act interpretation process, a more thorough analysis of illocutionary modalities and the role of context, and a better justification of the choice of primitive relations that appear in speech act types. Individual projects could include a detailed examination of several speech act types, or an application of the theory to some of the residual problems one encounters in actual discourse. Especially useful would be an explication of the relationship between the syntax of the segments of utterances and the interpretive constituents that those segments generate.

5.1. THE THESIS SUMMARIZED

Natural language is an object of wonderous complexities, and the determined efforts of thousands of scholars over a period of nearly fifty years (to date the "modern" era from Bloomfield (1933)) have yielded only an incomplete understanding of its mysteries. Even the highly formalized and constrained program begun by Chomsky, (1957, 1965) has resulted in detailed analyses of but a few fragments of a handful of natural languages.[1] Yet, for the most part, work during this period has focused on sentences in isolation, not on utterances as they occur in natural language discourse, where inherent complexities of linguistic structure are compounded by the complexities associated with perceiving, planning, and acting that are the cognitive prerequisites of intelligent interaction with the world. It is little wonder that theories of language use are in their intellectual infancy.

Nevertheless, one aspect of language use — the problem of speech acts — has been the subject of considerable research, and deserves to be formalized, if only to reveal the inadequacies of our understanding of the problem. This thesis represents an attempt at just such a formalization. The approach taken here has been dictated by a consideration of the kinds of phenomena to admit (and exclude) from the realm of speech acts, and by a commitment to computational simplicity. The result is a theory that is highly limited but still capable of offering explanations for a variety of complex phenomena and capable of making predictions that can serve as the basis of future research.

The theory as developed in Chapters 1 through 4 actually has several parts, each of which can be summarized briefly.

The first part focuses on semantic foundations. As this is a semantic theory, it is necessary to decide how to represent meaning and what formal apparatus to use. The decision taken here — to use a situation semantics — is based on the argument, presented forcefully in Barwise and Perry (1981b, c), that more traditional (i.e., Fregean) approaches to meaning representation are inadequate to deal with the intuitive relations (beyond simple truth-conditions) expressed by words as they occur in a variety of natural language contexts, and that the most influential recent developments in semantics, taking possible worlds as primitives, are computationally undesirable. Coupled to this is the need to regard discourse situations as distinguished entities composed of objects (in particular, speakers and addressees), properties, and relations, that together exhaustively delimit the context of utterance interpretation.

The representation-construct exploited in the theory is the situation-type, which encodes information about a partial state of situations, given some constellation of primitive objects, properties, or relations, by indicating whether that constellation holds in a particular situation.[2] Using situation-types, we can express the content of an utterance in terms of the constraints it effects on the set of situations that the utterance characterizes. There is no loss of expressive power by choosing situation-types, with objects, properties, and relations as primitives, over, say, a semantic formalism in which possible-worlds (situations) are taken as primitives. There is, however, the ontological problem of how to choose primitives, which is here left unresolved except to the extent that several "discourse-relation" primitives are distinguished which play an important role in defining the end-states that utterances can achieve.

The principal relation encountered repeatedly is the relation given by **believe**. This reflects the decision to regard the structure of discourse situations as expressible, indeed knowable, only in terms of the belief-states conventionally manifested in the information that utterances introduce. While this may be a mis-orientation — while belief may not be primitive at all — the decision to regard belief as primitive has consequences for the whole theory. Specifically, a number of speech act effects, ranging from simple assertion to ironic statement and sarcastic comment, are distinguished primarily in terms of the different constraints imposed on belief-states compatible with the discourse situation in which such acts occur.

The second part considers the problem of deciding what phenomena to include under the label "speech act." The most important observation is that it is impossible to link speech act generating segments with any simple syntactic or semantic constituents. Rather, speech acts seem to be effected both by subutterance and by suprautterance stretches of discourse, and are sensitive to the content of the discourse situation. In designing a theory that is capable of accounting for both extremes, it is necessary to separate the ways in which the simplest constituents of an utterance can be used from the conditions on the discourse end-states that can be effected. This is accomplished by allowing even the smallest meaningful constituents of an utterance to give rise to speech acts by assuming that all such constituents are issued in a finite number of "illocutionary modes," whose effect is to introduce the speaker, addressee, and the information contained in the constituent into the discourse situation in some primitive relationship; and further, by deciding to regard as a speech act only those sets of relationships which combine to achieve well-defined discourse end-states. These end-states are given in terms of speech act types which can be regarded as partial functions that map ·discourse situations into discourse situations, with each type corresponding to the effects of a particular kind of speech act.[3]

One consequence of this separation of illocutionary modality from speech act type is the ability to define complex speech acts in terms of simple constituent propositions. This also enables us to account for suprautterance effects that depend on complex conditions of context but are achieved by single utterances.

Another consequence of this division of speech act generation into two parts is the ability to make speaker intentionality a reflex of the speech act interpretation process. In effect, the speaker can intend to achieve (vis-a-vis an addressee) only those end-states which are mutually recognized to be among the set of (partial) end-states which his dialect admits as legitimate speech act types. The paths that might be taken to a particular end-state can sometimes by varied, but the speech act effect will be the same.

This two-step generation/interpretation process is made possible, in part, by choosing to regard discourse as proceeding in a discrete step-by-step fashion, where each step is determined by the addition (or removal) of a finite amount of information. This permits us a very fine-grained analysis of changes in the discourse situation and of the effects of even the simplest of speech acts.

The third part of the thesis consists of the formalization of a theory of speech act interpretation. This involves the isolation of interpretive constituents — the meaningful, well-formed utterance parts that are input to the speech act generation process — and a series of steps designed to convert the interpretive constituents into propositions, at the level of the discourse situation, that can combine to yield speech acts. The first step is the application of illocutionary mode functions to the interpretive constituents to produce a series of candidate propositions in which the speaker, addressee, and information contained in the interpretive constituents are represented as being in some particular discourse-level relationship. The second step involves the reconciliation of candidate propositions with existing propositions (facts) in the discourse situation. Broadly speaking, this step represents the effects of context on speech act interpretation, though, here, those effects are limited to a special treatment for candidate propositions that are redundant or contradictory vis-a-vis the set of already existing propositions that give the discourse situation. The third step involves the matching of combinations of candidate propositions with available speech act types, and the decision to choose one or more matched types for implementation.[4]

Several assumptions inform this aspect of the thesis which bear repeating. Foremost is the assumption that discourse involves a variety of cognitive processes, some of which are properly outside the bounds of formal linguistics.

In making decisions concerning which of several speech act interpretations to give an utterance, an addressee accesses information about perceived plans and goals, as well as information about what actual speech acts could be performed by the utterance. There are areas in which such planning can become conventionalized, as when particular discourse genres become associated with particular kinds of speech act choices; but there are also many instances when a choice can be determined only after an analysis of the discourse as part of a complex planning network. In such cases, generalized planning mechanisms, including knowledge of scripts, knowledge of rules of socio-cultural interaction, and knowledge of an individual speaker's or addressee's predisposition to act in certain ways, may all be relevant.

More properly within the bounds of the linguistic aspects of speech act interpretation, there are several levels at which decisions can be made. First, we can appeal to our knowledge of discourse-pragmatic functions of utterances to define a series of direct interpretations that utterances can effect. In many ways these direct interpretations correspond to the semantic presuppositions of the utterance, as when the use of a definite article can be interpreted to mean that the speaker is referring to old information. But some of these interpretations, such as when the speaker can be understood to be characterizing a referent as of a certain class — and thereby be understood to express an attitude toward the referent — are not semantic presuppositions, but are discourse functional. Second, we can identify a number of conventional syntactico-lexical structures that preempt choices in the interpretation process. For example, subject-auxiliary inverted syntax combined with literal question intonation might be associated with requestives of various kinds; and words and phrases that are highly regulated by context (e.g., *How do you do?*) could trigger preferred speech act interpretations that are directly part of their semantic descriptions.[5]

Finally, in the fourth part of the thesis, the relationship between truth-conditions and speech acts is explored. An important distinction is drawn between the truth-conditions on the sets of propositions that speech acts introduce to the discourse situation — which express the necessary truth-value relations that must obtain in the discourse situation — and the truth-conditions that apply to those same propositions when evaluated outside the scope of the discourse situation. This problem of orientation can be regarded as properly outside the domain of the theory of speech acts but of considerable interest to the theory of semantics that underlies the theory of speech acts. Here a number of examples involving the effects of constatives and requestives are examined and it is shown that the question of truth and meaning cannot be subsumed under any one aspect of utterance-interpretation, but rather is affected by interaction of several components of the interpretation process, including conventions related to cooperation.

In sum, certain features of discourse related to speech act generation, interpretation, and effect seem amenable to a formal semantic treatment, but there are limitations in the ability of any semantics — in isolation from a comprehensive model of the interaction that obtains in actual discourse, with attendant inferencing schemata — to capture all aspects of natural language discourse. The extent to which the present theory succeeds in establishing a formal semantic framework for treatment of speech act phenomena is examined in the following section.

5.2.   THE THESIS EVALUATED

In section 1.4, desiderata for a theory of speech acts were presented, based on considerations both of the prerequisites of formal theories, in general, and of the kind of phenomena that fall within the realm of speech acts. We might briefly evaluate the theory developed here in terms of those desiderata. Taking each point in turn, we could make the following observations:

The theory is formal enough to offer explanations (for example, of the differences between the effects of assertions and reaffirmations, etc.) and make predictions (for example, to suggest the existence of a TESTIFY (TO)/CONFIRM speech act type) (cf. (25i.)), though it requires a more complete elaboration than was possible here.

The theory is capable of assigning multiple speech act interpretations to an utterance (cf. (25ii.)). Indeed, the speech act interpretation process proceeds by overgeneralizing interpretations, then reducing the candidate set.

The theory is capable of capturing subutterance and suprautterance speech act phenomena (cf. 25iii.)). Subutterance phenomena are accommodated by providing for speech act effects to be based on interpretive constituents, which can be small sub-parts of utterances, rather than on some arbitrary syntactic unit. Suprautterance phenomena are accommodated by separating illocutionary modality (which operates on interpretive constituents) from speech act types, which are constrained, in part, by sometimes complex conditions that make reference to simple propositions created by the interpretive constituents under some illocutionary modality. A suprautterance effect is achieved only when all the conditions are satisfied in the discourse situation, which can require many steps.

The theory is explicit about some of the kinds of inferencing it requires and the rules that govern such inferencing (cf. (25iv.)), but it could expand upon this point. At present, the most elaborate example involves discourse genre-mediated choices for speech act interpretations, and what rules govern proposition negation. At least there is nothing in the theory that is incompatible with a more highly elaborated set of inferencing rules.

The theory is computationally feasible and does utilize simple mechanisms (cf. (25v.)), by basing itself on a semantics (situation semantics) that is computationally tractable, and by requiring nothing more complex than relatively simple pattern-matching and an ATN-like bookkeeping program, where the transitions are between states of a discourse situation, not nodes in a syntactic parse-tree.

The theory is specific about the role of extra-theoretic information and processes (cf. (25vi.)), to the extent that it defines the role that such processes must play. For example, the generation of interpretive constituents is based, in part, on the output of a "black box" syntactic/semantic analyzer, which interfaces with the theory only at the beginning of the interpretation process. Similarly, the theory provides for interaction with various kinds of planning mechanisms at the point where choices for implementation must be made.

The theory is capable of representing and utilizing contextual information in giving derivations for speech acts (cf. (25vii.)), though the operation of the reconciliation function, X, was limited to the simple cases of repeated and contradictory candidate propositions. Still, the effects of context are clearly evident in the conditions on the speech act types, so even though the interactive role of context on speech act interpretation is only cursorily represented, the effects of context as a source of information about what speech act types are matched by any particular utterance are always present.

The theory is sensitive to the role of prosodic information (cf. (25viii.)), by providing for preemptive speech act interpretations or illocutionary mode choices that are associated with certain kinds of (conventional) prosody. The theory does not elaborate on the role of non-verbal information, but can accommodate it in much the same way as the prosodic information, by allowing certain kinds of gestures either directly to introduce interpretive constituents (such as would be the case of a deictic gesture being associated with the interpretive constituent "\$ is referring to [[$\langle \nearrow \rangle$]] (= some object, etc.)") or to preempt speech act interpretations (as when a shrug of the shoulders introduces the information that the speaker doubts what he is saying).

The theory is flexible enough to account for some kinds of indirect speech acts (cf. (25ix.)), especially where the utterance contains constituents that manifest the semantic relationships that are focused on in the indirect act, but does not provide for other kinds of indirect speech act phenomena.

Finally, the theory is generalizable to multiple speakers and addressees (cf. (25x.)), though, for convenience, the special case of two-person discourse is used in most of the examples.

The principal advantage that this theory offers over previous theories (besides its formal grounding) is its ability to deal with subutterance and suprautterance speech act phenomena with the same mechanisms. And those same mechanisms — the isolation of interpretive constituents issued in an illocutionary modality from the speech act types that utilize the resulting propositions — provide a natural treatment for certain kinds of indirect speech acts, typified by the "whimperatives" (Sadock (1970)), "impositives" (Green (1973)), and "requestions" (Sadock (1974)).[6]

Whimperatives are syntactic questions that query the ability of the addressee to do something, with the intention of making a request. For example, a question like

(346) *Can you open the door?*

when used to ask the addressee to open the door, is a whimperative. Impositives have the form of questions about some activity, but are used to suggest or request that the activity be done. For example,

(347) *Why don't we leave?*

(348) *Shouldn't we leave?*

(349) *How about leaving?*

all literally ask about leaving, with the intention of requesting an addressee to join the speaker in leaving. Finally, requestions indirectly request that an addressee supply the missing element in a statement as an answer to a question, as in

(350) *The Japanese bombed Pearl Harbor on?*

What these three types of indirect speech acts have in common is that the desired (indirect) effect can be constructed out of elements that are overtly part of the utterance. Just as the utterance *I think that you should leave* was analyzable, in part, as both an assertion (statement of belief) and a request to leave (cf. sec. 3.2), because the interpretive constituents of the utterance, when input to the illocutionary mode functions for constatives and requestives, served to generate candidate propositions that satisfied the description for the speech act types ASSERT and REQUEST ACTION, so the utterances in (346) - (350) have interpretive constituents that can be analyzed as being issued in a variety of illocutionary modes.

Whimperatives and impositives contain interpretive constituents that can be directly input to the illocutionary mode function for requestives (L_2). For example, among the interpretive constituents of (346) is

(351) @ open the door;

and among the interpretive constituents of (347) and (348) is

(352) $ and @ leave.

Both can become embedded in **want** and **request** candidate propositions to qualify as requests — provided nothing in the context blocks such an interpretation.

Requestions are issued with rising (question) intonation on the missing element. Under one analysis, such intonation is conventionally preemptive for requestives. The balance of the utterance contributes information that represents the presuppositions of a request for information. The fact that the speaker immediately relinquishes his turn indicates that a response is desired (cf. sec. 2.2, (39a.) and (39c.)), and an appropriate response to an incomplete proposition is to supply the completing element.

There are indirect speech act phenomena, however, that are not handled by the decomposition of an utterance into interpretive constituents, analyzed as being issued in a variety of illocutionary modes. Indeed, the theory developed here would suggest a division of indirect speech act phenomena into two broad classes: those "indirect" effects that are derivable from the information overtly present in the utterance, and those effects that result only from a chain of inferencing that begins with information present in the utterance, but is only remotely related to that information. In a sense, the theory would eschew the label "indirect" for the first class of effects, since they can be generated directly. The second class of effects would be treated as outside the theory proper (or at least, on its fringes), and regarded as falling in the domain of interactive planning that is necessary for discourse, in general.

Typical of this second class of indirect effects are those produced by utterances such as the following:

(353) *Here's a chair.* (for: *Please take a seat.*)

(354) *It's a bit warm in here.* (for: *Open the window!*)

(355) *I'm trying to listen to this program.* (for: *Shup up or get out!*)

In each of these cases the desired interpretation is not generable from the use of overt interpretive constituents[7] under the application of illocutionary mode functions above. Rather, each can be regarded as initiating patterns of inferencing, some of which converge on the desired interpretation.

A principal shortcoming of the present theory is that it does not provide the rules that would be necessary to link the speech act generation/interpretation process with the remote effects that speech acts can have. The theory does suggest what mechanisms might be involved, e.g., discourse genre types, scripts, and a general planning mechanism, but is not explicit about how they should interact with other components of the theory (except to the limited extent that genre types are used (cf. sec. 3.4)).

On a more fundamental level, the theory suffers from the absence of strong arguments for its choice of illocutionary mode primitives. In particular, the decision to use belief as the basis of information in discourse requires further justification. However, it should be possible, regardless of the choice of primitives, to retain the formal apparatus that the theory introduces. The actual choice of primitives made here has served to illustrate the function of that formal apparatus.

Yet another fundamental problem concerns the absence of a specific mechanism to provide syntactic-semantic parsings of an utterance that can serve as the basis of interpretive constituent generation. The device used here — a "black box" — serves as a metaphor for a large body of work (outside the realm of speech act theory, *per se*) that has grappled with this problem. While we should not be responsible for a solution, we should recognize that the theory developed here must remain incomplete until one is found.

5.3. DIRECTIONS FOR FUTURE RESEARCH

The theory developed in this thesis has many "loose ends" that should be given a more thorough treatment. To consider, again, just the problems cited in the previous section, we can see the need for future work to provide explicit rules of inferencing that link the various components in the theory; to investigate the ontological status of illocutionary mode primitives; and to clarify the operations of the "black box" linguistic analyzer. In addition, only the simplest and most straight-forward of contextual effects were considered in defining the conditions on the reconciliation function, X. This may be excusable given the limited scope of this thesis — to provide a "first-pass" description of a theory of speech acts — but cannot be forgiven in future work. Furthermore, in presenting illocutionary mode functions, only two — those for constatives and requestives — were used. A complete theory would require a complete list of such functions, for directives, expressives, commissives, and perhaps other (yet to be identified) illocutionary modes. In short, in almost every aspect of the theory presented there is room for expansion and further research.

However, I would like to suggest two areas, in particular, which would profit from future work and would serve to extend and test the theory. The first concerns the set of speech act types, and the second focuses on some problems of natural language discourse that might prove amenable to solution within the theory of speech acts.

The score or so speech act types that appear in this dissertation have the immediate, pragmatic function of providing concrete instances of a component that is absolutely essential to the design of the theory of speech acts. Yet they suffer both from an incomplete justification of their details, and from the absolute limitation of their numbers. Since the speech act types represent — in a highly condensed, and highly constrained fashion — the socio-cultural and pragmatic information (as well as the discourse-semantic information) that competent speakers must share in order to engage in interactive discourse, there is in them a great potential for describing and explaining cross-dialect and cross-cultural linguistic variation as manifested at the level of discourse.

To take but one example, according to Taylor (1971), rural Japanese have no notion of what it is to negotiate. Presumably, such Japanese do understand the individual utterances that might occur in a negotiation dialogue, but they fail to distinguish the state of the discourse situation that is achieved when a negotiation reaches its (successful) conclusion. This failure cannot be attributed to any feature of the Japanese language (their urban counterparts clearly suffer no such deficiency), but could be explained in terms of speech act typology. Just as a refutation can be regarded as a suprautterance speech act phenomenon, so, too, a negotiation can, in part, be viewed as a suprautterance effect. The discourse situation is changed incrementally by the effects of individual (lesser) speech acts until all the preconditions are met for the speech act type COMPLETE NEGOTIATION to be matched.[8] It would be an interesting exercise to attempt to characterize the differences between the rural Japanese dialect(s) and the urban Japanese dialect(s) in terms of the sets of speech act types that each recognizes.

The second area concerns some features of natural language discourse that present problems for more traditional syntactic and semantic theories. A number of these problems are presented in G. Lakoff (1978), including the first four items in the following list:

(356) a. Amalgams (G. Lakoff (1974))
I invited you'll never guess how many people to God knows what kind of a party.
b. Interjections (James (1973))
John threw the ball — oh — up.
c. Correcting and editing devices (G. Lakoff (1978))
I looked up her dress — I mean, address.
d. Speech formulas (Becker (1975))
Your place or mine.
e. Discourse prosody
John is probably at school...although I told him to stay home... (*so maybe he didn't go.)
versus:
John is probably at school...althoouugh I told him to stay home... (so maybe he didn't go.)
f. Multimodal sequences
I thought you were referring to (↖) not to (↗).

All the phenomena represented by the examples under (356) — except speech formulas — have several features in common. First, all involve subutterance effects that alter the interpretation that we give to the larger syntactic structures (clauses/sentences) in which they appear. Second, any parser that would analyze these utterances properly would have to be sensitive to the status of the discourse situation as determined by the interpretation of constituent parts of the utterance up to the point when the phenomenon occurs. Finally, all seem to involve illocutionary effects different from the illocutionary effect of the utterance as a whole in which they are embedded. In short, in all these cases, the effect is achieved by exploiting an interpretive constituent, issued in some illocutionary mode, that has speech act status in the discourse situation.

As the language of the previous sentence indicates, there is a conceptual apparatus in the theory presented in this dissertation that affords a framework for interpreting such phenomena. The outstanding questions are what the speech act types associated with each should be, and, more importantly, what rules of syntax (and semantics) we must admit into the theory to accommodate interpretive constituent generation. This latter problem straddles the boundary between "black box" and rules of interpretation for constituent use, and raises the further question whether existing syntactic theories that make no provision for distinguished discourse-functional units (other than, say, a sentence) can be regarded as useful in dealing with natural language discourse. In any case, the theory would benefit from any attempt to extend it to cover these problems.

The remaining phenomenon, that of speech formulas, raises the question of what role conventionalized speech act effects have in the semantic description of such words and phrases. There is a place in the theory for conventional interpretations of at least two kinds: those that preempt illocutionary mode choices, and those that select speech act types directly. But the two or three cases that were used for illustration do not constitute a survey of the phenomenon, and the theory would profit from a more complete investigation.

In sum, these two broad problem areas — the role of speech act typology in defining dialects and cultures, and the role of utterance constituent use as it occurs in natural language discourse — offer a challenge to the theory of speech acts presented in this dissertation, and an opportunity to refine and rework the components that comprise that theory. The goal of the thesis developed here is to demonstrate that one essential aspect of language use — the effects of speech acts — can be given a formal semantic treatment that is both straight-forward and powerful enough to explain some of the interesting illocutionary phenomena of natural language interaction. But this represents only a first step toward a formal semantics of discourse. The goal of future work should be to extend the kind of semantic treatment begun here to other aspects of language use. Only when that is accomplished can we hope to have a complete linguistic theory of natural language.

NOTES

NOTES TO CHAPTER 1

1. This "Law" was a cornerstone of Renaissance philosophy and can be paraphrased as *God abhors a vacuum.*

2. At the sub-atomic level, of course, the observation process itself gravely affects the situation observed, so we might regard the limitations in our ability to extract information at this level as an inherent limitation on situations defined at that level.

3. An important problem for situation semantics is the ontological question of what individuals, properties, and relations are primitive (in the sense of "irreducible"), and what ones are composite. There is no attempt made in this thesis to distinguish among primitive and composite elements which occur in examples, and it is clearly beyond the scope of the brief introduction to situation semantics that this section represents to do so. Only in the relationships that arise in discourse situations as a result of utilizing certain illocutionary modes in interpreting utterances do primitives appear that have consequences for the theory of speech acts; and those primitives are presented in some detail. Generally, individuals, properties, and relations that appear in situation-types can be regarded as shorthand notations for whatever collection of primitive individual-, property-, and relation-concepts would be necessary to define the corresponding English words of which the selected items are glosses. Such items are given in boldface (e.g., **contain**), and are distinguished from the illocutionary mode primitives which are given in boldface and underlined (e.g., **say**).

4. We should understand the scope of rule government to be quite wide, ranging from the assumption (convention?) that speaker and addressee will share a language (or languages) whose rules of phonology, syntax, semantics, etc., they will obey, to the kinds of principles of cooperation that are given by the Gricean Maxims (cf. Grice (1975)). Furthermore, any specific rules of interpretation that speaker and addressee must share to facilitate communication should also be included under this point. Such special rules might encompass conventions associated with the use of discourse genres, or with transformations of the discourse situation, as when we play-act, or (from the other point of view) watch a play. Indeed, one special set of rules which is absolutely essential to the successful interaction of interlocutors is that set giving the

rules of speech act interpretation, the explication of which is the object of this dissertation.

5. The **believe** relation used here is a relation between an individual and some proposition, given as a situation-type. The content of a proposition will be denoted by ": =", with the name of the proposition appearing on the left, and the situation-type on the right. As a notational convenience in subsequent reference, the situation-type expression, d(**be-in**, a, D) = 1, will be abbreviated as (a∈D), for some individual or proposition a; and the situation-type expression, d(**have-value**, x, a) = 1, will be abbreviated as d(x=a) = 1, for some x ∈ {\$, @} and some individual a.

6. Arguments for the need for such assumptions can be found in Lewis (1969) and Schiffer (1972).

7. Content as it is used here subsumes the three major interpretations given to context found by Clark and Marshall (1981) (or, alternatively, in Clark and Carlson (1981)): community membership, linguistic text, and physical co-presence.

8. As stated in the Preface, this work does not present an exegesis of traditional speech act theory. While individual points might be discussed explicitly in the context of a traditional perspective, it is for the most part assumed that the reader is familiar with the speech acts literature. A limited set of references, reflecting my personal tastes, is the following: Allen (1979), Austin (1962), Bach and Harnish (1979), Cohen (1978), Cole (1978), Cole and Morgan (1975), Clark and Carlson (1982a, b), Gazdar (1981), Katz (1977), Perrault, et al. (1978), Sadock (1974), Searle (1969, 1975a, b, c), and Strawson (1964).

9. This approach to the representation of discourse is not new, but follows the practices of Bar-Hillel (1954) and others, most notably Gazdar (1979).

10. This particular example was first brought to my attention by Terry Winograd.

11. Here and elsewhere, the terms *marked* and *unmarked* are used, as in standard linguistic practice, to distinguish among items (at a phonological, syntactic, or semantic level, for example) that contrast in a particular context. The marked item or items are regarded as bearing distinctive features (information) that sets them apart from the unmarked item(s), which are thought of as simpler or primary in the contrast relationship.

12. Note: this should not be read without the comma as *You'll never guess who I met at the ballpark*, which, of course, is perfectly acceptable.

NOTES TO CHAPTER 2

1. Others, including Searle, and Bach and Harnish, have found problems with Austin's distinctions. Searle's solution is to collapse some of the locutionary with the illocutionary. Bach and Harnish expend some effort in separating illocutionary effects from perlocutionary ones.

2. This, of course, leaves untouched the distinction between effects that come from inferences (of any kind) and those that come from reflexes in situations. We might succeed in frightening someone by sneaking up behind him and yelling *Boo!* (as we might by yelling *I love you!*) because we exploit a situational reflex and not a discourse situation.

3. Actually, in cases where a wishes to create a special effect, or to speak ironically or sarcastically, he might very well violate the cooperative principle, but in such a way as to reveal the significant difference between his own understanding of the discourse situation and his interlocutor's.

4. These are designed to be similar to the "conversational postulates" of Gordon and Lakoff (1971), though they focus on a different level of discourse interaction and are given only informally.

5. *Backchanneling* refers to the use of minimal utterances (typically *uh-huh*) by an interlocutor to indicate that he is following the speaker.

6. *Fragmentary* should be understood as semantically incomplete with respect to the information available in the discourse situation, for example as in *So (I) ...; but ...; and ...; anyway ....*

7. These dialogues were adapted from an actual conversation transcribed from video tape. For the curious, (41) is a more accurate rendering of the original than (40).

8. There has been a great deal of work in artificial intelligence and cognitive science that attempts to rationalize conversational interaction in terms of more general sorts of problem solving involving the elaboration and enactment of plans in the service of discourse goals. Regrettably, it is not possible to include a discussion of this work in the scope of this thesis. For a good general introduction to the methodology and many of the assumptions of this literature, one should consult Beaugrande (1980). More specific works include Shank and Abelson (1977), Allen (1979),

Cohen (1978), Bruce and Newman (1978), Perrault, et al. (1978), Hobbs (1976), and Hobbs and Evans (1980).

9. Several taxonomies of speech acts have been proposed, including those in Searle (1975a) and Bach and Harnish (1979). While the structure of the speech act types given here differs both in general design and also specific detail, many of the distinctions among speech act types, and their names and families, owe much to this previous work.

10. Again, this should be understood with the earlier caveat in mind, namely, that there might be other primitive relations that better capture the essential features of representations of states of affairs. A discussion of some of the alternative primitives is presented in Barwise and Perry (1981b), where belief is regarded as epistemologically complex.

NOTES TO CHAPTER 3

1. There are, of course, alternative interpretations of these and earlier examples, especially as they are offered without context. Probably any set of four different interpretations could be used to make the point developed here.

2. An interesting example of the ability of situation semantics to preserve compositionality while allowing alternative parsings of this kind of constituent is given in Barwise (1981), where the Det-Nom and NP-Rel analyses of nominals are contrasted.

3. Interpretive constituents as understood here are similar to the "constituents" of Lieb (1979:358), which designate immediate constituent-like units derived from surface structure.

4. As a first approximation, one might regard the output of this black box as giving the "null context" (Katz and Fodor (1963)) interpretation of the utterance, though, in fact, every interpretation of an utterance is parasitic on some elements of context.

5. This approach repeats that taken by Montague and others who have continued his program (cf. Montague (1974) and Partee (1976)).

6. This illustration is adapted from the treatment given the fragment presented in Barwise and Perry (1981a: Chapter 4).

7. I translate the deontic operator here into an explicit implication, in a form that is compatable with the glosses given in the speech act types where obligation is a factor.

8. It would be necessary, of course, to propose a discourse situation-

type that utilized these propositions to give such an interpretation. To do so would be a straight-forward exercise using the speech act types in Chapter 2 as models.

9. A distinction is made here between two kinds of inferences "$\Rightarrow$" and "$\models$". The rules which enable inferences from the "$\Rightarrow$" form are many and varied, including rules that operate on and generate derived facts (as opposed to the framing and immediate facts) of the discourse situation. Rather than attempt to define these rules, we might simply accept that different rules can apply in different situations to enable inferences, and regard "$\models$" as shorthand notation for this.

10. There are genuine problems with the simple versions of proposition negation given in (164) - (168), which form the basis of the test for inconsistency. In these cases only negation of an atomic proposition is discussed, but there are clearly many kinds of negation or of entailment relations that lead to negation that are not covered by such a schematization. Indeed, it may not be possible to give a single schematization of these more general kinds of negation. Nevertheless, some means of evaluating the potential effects of candidate propositions is necessary in any theory of speech acts that strives to account for the interaction of context with utterance interpretation. I offer this simplified version of proposition negation both to illustrate the limited operations of the reconciliation function, X, and also to suggest how one facet of the considerably larger problem of general proposition negation might be handled by the theory.

11. This joke was first brought to my attention by Geoff Nunberg.

12. Specifically, different genres might have different type preference hierarchies associated with them.

13. A planning mechanism is defined in Hobbs and Evans (1980), where application to discourse analysis is discussed.

14. To the extent discussed above, where implicational hierarchies might are used, the theory might make choices for us.

15. As speech act types we might give the following:

REFUTE φ (D_i)
1: $d(\underline{say}, \$, \psi) = 1$
2: $d(\underline{believe}, \$, \psi) = 1$
3: $d(\underline{believe}, \$, \xi) = 1$
4: $d(\underline{refute}, \$, \varphi) = 1$
5: $d(\underline{believe}, \$, (NOT \varphi)) = 1$

where φ, ψ, ξ are propositions
such that $\psi \models \text{NOT } \varphi$,
and $\xi := d(\psi \models \text{NOT } \varphi) = 1$,
and 1, 2, 3, 4, 5 $\in D_{i+1}$.

MAKE IRONIC JOKE S (D_i)

1: $d(\underline{\text{say}}, \$, \varphi) = 1$
2: $d(\underline{\text{believe}}, \$, \varphi) = 0$
3: $d(\underline{\text{believe}}, \$, \psi) = 1$
4: $d(\underline{\text{believe}}, \$, \xi) = 1$
5: $d(\underline{\text{believe}}, \$, \zeta) = 1$

where $\varphi_{-n}, \dots, \varphi_{-1}, \varphi, \psi, \xi, \zeta$ are propositions
and S is a situation, of type s,
such that $s(\varphi_{-n}) = 1, s(\varphi_{-n+1}) = 1, \dots, s(\varphi_{-1}) = 1,$
$s(\varphi) = 1,$
and $s(\underline{\text{believe}}, @, (S \subseteq W)) = 1$
and $\psi := d(S \subseteq W) = 0$
and $\xi := [d(\underline{\text{believe}}, @, (S \subseteq W)) = 1 \gg d(\text{be-fool},$
$@) = 1]$
and $\zeta := s(\text{be-humorous}) = 1,$
and $3 \in D_i,$
and 1, 2, 3, 4, 5 $\in D_{i+1}$.

16. This is not always the case. Speakers can construct ironic jokes that depend only on having the punch line interpreted correctly in order to achieve the whole effect. But the fact that some ironic jokes exist that require more suffices to establish the point.

17. It is worth noting that in a society where such a speech act type does not occur, for example, among the Japanese, no amount of announcing of intentions can affect an appreciation of the finished product.

18. To be more precise about the operation of C we might consider the following schematicized case:

Assume we have an unordered set of candidate speech acts,

$$T^* = \{t_{10}^*, t_{25}^*, t_7^*, t_{59}^*\},$$

and a set of discourse genre types compatible with the current discourse situation,

$$G' = \{g_6, g_{31}, g_{15}\},$$
where g_6: $\langle [1: t_{10}, 2: t_{65}, 3: t_{59}], h_6 \rangle$
g_{31}: $\langle [1: t_{103}, 2: t_7], h_{31} \rangle$

$$g_{15}: \quad \langle \; [1: t_{59}, \; 2: t_{61}], \; h_{15} \; \rangle$$

C effects the application of each $g_j \in G'$ to T^*. Thus, applying g_6 to T^*, h_6 makes the following assignments:

$$t_{10}{}^*{:}1, \; t_{25}{}^*, \; t_7{}^*, \; t_{59}{}^*{:}3$$

Applying g_{31} to T^*, h_{31} makes the assignments:

$$t_{10}{}^*, \; t_{25}{}^*, \; t_7{}^*{:}2, \; t_{59}{}^*$$

Applying g_{15} to T^*, h_{15} makes the assignments:

$$t_{10}{}^*, \; t_{25}{}^*, \; t_7{}^*, \; t_{59}{}^*{:}1$$

These assignments can be consolidated as follows:

$$t_{10}{}^*{:}1, \; t_{25}{}^*, \; t_7{}^*{:}2, \; t_{29}{}^*{:}1, \; 3$$

The determination of relative rank in T^{**} is based on the value and number of indices each candidate bears. Candidates with lower indices outrank candidates with higher indices; and candidates with equivalent values on indices are discriminated according to total number indices, with greater number of indices outranking lesser number of indices. Thus, for the above set, the ranked output of C would be:

$$T^{**} \; = \; \{t_{59}{}^*{:}1, \; 3; \; t_{10}{}^*{:}1; \; t_7{}^*{:}2; \; t_{25}{}^*\}$$

NOTES TO CHAPTER 4

1. For relevant citations of Frege's work, and that of the others mentioned in this section, consult the bibliography.

2. The choice of these six authors is not intended as a complete listing, rather only is intended to illustrate difference in style of approach.

3. Cf. Perry (1980a, b) for a discussion of the different uses to which one can put revealed beliefs, and also, therefore, the different intentions that can be served in revealing beliefs.

4. One might view directives of all kinds as involving just such manipulation of the facts of the discourse situation. For example, in issuing an order, a speaker introduces a fact (viz. the consequence of not following the order) that directly impinges on the addressee, whose existence (some function of relationships in the actual world) is thereby changed.

5. For example, (201) could be part of the following:

It's four thirty and I've got to be home by five. It's raining

181

and there are no buses to be found anywhere. I keep telling myself "I'm not gonna make it."

6. Here, it is assumed that it is a meterological impossibility for any situation to have, simultaneously, both predicates **be-raining** and **be-dry** be true. This assumption is clearly false for an Alice-in-Wonderland world (or discourse situation), so an added condition on (semi-) fictional discourse situations must be given. Specifically, we could say that any discourse situation inherits from the world all the conventional and empirical laws that are related to predicates that hold of the discourse situation except in just those cases where such laws are explicitly suspended. In Alice's Wonderland, it is not so much the case that certain laws are suspended as that there are no laws at all.

7. This term is taken from Hobbs (1980), where the importance of completing chains of inferences linked to the predicates overtly introduced is discussed.

8. While this term is taken from Katz and Fodor (1963), it is intended here to represent the set of situation-types which an utterance's interpretive constituents determine, free of any illocutionary modality or frame of reference, including the current discourse situation.

9. Compare this with responses such as *Oh, a little busy, I guess. Why?* or *OK, I guess.* which invite queries and can preempt from the initiator the right to direct the course of further interaction.

10. Stalnaker pointedly states that he does "not propose an analysis of assertion" but intends rather to "make some modest claims about the way assertions act on the contexts in which they are made, and the way contexts constrain the interpretation of assertions." (1978:315)

11. Since the theory distinguishes among types of constatives — including one labeled ASSERT — and since discussion of Stalnaker (1978) necessarily involves a contrast of Stalnaker's and my usage of the notion of assertion, I employ the term "constative" at this point to avoid prejudicing the case.

12. Consult Barwise (1981) and Barwise and Perry (1980) for a more complete discussion of the differences between situation semantics and possible world semantics. Besides the obvious and very great ontological differences (including the use of possible worlds (situations) as primitives in one case; the use of objects, properties, and relations as primitives in the other), a principal distinction in the two systems is in computability. There are straightforward ways to guarantee effective computability in a situation semantics that are not available to possible worlds systems.

182

Nevertheless, this issue in no way affects Stalnaker's remarks or comparisons with the theory.

13. This is misleading since the sets determined by a proposition in both systems are potentially infinite.

14. This, of course, is true of sets of propositions as well. The set of situations (or possible worlds) determined by the proposition expressed in *It is hot and dry (here)*. will be a proper subset of and further restriction on the set of situations determined by the proposition expressed in *It is hot (here)*.

15. The exact case Stalnaker considers (1978:317ff) involves the use of *You are a fool*. Since it is important to contrast the way the world actually is with alternative descriptions of the world (as represented in some interpretations of the proposition), I have chosen a case with a less subjective condition than foolhood. Furthermore, instead of the proper names Stalnaker uses, I distinguish the interlocutors as a, b, and c, to eliminate one possible, but here irrelevant, confusion resulting from the interpretation of proper names as individuals.

16. The passage given is a paraphrase of Stalnaker's (1978:317) description of his own example, with appropriate substitutions to accommodate the difference between it and the modified version I give.

17. For the sake of simplicity, I have endeavored to suppress notational gargoyles whenever possible. This policy is reasonable with respect to the discussion of speech act effects, since temporal and referential indices are largely subsumed in the speech act types, and since the action of speech acts proceeds in a step-by-step fashion. But such a practice cannot be long maintained when one wishes to express precisely the interpretation of the propositions encoded in the interpretive constituents of an utterance (as opposed, say, to the interpretation of the <u>use</u> of the interpretive constituents, which is the domain of speech act theory). Thus, there is a glaring inadequacy in the interpretive gloss in (243) and (249) since the interpretation of *you* must be anchored by a variety of facts, including who is in the discourse situation, and whether the referent is co-present (as would be the case in normal usage) or a referent in a remote situation (as would be the case if *you* were used quotatively, or in a narrative, etc.). Minimally, then, we would have to index the interpretation to the current facts of the discourse situation and to the role *you* as a constituent plays in the interpretive constituents of the utterance, perhaps as follows: $_{d,i}[[you]]_S$. The interpretation we give in (243) and (249) represents the case where the situation-type invoked

183

by the interpretive constituents is supposed to be a situation-type of the discourse situation, in short, where S = d. Hence, *you* is interpreted to be just the addressee in d at time i.

18. Note, to repeat, b can (and must) recognize a's position without necessarily agreeing. We can, no doubt, think of many conversations where the operative principle has been to "agree to disagree" about some issue. Such a condition does not block communication, but, on the contrary, makes it more efficient.

19. Clearly, it is no simple matter determining the correct interpretation of *that*, in (277). In its full anaphoric range are an infinite number of possible referents. We can assume here that a variety of constraints, or selective inferences, aid us in deciding that the intended referent is one of φ_1' - φ_3', and that, of those, φ_3' is the most likely. The kinds of constraints that would come into play include our knowledge that *true* (or *false*) can be predicated only of propositions; that the most recently introduced propositions are the ones that entered the discourse situation via the speech act, of which only the ones expressing a's beliefs are contradictable; and that the proposition expressing a's beliefs have given rise to the introduction of φ_1' - φ_3', indirectly, via the metarule. Either b is saying that a doesn't believe what he purports to believe, or b is saying that some (or all) of φ_1' - φ_3' are false. In this latter case, only φ_3' seems likely to be subject to question (from b's point of view) since b should be able to perceive directly that he is wearing something (φ_1') and that what he's wearing is a hat (φ_2'), but he might not know (or remember) its color (φ_3').

20. In fact, according to the theory, this situation would match a CONTRADICT speech act type, since the essential precondition of explicit or derived contradictory propositions in the discourse situation can be met. It does not affect the discussion or argument, however, to speak of this act as a simple assertion.

21. Stalnaker's original example might not be subject to this criticism, since the proposition expressed by a does not involve multiple interpretive constituents, as given. (Recall, a merely says: *You are a fool.*)

22. The example is reproduced in a format that is designed to facilitate future reference, so numbering has been changed.

23. This last point is not a necessary one, but in the example ((285)) B does respond, and we may perhaps assume that there are numerous cues, even in the least felicitous of cases, that indicate to an interlocutor

that a response is being requested.

24. Recall that such conventional interpretations (given in capitals) short-circuit the speech act interpretation process by forcing the application of specific illocutionary mode functions, in some cases, or by forcing the matching of specific speech act types.

25. The use of "script" here follows that in Shank and Abelson (1977), though the format for presenting the information contained is modified.

26. Note that we have assumed that, under the interpretation of *the time*, there is an ellipted argument — some activity, α — that is lexically/semantically invoked, and that the identity of that activity is available in the discourse situation. Here we might assume that the identity of A and B as prostitute and john, respectively, in addition to the kinds of activities mentioned in the co-present solicitation script, establishes a limited set of unmarked choices of interpretation. Observe, also, that when the activity is not mutually known, the addressee often responds with *For what?*

27. Figure 4 is not intended to be a complete schematization of the interaction of interpretations and responses, merely to be illustrative of some of the relations.

28. It would be wrong to propose that the rules governing interaction at this level are linguistic (pragmatic) universals. If B were a Warm Springs Indian, for example (cf. Philips (1976)), he would not have a rule linking the surrendering of a turn at talk with a request for a response.

29. A complete discussion of this dialogue from the point of view of Socrates' role and use of irony can be found in Kierkegaard (1965:74ff).

30. As quoted from Plato's *Apology* in Kierkegaard (1965:197), the meaning is: "Human wisdom is worth little or nothing... He among you is the wisest who, like Socrates, knows that this wisdom is really worth nothing at all."

31. Coleman and Kay discuss one kind of expressive which they term "the social lie" (Coleman and Kay (1981:29)), in which the same conditions apply. They claim that there is no deception involved in such cases, but in light of the foregoing comments the notion of deception might need qualification. Clearly, in following social convention one expects to bring about a discourse situation in which speaker and addressee are regarded as holding the beliefs they profess. One might disingenuously say to a host: *This has been a wonderful party. I've*

enjoyed myself very much. (assuming the performance of the utterance is "normal" in other respects), and fully expect the host to respond with an appropriate expressive (e.g., *Well, I'm glad you had a good time.*) The propositions expressed are consistent within the context of a discourse situation in which speaker and addressee have the beliefs attributed to them by the expressives. The deception would occur only if the host chose to regard the utterance not as an expressive (with limited scope of truth), but as an assertion oriented toward the actual world.

32. For a complete discussion of the design of the experiment, consult Coleman and Kay (1981:30ff).

33. The chart in (328) summarizes information presented by Coleman and Kay in their Table 2. and Figure 2. (Coleman and Kay (1981:33))

34. There are, of course, many "other things" going on in cases like these. In (336), for example, there is an emphatic REQUEST FOR RESPONSE, perhaps also a threat, if only implicit, in an ORDER TO ANSWER. In (337), there may be a REQUEST TO DESIST (some activity, such as complaining or badgering), and pleading.

NOTES TO CHAPTER 5

1. The negative tone of this statement should not be understood as intended to deprecate the significance of this work. That work represents a monumental achievement, whose absolute limitations serve to underscore the enormity of a complete solution.

2. The formal definitions of a situation-type and of the other concepts that play a role in the development of the foundations of the theory are collected in Appendix A.

3. All the speech act types used for illustration in earlier sections of the thesis have been organized under families of types in Appendix B.

4. The formal constructs for this and related earlier parts of the thesis are collected in Appendix C to facilitate reference.

5. For an interesting collection of some of these words and phrases, consult Becker (1975).

6. For a discussion of these classes of indirect speech acts, consult Sadock (1974: Chapter 6) and a related discussion in Bach and Harnish (1979:174ff).

7. A further qualification is actually necessary, especially in the case of (353) and (355), if we are to claim that there are no interpretive

constituents present that lead (directly) to the desired interpretation. Namely, we must assume that (353) is issued without an accompanying gesture (such as a sweep of the hand toward a seat, which might be associated with a conventional request to sit down), and that (355) is issued with intonation appropriate for assertions, and not in a "plaintive" manner (which could have a conventional interpretation as a request to desist).

8. This description of the effects of speech acts on the discourse situation as a process in which simple operations on a state can effect changes that incorporate the effects of the operations, while preserving the integrity of the state comes, in part, from treating speech acts as STRIPS-like operators (cf. Fikes and Nilsson (1971)).

BIBLIOGRAPHY

Allen, J. (1979) *A plan-based approach to speech act recognition.* Technical Report No. 131/79, Department of Computer Science, University of Toronto.

Austin, J. L. (1962) *How to do things with words.* Cambridge, Mass.: Harvard University Press, and London: Clarendon Press.

Bach, K. and R. M. Harnish (1979) *Linguistic communication and speech acts.* Cambridge, Mass.: The MIT Press.

Bar-Hillel, Y. (1954) Indexical expressions. *Mind* 63, 359-379.

Barwise, J. (1980) Scenes and other situations. In Barwise, J. and I. A. Sag (Eds.), *Stanford Working Papers in Semantics 1*, Stanford, Ca.: Stanford Cognitive Science Group, Part B.

Barwise, J. (1981) Some computational aspects of situation semantics. *Proceedings of the 19th Annual Meeting of the Association for Computational Linguistics*, Stanford, Ca.: The Association for Computational Linguistics, 109-111.

Barwise, J. and J. Perry (1980) The situation underground. In Barwise, J. and I. A. Sag (Eds.), *Stanford Working Papers in Semantics 1*, Stanford, Ca.: Stanford Cognitive Science Group, Part D.

Barwise, J. and J. Perry (1981a) *Situation semantics: A theory of linguistic meaning.* Unpublished manuscript.

Barwise, J. and J. Perry (1981b) Situations and attitudes. *Journal of Philosophy* 78, No. 11.

Barwise, J. and J. Perry (1981c) Semantic innocence and uncompromising situations. *Midwest Studies in Philosophy* 6, 387-403.

Beaugrande, R. de (1980) *Text, discourse, and process.* Norwood, N. J.: Ablex Publishing Corporation.

Becker, J. (1975) The phrasal lexicon. In Nash-Webber, B. L. and R. C. Shank (Eds.), *Theoretical issues in natural language processing*, Cambridge, Mass., 60-63.

Belnap, N. D. and T. B. Steel, Jr. (1976) *The logic of questions and answers.* Bibliography compiled by Urs Egli and Hubert Schleichert. New Haven and London: Yale University Press.

Bloomfield, L. **(1933)** *Language.* New York: Holt, Rinehart and Winston.

Bruce, B. and D. Newman **(1978)** Interacting plans. *Cognitive Science 2,* 195-233.

Chomsky, N. **(1957)** *Syntactic structures.* The Hague: Mouton and Co.

Chomsky, N. **(1965)** *Aspects of the theory of syntax.* Cambridge, Mass.: The MIT Press.

Clark, H. H. **(1979)** Responding to indirect speech acts. *Cognitive Psychology 11,* 430-477.

Clark, H. H. and T. B. Carlson **(1981)** Context for comprehension. In Long, J. and A. Baddeley (Eds.), *Attention and Performance 9,* Hillsdale, N. J.: Lawrence Erlbaum Associates, 313-330.

Clark, H. H. and C. R. Marshall **(1981)** Definite reference and mutual knowledge. In Joshi, A., B. Webber, and I. A. Sag (Eds.), *Elements of discourse understanding,* Cambridge: Cambridge University Press.

Clark, H. H. and T. B. Carlson **(1982a)** Hearers and speech acts. *Language 58.*

Clark, H. H. and T. B. Carlson **(1982b)** Speech acts and hearer's beliefs. In Smith, N. V. (Ed.), *Mutual knowledge,* London: Academic Press.

Cohen, P. R. **(1978)** *On knowing what to say: Planning speech acts.* Technical Report No. 118, Department of Computer Science, University of Toronto.

Cole, P. (Ed.) **(1978)** *Syntax and semantics 9: Pragmatics.* New York: Academic Press.

Cole, P. and J. L. Morgan (Eds.) **(1975)** *Syntax and semantics 3: Speech acts.* New York: Academic Press.

Coleman, L. and P. Kay **(1981)** Prototype semantics. *Language 57,* 26-44.

Cooper, R. **(1975)** *Montague's semantic theory and transformational syntax.* Unpublished doctoral dissertation, University of ·Massachusetts.

Cooper, R. **(forthcoming)** *Quantification and syntactic theory.* Dordrecht, Holland: D. Reidel Publishing Company.

189

Davidson, D. (1967) Truth and meaning. *Synthese 17*, 304-323.

Dore, J. (1977) Children's illocutionary acts. In Freedle, R. O. (Ed.), *Discourse production and comprehension*, Norwood, N. J.: Ablex Publishing Corporation, 227-244.

Dore, J. and R. McDermott (to appear) Linguistic indeterminacy and social context in utterance interpretation. *Language*.

Ervin-Tripp, S. and C. Mitchell-Kernan (Eds.) (1977) *Child discourse*. New York: Academic Press.

Fikes, R. and N. J. Nilsson (1971) STRIPS: A new approach to the application of theorem proving to problem solving. *Artificial Intelligence 2*, 189-208.

Fraser, B. (1974) An analysis of vernacular performative verbs. Distributed by The Indiana University Linguistics Club, Bloomington, Indiana.

Freedle, R. O. (Ed.) (1977) *Discourse production and comprehension*. Norwood, N. J.: Ablex Publishing Corporation.

Frege, G. (1968) The thought: A logical inquiry. In Klemke, E. D. (Ed.), *Essays on Frege*, Urbana, Ill.: Illini Books, 507-535.

Gazdar, G. (1979) *Pragmatics*. New York: Academic Press.

Gazdar, G. (1981) Speech act assignment. In Joshi, A., B. Webber, and I. A. Sag (Eds.), *Elements of discourse understanding*, Cambridge: Cambridge University Press, 64-83.

Goffman, E. (1976) Replies and responses. *Language and Society 5*, 257-313. Also reprinted in Goffman, E. (1980) *Forms of talk*, Philadelphia: University of Pennsylvania Press, 5-77.

Goffman, E. (1980) *Forms of talk*. Philadelphia: University of Philadelphia Press.

Goody, E. (1972) "Greeting," "begging," and the presentation of respect. In Fontaine, J. S. (Ed.), *The interpretation of ritual*, London: Taristock, 39-71.

Gordon, D. and G. Lakoff (1971) Conversational postulates. In *Papers from the Seventh Regional Meeting, Chicago Linguistic Society*, Chicago: Chicago Linguistic Society, 63-84. Also reprinted in Cole, P. and J. L. Morgan (Eds.) (1975) *Syntax and semantics 3: Speech acts*, New York: Academic Press, 83-106.

Green, G. M. (1973) How to get people to do things with words. In

Shuy, R. W. (Ed.), *New directions in linguistics*, Washington, D. C.: Georgetown University Press, 51-81.

Grice, H. P. **(1975)** Logic and conversation. In Cole, P. and J. L. Morgan (Eds.), *Syntax and semantics 3: Speech acts*, New York: Academic Press, 41-58.

Grosz, B. **(1978)** *The representation and use of focus in dialogue understanding.* Technical Note 151, SRI International, Menlo Park, California.

Gumperz, J. J. **(1977a)** Contextualization in interaction. Unpublished manuscript.

Gumperz, J. J. **(1977b)** Sociocultural knowledge in conversational inference. In Saville-Troike, M. (Ed.), *28th Annual Round Table Monograph Series on Language and Linguistics*, Washington, D. C.: Georgetown University Press.

Hobbs, J. R. **(1976)** *A computational approach to discourse analysis.* Research Report No. 76-2, Department of Computer Sciences, City College, City University of New York.

Hobbs, J. R. **(1980)** Selective inferencing. *Proceedings of the Third National Conference of the Canadian Society for Computational Studies of Intelligence*, Victoria, B. C., 101-114.

Hobbs, J. R. and D. A. Evans **(1980)** Conversation as planned behavior. *Cognitive Science 4*, 349-377.

Jackendoff, R. S. **(1972)** *Semantic interpretation in generative grammar.* Cambridge, Mass.: The MIT Press.

James, D. **(1973)** *Some aspects of the syntax and semantics of interjections in English.* Unpublished doctoral dissertation, University of Michigan.

Johnson-Laird, P. N. **(1980)** Mental models in cognitive science. *Cognitive Science 4*, 71-115.

Joshi, A., B. Webber, and I. A. Sag **(Eds.)** **(1981)** *Elements of discourse understanding.* Cambridge: Cambridge University Press.

Kamp, H. **(1981)** A theory of truth and semantic representation. In Groenendijk, J. A. G., T. M. V. Janssen, and M. B. J. Stokhof (Eds.) *Formal methods in the study of language*, Amsterdam: Mathematisch Centrum, 277-322.

Katz, J. J. **(1977)** *Propositional structure and illocutionary force.* New York: Thomas Y. Crowell, Inc.

Katz, J. J. and J. A. Fodor (1963) The structure of a semantic theory. *Language* 39, 170-210.

Kierkegaard, S. (1965) *The concept of irony.* New York: William Collins Sons and Co., and Harper and Row.

Klein, E. (1981) Kamp's discourse representation structures and generalized phrase structure grammar. Talk given at the Stanford Sloan Workshop on Non-transformational Syntax, June, 1981.

Klemke, E. D. (Ed.) (1968) *Essays on Frege.* Urbana, Ill.: Illini Press.

Labov, W. and D. Fanshel (1977) *Therapeutic discourse.* New York: Academic Press.

Lakoff, G. (1974) Syntactic amalgams. In La Galy, M. W., R. A. Fox, and A. Bruck (Eds.), *Papers from the Tenth Regional Meeting, Chicago Linguistics Society*, Chicago: Chicago Linguistics Society, 321-344.

Lakoff, G. (1978) Some remarks on A. I. and linguistics. *Cognitive Science* 2, 267-275.

Lewis, D. K. (1969) *Convention.* Cambridge, Mass.: Harvard University Press.

Lieb, H.-H. (1979) Principles of semantics. In Heny, F. and H. S. Schnelle (Eds.) *Syntax and semantics 10: Selections from the Groningen Round Table*, New York: Academic Press, 353-378.

Montague, R. (1974) *Formal philosophy: Selected papers of Richard Montague,* edited by R. H. Thomason. New Haven and London: Yale University Press.

Ochs, E. and B. Schieffelin (Eds.) (1979) *Developmental pragmatics.* New York: Academic Press.

Partee, B. H. (Ed.) (1976) *Montague grammar.* New York: Academic Press.

Perrault, R. C., J. Allen, and P. R. Cohen (1978) Speech acts as a basis for understanding dialogue coherence. In *Proceedings of the Second Conference on Theoretical Issues in Natural Language Processing*, Champaign-Urbana, Ill.

Perry, J. (1980a) Belief and acceptance. *Midwest Studies in Philosophy* 5, 533-542.

Perry, J. (1980b) A problem about continued belief. *Pacific Philosophical Quarterly* 61, 317-332.

Philips, S. U. (1976) Some sources of cultural variability in the regulation of talk. *Language and Society* 5, 81-95.

Quine, W. V. O. (1966) *The ways of paradox.* New York: Random House.

Quine, W. V. O. (1970) *Philosophy of logic.* Englewood Cliffs, N. J.: Prentice-Hall.

Russell, B. (1919) *Introduction to mathematical philosophy.* London: George Allen and Unwin.

Sadock, J. M. (1970) Whimperatives. In Sadock, J. M. and A. L. Vanek (Eds.), *Studies presented to Robert B. Lees by his students,* Edmonton, Canada: Linguistic Research, 223-239.

Sadock, J. M. (1972) Speech act idioms. In Peranteau, P. M., J. N. Levi, and G. C. Phares (Eds.), *Papers from the Eighth Regional Meeting, Chicago Linguistics Society,* Chicago: Chicago Linguistics Society, 329-340.

Sadock, J. M. (1974) *Toward a linguistic theory of speech acts.* New York: Academic Press.

Sag, I. A. and M. Liberman (1975) The intonational disambiguation of indirect speech acts. In Grossman, R. E., J. L. San, and T. J. Vance (Eds.), *Papers from the Eleventh Regional Meeting, Chicago Linguistics Society,* Chicago: Chicago Linguistics Society, 487-497.

Schiffer, S. R. (1972) *Meaning.* Oxford: Oxford University Press.

Searle, J. R. (1969) *Speech acts: An essay in the philosophy of language.* Cambridge: Cambridge University Press.

Searle, J. R. (1975a) A taxonomy of illocutionary acts. In Gunderson, K. (Ed.), *Language, mind, and knowledge, Minnesota studies in the philosophy of science* 3, Minneapolis, Minn.: University of Minnesota Press, 344-369. Also reprinted in Searle, J. R. (1979) *Expression and meaning,* Cambridge: Cambridge University Press, 1-29.

Searle, J. R. (1975b) Meaning, communication and representation. Unpublished manuscript.

Searle, J. R. (1975c) Indirect speech acts. In Cole, P. and J. L. Morgan (Eds.), *Syntax and semantics* 3: *Speech acts,* New York: Academic Press, 59-82.

Searle, J. R. **(1979)** *Expression and meaning.* Cambridge: Cambridge University Press.

Schiffrin, D. **(1977)** Opening encounters. *American Sociological Review 42,* 679-691.

Shank, R. C. and R. Abelson **(1977)** *Scripts, plans, goals and understanding.* Hillsdale, N. J.: Lawrence Erlbaum Associates.

Stalnaker, R. C. **(1978)** Assertion. In Cole, P. (Ed.), *Syntax and semantics 9: Pragmatics,* New York: Academic Press, 315-332.

Strawson, P. F. **(1950)** On referring. *Mind 59,* 320-344.

Strawson, P. F. **(1964)** Intention and convention in speech acts. *The Philosophical Review 73,* 439-460.

Taylor, C. **(1971)** Interpretation and the science of man. *The Review of Metaphysics 25,* 3-51.

Winograd, T. **(1980)** What does it mean to understand language? *Cognitive Science 4,* 209-241.

APPENDIX A DEFINITIONS OF CONCEPTS

The following terms/concepts play an important role in the theory developed in this thesis, though the list is not exhaustive. Items are presented in the order in which they appear in the dissertation, and are defined by exerpting their original context.

Situation-type:

In situation semantics, we define a situation-type to be a partial function characterizing various kinds of situations. More precisely, if we let A represent the set of objects, $\{ a_0, a_1, a_2, ... \}$, and R the set of sets of n-place relations, $\{ R^0, R^1, R^2, ... \}$, with R^0 being the set of 0-place relations (one of which might give, for example, the state of it raining); R^1, the set of properties, or 1-place relations (including, for example, the property of being green); R^2, the set of 2-place relations (including, for example, the relation of one person hitting another person); etc.; then we can define a situation-type, s, to be a partial function which returns the values 0, 1, or *undefined* for any relation and set of objects depending on whether that relation holds of that set of objects for the situations of which s is the type. We write:

(1) $s(r^n, a_1, ... , a_n) = 1$ iff $a_1, ... , a_n$ are in the relation r^n in the set of situations given by s,

$s(r^n, a_1, ... , a_n) = 0$ iff $a_1, ... , a_n$ are not in the relation r^n in the set of situations given by s, and otherwise

$s(r^n, a_1, ... , a_n) =$ undefined.

W:

For example, the situation-type

(6) $s(\text{want}, \textbf{Brynn}, \textbf{the-ball}) = 1$

gives just those situations in which the person designated by *Brynn* (i.e. **Brynn**) is in a **want** relationship to the person or object designated by *the ball* (i.e. **the-ball**). Whether or not there are, in fact, situations which have this type is an empirical matter. Conventionally, in situation semantics, the problem is whether or not S, the set of situations having s as their type, is contained in **W**, the set of situations that obtain in the world. If $S \subseteq W$, then (6) gives the type of a set of real situations; if not, then (6) gives the type of a set of imaginary situations.

The framing facts of a discourse situation:

We might list some of the features of discourse situations that distinguish them from other situations as follows:

(8)   a.   There is a speaker
         b.   There is at least one addressee
         c.   All parties to the situation recognize that they are in a discourse situation
         d.   The purpose is semiotic (meaning that the speaker engages in symbolic representation of situations for a purpose, designed so the addressee(s) can discover the purpose)
         e.   The process is rule-governed

The situation that a speaker and addressee find themselves in is similar to all other situations involving mutual activity, but is distinguished by having all the characteristics given in (8). These characteristics represent the <u>framing facts</u> of a discourse situation.

Immediate and derived facts:

There are, of course, other facts that are part of any discourse situation, and these will consist of two kinds, <u>immediate</u> and <u>derived</u>. Immediate facts include what one sees, hears, smells, etc., in the physical environment — those facts that are directly accessible to perception — of which all the participants can be aware. In addition, we can consider the direct effects of utterances — including the meanings of the subparts of the utterance, and their speech act effects — to be part of the set of immediate facts. Derived facts, on the other hand, are any facts introduced to the discourse situation through processes of inferencing that begin with framing facts or immediate facts. For example, if it is a fact that a is the speaker, and b the addressee, in a discourse situation, we might infer that a believes he is the speaker in that discourse situation; and we might utilize this inference in yet other inferences about what a should do or think if he does, in fact, hold such a belief. But while such an inference might seem natural and even essential under normal conventions of interaction, it is in no way necessary. The speaker might not believe that he is the speaker is a discourse situation that includes b: he might think he is talking to himself; or he might be speaking deliriously to an imaginary interlocutor. So, while derived facts may be very important constituents of the discourse situation, we should be cautious, in writing rules, to distinguish between them and the other, more immutable framing and immediate facts.

Metarule of mutual belief:

(13') **Metarule of Mutual Belief (Optional)**

If f is a framing fact or immediate fact of the discourse situation consisting of participants a and b, then the following are derived facts of the discourse situation:

a. $d(believe, a, f) = 1$
b. $d(believe, b, f) = 1$
c. $d(believe, a, \varphi) = 1,$
where $\varphi := d(believe, b, (13'a.)) = 1$
d. $d(believe, b, \psi) = 1,$
where $\psi := d(believe, a, (13'b.)) = 1$

The discourse situation as a function of speech act interpretation:

...significant incrementations to the content of the discourse situation can be made as a result of the interpretation of smaller than utterance segments as well as larger than utterance stretches of discourse. To accommodate this aspect of discourse we should revise (14) as follows:

(23) $\quad D_{i+1} = I(f_u, D_i)$

Here, U, in the expression $I(U, Di)$, has been replaced by f_u, which stands for some constituent (not necessarily proper) subpart of an utterance that can be given an interpretation effecting a change in the content of the discourse situation. As before, the expression $I(f_u, D_i)$ represents the speech act.

Speech act:

(36) A **Speech Act** is the use of an utterance directed at an addressee in the service of a set of intentions, namely,
i. the intention to produce a certain illocutionary effect in the addressee;
ii. the intention to produce this effect by getting the addressee to recognize the intention to produce the effect; and
iii. the intention to produce this recognition by means of

the addressee's knowledge of the rules governing the utterance.

Here *speech act* can be understood as *illocutionary act*, that aspect of the utterance which produces *illocutionary* effects. Illocutionary effects are related to intentions which are realized in their recognition. Recognition of intention, in turn, is affected by rules governing the utterance.

Speech act type:

In order to speak precisely about the effects of utterances on discourse situations, we need a device to capture the (partial) information that speech acts add to discourse situations and to express the (partial) constraints on the discourse situations in which speech acts of a certain type can take place. That device is a speech act type.

Formally, a speech act type can be regarded as a partial mapping between discourse situations. A given speech act type, applied to a particular discourse situation, in which the variables of the speech act type are defined and the conditions of the speech act type are met, returns a new discourse situation. Specifically, it returns a new discourse situation containing a finite number of new facts and all the facts of the old discourse situation unchanged except where specified in its conditions.

Illocutionary mode functions:

Illocutionary mode functions convert bare interpretive constituents into propositions that relate the speaker and addressee to the information in the interpretive constituents. Put another way, the illocutionary mode functions generate partial interpretations of utterances that correspond to the use of the interpretive constituents of the utterance with a particular illocutionary force.

More formally, each illocutionary mode function, $L_i \in L$, is defined for certain types of interpretive constituents of an utterance, $f_j \in F_u$, such that if an interpretive constituent, f_j, is accepted by an illocutionary mode function, L_i, a set of candidate propositions, $L_i(f_j)$, is returned, given schematically as follows:

$$(106) \quad \{ \quad d(r^{m+1}_{Li_1}, a_1, \ldots , a_m, f_j) = \delta_1,$$

$$d(r^{k+1}_{Li_2}, a_1, \ldots , a_k, f_j) = \delta_2, \ldots ,$$

$$d(r^{g+1}_{Li_n}, a_1, \ldots , a_g, f_j) = \delta_n \quad \},$$

$$\text{where } \delta_1, \delta_2, \ldots , \delta_n \in \{0, 1\}$$

The predicates in these expressions have superscripts giving the number of argument places and subscripts giving their serial order with respect to the other predicates associated with the illocutionary mode function, L_i. Note that one of the arguments of each predicate is obligatorily the interpretive constituent f_j. The predicates, themselves, and the arguments other than the interpretive constituent, f_j, provide the information that converts the interpretive constituent into a discourse-level, candidate proposition. These are <u>candidate propositions</u> because without reference to context it cannot be determined whether a particular expression in this form should have status as a proposition in the discourse situation.

APPENDIX B   THE SPEECH ACT TYPES

The following speech act types, arranged here under families of types, appeared throughout the dissertation. They are collected here for convenient reference.

Constatives:

(44) ASSERT φ (D_i)
    1: d(<u>say</u>, \$, φ) = 1
    2: d(<u>believe</u>, \$, φ) = 1
        where φ is a proposition
        and 1, 2 $\in$ D_{i+1}

(45) INFORM φ (D_i)
    1: d(<u>say</u>, \$, φ) = 1
    2: d(<u>believe</u>, \$, φ) = 1
    3: d(<u>believe</u>, @, φ) = 1
        where φ is a proposition
        and 1, 2, 3 $\in$ D_{i+1}

(46) RETRACT φ (D_i)
    1: d(<u>say</u>, \$, φ) = 1
    2: d(<u>say</u>, \$, ψ) = 1
    3: d(<u>believe</u>, \$, ψ) = 1
    4: d(<u>believe</u>, \$, φ) = 1
    5: d(<u>believe</u>, \$, φ) = 0
        where φ, ψ are propositions
        s. t. ψ $\Rightarrow$ d(<u>believe</u>, \$, φ) = 0,
        and 1, 4 $\in$ D_i, $\notin$ D_{i+1}
        and 2, 3, 5 $\in$ D_{i+1}

(47) (SELF-) CONTRADICT φ (D_i)
    1: d(<u>say</u>, \$, φ) = 1
    2: d(<u>say</u>, \$, ψ) = 1
    3: d(<u>believe</u>, \$, φ) = 1
    4: d(<u>believe</u>, \$, ψ) = 1
        where φ, ψ are propositions such that ψ $\Rightarrow$ NOT φ,
        and 1, 3 $\in$ D_i, $\notin$ D_{i+1}

(133) REITERATE φ (D_i)
1: [d($\underline{say}$, \$, φ) = 1]*
2: [d($\underline{believe}$, \$, φ) = 1]*
where φ is a proposition,
and 1, 2 $\in$ D_{i+1}

(134) REAFFIRM φ (D_i)
1: d($\underline{say}$, \$, φ) = 1
2: [d($\underline{believe}$, \$, φ) = 1]*
where φ is a proposition,
and 1, 2 $\in$ D_{i+1}

(145) TESTIFY (TO)/CONFIRM φ (D_i)
1: [d($\underline{say}$, \$, φ) = 1]*
2: d($\underline{believe}$, \$, φ) = 1
where φ is a proposition,
and 1, 2 $\in$ D_{i+1}

(181) SARCASTICALLY ASSERT φ (D_i)
1: d($\underline{say}$, \$, ψ) = 1
2: [d($\underline{believe}$, \$, ψ) = 0]*
3: d($\underline{believe}$, \$, φ) = 1
where φ, ψ are propositions
such that ψ $\models$ NOT φ,
and 3 $\in$ D_i,
and 1, 2, 3 $\in$ D_{i+1}

(182) IRONICALLY ASSERT φ (D_i)
1: d($\underline{say}$, \$, ψ) = 1
2: [d($\underline{believe}$, \$, ψ) = 0]*
3: d($\underline{believe}$, \$, φ) = 1
4: d($\underline{believe}$, \$, ξ) = 1
5: d($\underline{believe}$, \$, ζ) = 1
where φ, ψ, ξ, and ζ are propositions
such that ψ $\models$ NOT φ,
and ξ := [$\exists$s s. t. [s($\underline{say}$, \$, ψ) = 1 $\Rightarrow$
[s($\underline{believe}$, \$. ψ) = 0 and s($\underline{believe}$, \$, φ) = 1]]
and [s($\underline{believe}$, @, ψ) = 1 $\Rightarrow$ s($\underline{be\text{-}fool}$, @ = 1]]
and ζ := (s=d)
and 3, 4, 5 $\in$ D_i,
and 1, 2, 3, 4, 5 $\in$ D_{i+1}

Requestives:

(51) REQUEST INFORMATION (D_i)
1: $d(\underline{want}, \$, @, \langle\alpha, q(x)\rangle) = 1$
2: $d(\underline{request}, \$, @, \langle\alpha, q(x)\rangle) = 1$
3: $d(\underline{know}, \$, \langle\alpha, q(x)\rangle) = 0$
4: $d(\underline{believe}, \$, \varphi) = 0$
where α is a reply such that $\lambda x[q(x)]\ [[\alpha]]$
is a well-formed and complete expression,
where $\lambda x[q(x)]$ represents the partial information of
the presuppositions of the question,
and $\varphi := d(\underline{know}, @, \langle\alpha, q(x)\rangle) = 0$,
and $1, 2, 3, 4 \in D_{i+1}$

(52) REQUEST PERMISSION (for γ) (D_i)
1: $d(\underline{want}, \$, @, \alpha) = 1$
2: $d(\underline{request}, \$, @, \alpha) = 1$
3: $d(\underline{believe}, \$, \varphi) = 0$
4: $d(\underline{believe}, \$, \psi) = 0$
5: $d(\underline{believe}, \$, \xi) = 1$
6: $d(\underline{want}, \$, @, \gamma) = 1$
where α is a reply
s. t. $[d(\underline{permit}, @, \$, \gamma) = 1] \in [[\alpha]]$
and γ is an action or a state,
and $\varphi := d(\underline{be\text{-}able\text{-}to\text{-}do}, @, \zeta) = 0$,
where $\zeta := d(\underline{permit}, @, \$, \gamma) = 1$,
and $\psi := [d(\underline{permit}, @, \$, \gamma) = 0] \notin D_{i+n},\ n \geq 1$,
and $\xi := d(\underline{exist}, \beta) = 1$,
where $\beta := [[d(\underline{do}, \$, \gamma) = 1] \gg$
$\qquad\qquad d(\underline{suffer\text{-}neg.\text{-}conseq.}, \$) = 1]$,
and $1, 2, 3, 4, 5, 6 \in D_{i+1}$

(57) REQUEST ACTION (γ) (D_i)
1: $d(\underline{want}, \$, @, \varphi) = 1$
2: $d(\underline{request}, \$, @, \varphi) = 1$
3: $d(\underline{believe}, \$, \psi) = 0$
where γ is an action,
and $\varphi := d(\underline{do}, @, \gamma) = 1$,
and $\psi := d(\underline{be\text{-}able\text{-}to\text{-}do}, @, \gamma) = 0$,
and $1, 2, 3 \in D_{i+1}$

(298) REQUEST POLARITY OF φ (D_i)
1: $d(\underline{want}, \$, @, \langle\alpha, \varphi\rangle) = 1$
2: $d(\underline{request}, \$, @, \langle\alpha, \varphi\rangle) = 1$
3: $d(\underline{know}, \$, \langle\alpha, \varphi\rangle) = 0$
4: $d(\underline{believe}, \$, \psi) = 0$
where φ is a proposition of the form
$$d(r^n, a_1, \ldots, a_n) = \delta,$$
with $\delta \in \{0, 1\}$,
and α is a reply s. t. $[[\alpha]] = \delta$,
and $\psi := [d(know, @, \langle\alpha, \varphi\rangle) = 0]$,
and 1, 2, 3, 4 $\in D_{i+1}$

(317) REQUEST STATE (α) (D_i)
1: $d(\underline{want}, \$, @, \alpha) = 1$
2: $d(\underline{request}, \$, @, \alpha) = 1$
3: $d(\underline{believe}, \$, \varphi) = 1$
where α is a state,
and $\varphi := [d(\underline{be\text{-}able\text{-}to\text{-}be\text{-}in}, @, \alpha) = 1]$,
and 1, 2, 3 $\in D_{i+1}$

(318) REQUEST ACTIVITY (α) (D_i)
1: $d(\underline{want}, \$, @, \alpha) = 1$
2: $d(\underline{request}, \$, @, \alpha) = 1$
3: $d(\underline{believe}, \$, \varphi) = 1$
where α is an activity,
and $\varphi := [d(\underline{be\text{-}able\text{-}to\text{-}do}, @, \alpha) = 1]$
and 1, 2, 3 $\in D_{i+1}$

Permissives:

(54) GRANT PERMISSION (for γ) (D_i)
1: $d(\underline{permit}, \$, @, \gamma) = 1$
2: $d(exist, \beta) = 1$
3: $d(\underline{believe}, \$, \varphi) = 1$
4: $d(\underline{believe}, \$, \psi) = 0$
where γ is an action or a state,
and $\beta := [[d(do, @, \gamma) = 1] \gg d(suffer\text{-}neg.\text{-}conseq., @) = 1]$,
and $\varphi := d(\underline{be\text{-}able\text{-}to\text{-}do}, \$, \xi) = 1$,
where $\xi := d(\underline{permit}, \$, @, \gamma) = 1$,

$$\text{and } \psi := d(\underline{want}, @, \$, \xi) = 0,$$
$$\text{and } 2 \in D_i, \notin D_{i+1},$$
$$\text{and } 1, 3, 4 \in D_{i+1}$$

(55) DENY PERMISSION (for γ) (D_i)
1: $d(\underline{permit}, \$, @, \gamma) = 0$
2: $d(exist, \beta) = 1$
3: $d(\underline{believe}, \$, \varphi) = 1$
   where γ is an action or a state,
   and $\beta := [[d(do, @, \gamma) = 1] \gg$
   $\qquad\qquad\qquad d(\text{suffer-neg.-conseq.}, @) = 1]$,
   and $\varphi := d(\text{be-able-to-do}, \$, \xi) = 1$,
   where $\xi := d(\underline{permit}, \$, @, \gamma) = 1$,
   and $2 \in D_i$,
   and $1, 2, 3 \in D_{i+1}$

Directives:

(58) ORDER ACTION (γ) (D_i)
1: $d(\underline{want}, \$, @, \varphi) = 1$
2: $d(\underline{order}, \$, @, \varphi) = 1$
3: $d(\underline{believe}, \$, \psi) = 0$
4: $d(\underline{believe}, \$, \xi) = 1$
5: $d(\underline{believe}, \$, \zeta) = 1$
   where γ is an action,
   and $\varphi := d(do, @, \gamma) = 1$,
   and $\psi := d(\text{be-able-to-do}, @, \gamma) = 0$,
   and $\xi := d(\text{have-authority-over}, \$, @, \gamma) = 1$,
   and $\zeta := [[d(do, @, \gamma) = 0] \gg$
   $\qquad\qquad\qquad d(\text{suffer-neg.-conseq.}, @) = 1]$,
   and $1, 2, 3, 4, 5 \in D_{i+1}$

Commissives:

(59) AGREE TO DO (γ) (D_i)
1: $d(\underline{say}, \$, \varphi) = 1$
2: $d(\underline{believe}, \$, \varphi) = 1$
3: $d(\underline{believe}, @, \varphi) = 1$
4: $d(\underline{believe}, \$, \psi) = 1$

5: $d(\underline{believe},\ @,\ \dot{\psi}) = 1$
where $\varphi := d(\underline{intend},\ \$,\ \xi) = 1$,
where $\xi := d(\underline{do},\ \$,\ \gamma) = 1$,
and $\psi := [[d(\underline{do},\ \$,\ \gamma) = 0] \gg$
$d(\underline{suffer\text{-}neg.\text{-}conseq.},\ \$) = 1]$,
and $1, 2, 3, 4, 5 \in D_{i+1}$

Discourse-pragmatic effects of constituent use:

(75) ISOLATE c (D_i)
   1: $d(\underline{want},\ \$,\ @,\ \varphi) = 1$
   2: $d(\underline{request},\ \$,\ @,\ \psi) = 1$
   where φ and ψ give states,
   $\varphi := d(\underline{notice},\ @,\ c) = 1$,
   $\psi := d(\underline{evaluate},\ @,\ c) = 0$,
   and $1, 2 \in D_{i+1}$

(77) REFER TO [[c]] (D_i)
   1: $d(\underline{be\text{-}referring\text{-}to},\ \$,\ [[c]]) = 1$
   2: $d(\underline{agree\text{-}to},\ \$,\ @,\ \varphi) = 1$
   where c is of category PN, and $[[c]] \in A$,
   and $\varphi := d(\underline{evaluate\text{-}as},\ c,\ [[c]]) = 1$,
   and $1, 2 \in D_{i+1}$

(79) ANAPHORICALLY REFER TO [[c]] (D_i)
   1: $d(\underline{be\text{-}referring\text{-}to},\ \$,\ [[c]]) = 1$
   2: $d(\underline{agree\text{-}to},\ \$,\ @,\ \varphi) = 1$
   3: $d(\underline{believe},\ \$,\ \psi) = 1$
   where c is of category PRO, and $[[c]] \in \mathbf{A}$,
   and $\varphi := d(\underline{evaluate\text{-}as},\ c,\ [[c]]) = 1$,
   and $\psi := d([[c]] \in D_i) = 1$,
   and $1, 2, 3 \in D_{i+1}$

(81) EXPRESS NUMBER [[c]] (D_i)
   1; $d(\underline{believe},\ \$,\ \varphi) = 1$
   2: $d(\underline{express},\ \$,\ \varphi) = 1$
   where c is of category DET,
   and [[c]] is a relation, r^1_k, giving the number-
   characteristics of the individual(s), a_j, in its scope,
   and $\varphi := d(r^1_k,\ a_j) = 1$,

205

and $1, 2 \in D_{i+1}$

(83) EXPRESS CLASS MEMBERSHIP [[c]] (D_i)
1: $d(\underline{\text{believe}}, \$, \varphi) = 1$
2: $d(\underline{\text{express}}, \$, \varphi) = 1$
where c is of category CN, and [[c]] is an equivalence class,
and $\varphi := [(\exists a_j)$ s. t. $[a_j \in [[c]]$ and $d(a_j \in D_i) = 1]]$,
and $1, 2 \in D_{i+1}$

Miscellaneous types:

(158) EVALUATE ALTERNATIVES, $\sigma_1, \sigma_2, \sigma_3, \ldots$ (D_i)
1: $d(\underline{\text{choose}}, \$, \sigma_i) = 1$
2: $d(\underline{\text{want}}, \$, @, \sigma_i) = 1$
where $\sigma_1, \sigma_2, \sigma_3, \ldots \in \Sigma$, a set of situation types,
and $\sigma_i \in \Sigma$,
and $1, 2 \in D_{i+1}$

REFUTE φ (D_i)
1: $d(\underline{\text{say}}, \$, \psi) = 1$
2: $d(\underline{\text{believe}}, \$, \psi) = 1$
3: $d(\underline{\text{believe}}, \$, \xi) = 1$
4: $d(\underline{\text{refute}}, \$, \varphi) = 1$
5: $d(\underline{\text{believe}}, \$, (\text{NOT } \varphi)) = 1$
where φ, ψ, ξ are propositions
such that $\psi \models \text{NOT } \varphi$,
and $\xi := d(\psi \models \text{NOT } \varphi) = 1$,
and $1, 2, 3, 4, 5 \in D_{i+1}$.

MAKE IRONIC JOKE S (D_i)
1: $d(\underline{\text{say}}, \$, \varphi) = 1$
2: $d(\underline{\text{believe}}, \$, \varphi) = 0$
3: $d(\underline{\text{believe}}, \$, \psi) = 1$
4: $d(\underline{\text{believe}}, \$, \xi) = 1$
5: $d(\underline{\text{believe}}, \$, \zeta) = 1$
where $\varphi_{-n}, \ldots, \varphi_{-1}, \varphi, \psi, \xi, \zeta$ are propositions
and S is a situation, of type s,
such that $s(\varphi_{-n}) = 1, s(\varphi_{-n+1}) = 1, \ldots, s(\varphi_{-1}) = 1,$
$$s(\varphi) = 1,$$

$$\text{and } s(\underline{\text{believe}}, @, (S \subseteq W)) = 1$$
$$\text{and } \psi := d(S \subseteq W) = 0$$
$$\text{and } \xi := [d(\underline{\text{believe}}, @, (S \subseteq W)) = 1 \gg$$
$$d(\underline{\text{be-fool}}, @ = 1]$$
$$\text{and } \zeta := s(\underline{\text{be-humorous}}) = 1,$$
$$\text{and } 3 \in D_i,$$
$$\text{and } 1, 2, 3, 4, 5 \in D_{i+1}$$

(325) *LIE (D_i)

1: $d(\underline{\text{say}}, \$, \varphi) = 1$
2: $d(\underline{\text{believe}}, \$, \varphi) = 1$
3: $d(\underline{\text{believe}}, \$, \psi) = 1$
4: $d(\underline{\text{believe}}, @, \xi) = 1$

where φ, ψ, and ξ are propositions such that φ is
actually false,
$$\text{and } \psi := [(d(\underline{\text{say}}, \$, \varphi) = 1) \Rightarrow$$
$$(d(\underline{\text{believe}}, @, \varphi) = 1)];$$
$$\text{and } \xi := (d \subseteq W);$$
$$\text{and } 1, 2, 3, 4 \in D_{i+1}$$

APPENDIX C   THE FORMAL APPARATUS

The following rules, conditions, and definitions play a role in the development of the formal theory presented in this dissertation. Items appear here in the order in which they are presented in the thesis.

The rules of constituent use:

(74) **RULE OF CONSTITUENT USE 1:**
If c is a constituent of an utterance, then one possible interpretation of the use of c in the utterance is that the speaker is calling attention to c.

(76) **RULE OF CONSTITUENT USE 2:**
If c is a constituent of an utterance of category PN, then one possible interpretation of the use of c in the utterance is that the speaker is referring to the individual designated by c (specifically: [[c]]).

(78) **RULE OF CONSTITUENT USE 3:**
If c is a constituent of an utterance of category PRO, then one possible interpretation of the use of c in the utterance is that the speaker is referring to an already present individual in the discourse situation.

(80) **RULE OF CONSTITUENT USE 4:**
If c is a constituent of an utterance of category DET, then one possible use of c in the utterance is that the speaker is expressing the proposition that the individual or individuals in the scope of the determiner have the number-characteristics associated with the interpretation of c.

(82) **RULE OF CONSTITUENT USE 5:**
If c is a constituent of an utterance of category CN, then one possible interpretation of the use of c is that the speaker is expressing the proposition that there is a referent in the discourse situation of the equivalence class given by the interpretation of c.

The reconciliation function, X:

Schematically, if we let $L_i(f)_k$ stand for the kth (in order) candidate proposition in the set of candidate propositions generated by the application of illocutionary mode function L_i to interpretive constituent f, we could show the effects of X as follows:

(125) $\quad X(L_i(f)_k) = [L_i(f)_k]^*$ or $L_i(f)_k$

A candidate proposition is returned by X as a "*"-marked candidate proposition when there is information in the discourse situation that is in conflict with or is especially affected by the information of the candidate proposition. A marked candidate proposition can go on to be implemented only under special circumstances. A candidate proposition is returned unmarked (unchanged) when there is no information in the discourse situation that would affect its being implemented.

> (132) CONDITION ON X:
> If p is a candidate proposition based on an interpretive constituent
> derived at time D_i, and $p \in D_i$, then $X(p) = p^*$.

> (179) CONDITION ON X (OPTIONAL)
> If p is a candidate proposition based on an interpretive constituent
> derived at time D_i, and $q \in D_i$ s. t. $p \models NOT\ q$, then $X(p) = p^*$.

The speech act interpretation process:

All of the operations ... of a speech act interpretation process, can be summarized formally with the aid of the following conventions:

> (191) Let P be a finite set of candidate propositions derived from the application of illocutionary mode functions $L_i \in L$, to the interpretive constituents of the utterance (or utterance fragment) under consideration.

> (192) Let D_i be the set of propositions which hold of the discourse situation at time i.

> (193) Let T be a finite set of speech act types, with each individual speech act type, t_i, composed of one or more

propositions in general form (i.e. with variables unevaluated) and one or more conditions on the discourse situation and the variables.

In addition we can define the following operations based on these conventions:

(194) A speech act type, t_i, is matched by a set of propositions, $P' = \{ p_j, ... , p_n \}$, in a discourse situation, D_i, if each $p_m \in P'$ is also $\in P \cup D_i$, and there is an evaluation of the variables in the speech act type such that each proposition under t_i is in P', and no proposition not under t_i is also in P', and all the conditions under t_i are met.

(195) A match function, M, returns matched speech act types given a finite set of speech act types, T, a finite set of candidate propositions, P, and a discourse situation, D_i:
$$M(T, P, D_i) = T^*,$$
where T^* is a set of matched speech act types, such that each
$t_i^* \in T^*$ is matched, relative to P and D_i, and all propositions under t_i^* are evaluated (i.e. variable-free).

After application of M there is a set of candidate speech acts (i.e. evaluated speech act types) which represent the potential speech act interpretation of the utterance (or fragment) under consideration. One or more of these candidates (t_i^*) must be chosen for implementation. [A] variety of factors can influence choice, including considerations of perceived speaker-addressee goals, and discourse genre. The effects of this last factor might be incorporated as follows:

(196) Let G be a finite set of discourse genre types, with each individual genre type, g_i, consisting of a partially ordered subset of speech act types and an assignment function, h_i. To any candidate speech act, $t_j^* \in T^*$, h_i assigns a number corresponding to the rank of the speech act type represented by t_j^* in the subset under g_i (with no assignment if there is no corresponding speech act type).

Then we can define a choice function as follows:

(197) A choice function, C, returns a partially ordered set of

matched speech act types, T^{**}, given a set of matched speech act types, T^*, a set of genre types, $G' \subseteq G$, and a discourse situation, D_i:

$$C(T^*, G', D_i) = T^{**},$$

where each $t_j^* \in T^{**}$ bears a rank number derived as a result of the
application of every $g_j \in G'$ to T^*, and each $g_j \in G'$ is compatible
with D_i.[18]

The last operation involves the derivation of the new discourse situation, given by the implementation of one or more speech acts. Depending on whether we allow branching models of the discourse situation, this can be simple or complex. For example, we might define an implementation function for non-branching models as follows:

(198) An implementation function, I, returns a new discourse situation upon being presented with an ordered set of candidate speech acts, T^{**}, and a discourse situation, D_i:

$$I(T^{**}, D_i) = D_{i+1},$$

where D_{i+1} represents the addition of the highest ranking candidate speech act in T^{**}, t_j^*, to D_i, such that all the conditions in t_j^* are met in D_{i+1}.

Alternatively, of course, more than one candidate speech act or even all could be implemented, depending on compatibility. If branching models are allowed, I could be redefined to return a <u>set</u> of new discourse situations, perhaps along the following lines:

(199) An implementation function, I, returns a set of new discourse situations upon being presented with an ordered set of candidate speech acts, T^{**}, and a discourse situation, D_i:

$$I(T^{**}, D_i) = D_{i+1}$$

where each $D_{i+1, j} \in D_{i+1}$ represents the addition of one or more candidate speech acts in T^{**}, to D_i, such that all the conditions on the speech acts are met in $D_{i+1, j}$.

Metarule of cooperation:

(258) METARULE OF COOPERATIVE DISCOURSE:
If d(<u>believe</u>, \$, φ) = 1, then d(φ) = 1,
unless d(<u>believe</u>, @, (NOT φ)) = 1,
or d(<u>believe</u>, @, φ) = 0.